STAIRWAY TO NOWHERE

Luke James

BRUMMIE
GIT
PRESS

Library of Congress Cataloging-in-Publication Data

Stairway To Nowhere by Luke James - 1st ed. 2010.

1. Personal Memoir - Fiction
2. Music business, UK, USA - Fiction
2. Comedy novelization - Fiction
3. Popular culture - Fiction

ISBN:978-0-615-35067-7

Written in the fiction factory. Names, characters, places, and incidents are either products of the authors imagination, personal memory, or are used fictitiously.

Printed in USA on dead trees

Brummie Git Press

Dedicated to
Miki Cottrell

Thanks to:
Karin Cornils, Roy James, Dik Davis. John Mulligan, Symiane Loora, Annette Rhodes, Callum Cottrell, Daniel Cottrell, Sid Cottrell, Jan Cottrell, Suzy Varty, Clive Litchfield, Gavin Lawson, Matthew Moon, Alan Black, Martin Degville, Jane Kahn, Patti Belle, Anthony Burnham, Alex Ogg, Stuart Vernon, Robert Mag, Vuk Pavlovic, Stephen Lester, Nick Byng, Jerry Lanchbury, Pedro, Whistling Pete, Bob Laul, Nick Jones, Kim Turner, Dan Neer, Paul Raven, Richard Jobson, Bryan Gregory, George Gimarc, Randall Wiliams

PHOTO/DESIGN CREDITS
Brummie Git logo picture: Graham Higgins
Page 3: Callum Cottrell
Page 5: Todd M. LeMieux
Page 11, 24: Molly Denean
Page 17: Luke Sky
Page 21, 43: John Mulligan
Page 31: Symiane Loora
Page 17, 101: Eugene Merinov
Page 58: Roy James
Page 71: Nigel Van Beek
Page 72: Suzy Varty
Page 116, 128: Gus Stewart
Page 197: Greg Dorsett

*Luke stepping around the stage like a vacant giraffe crooning
some of the finest vocals this side of Nat King Cole.*
Sounds (1979)

*In a fight I know I'd have taken Dik Davis over John Taylor.
The Durani might have lost a contact lens.*
Jerry Lanchbury of The Stop (2009)

*"Me and Dik (Davis) the drummer got beaten up by car
workers in the toilet before our first gig."*
Luke Sky, Sounds (1979)

*Fashion ... a wonderful, oddball punk/new wave trio.
Fronted by 6'9" singer/guitarist Luke, their music was the
perfect amalgam of punk snark, Krautrock attack and dub
reggae suss ...*
Big Takeover Magazine. (2009)

*... the lengthy Luke whose salient vocals and inventive guitar
playing has kept Fàshiön's music in motion ... From punk
buzzsaw to John Williams harmonics he's the most exciting
instrumentalist I've seen since the last time I said: "He's the
most exciting instrumentalist I've seen since..."*
Sounds, (1980)

*Formed in 1978 as Fàshiön Music, they played angular
post-punk with reggae undertones that echoed the likes of
Magazine, The Cure and Joy Division but remained defiantly
individual.*
Mike Davies, Brumbeat (2009)

"That's it, let's sign 'em."
Soundbyte after end of *Sodium Pentathol Negative* by
Fàshiön, last track on side 4, IRS Greatest Hits Vol 2&3
(IRS)

STAIRWAY TO NOWHERE

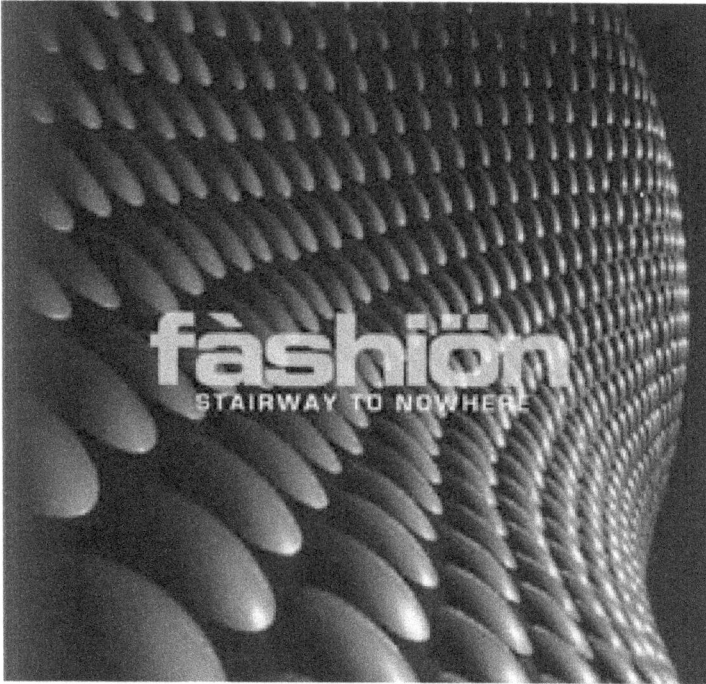

LUKE JAMES

None of this is true
Even if it did happen

Also by Luke James
Public House (fiction anthology)
Product Perfect (audio recording)
Stairway To Nowhere (audio recording)

CONTENTS

Chapter One
On The Stairway, Off The Stairway

"I'm worried about Dik." Mulligan says.

We're standing out in the alley that leads to the entrance of The Rum Runner. We rehearse in the Rum Runner, as do Duran Duran. The Beat filmed the video for *Mirror In The Bathroom* inside the mirrored tack of The Rum Runner. Mulligan and I are taking a break from another slog of a rehearsal, trying to come up with new material for the second album, and mostly failing. So, a quick breath of traffic fumes with our fags.

"Worried?" I ask. "Why?"

"I'm worried he might leave the band."

"Huh. You should worry more about me leaving."

"Yeah. But the difference is ... well, he might actually *do* it." Mulligan says.

Oh dear Jon, wrong thing to say, very wrong thing to say.

►►►►

"Goddamn it!" Miles yells and slams his fist down on the desk. "I've lost two bands this week! First this asshole kills himself. Then this other asshole steals his band's truck and all their gear and drives off into the desert. I got gigs lined up, radio, TV, all kindsa shit. I don't need this. This is not some goddamned game we're playing here!"

No, it isn't. It's people's lives. Their deaths even. And soon, soon you Yank git, there's going to be another one of your band's who are a singer/guitarist short of a full deck.

►►►►

"You sure about this?" Dad asks.

We're sitting in his black cab, parked round the corner from Outlaw Studios. I'm right back where Fàshiön recorded our first demo – was it only two years ago? It feels like bloody years, and all of them stacked on my back. I stare out at the grey veil of drifting rain.

"Yeah Dad. I'm sure." I turn and smile at him, an expression devoid of any warmth, "Fuck the music business, eh."

"But I thought the tour with that Irish band went well."

"U2? Great band. Far as I'm concerned, fucking disastrous tour for us though. If you can call a dozen small clubs a tour."

"Well, long as you're sure."

"Yeah." I say. "I am. Just don't want to be in the music business any more."

On the way into town, we detour along the Kings Norton Road and park outside Annette's house. I'm a bit nervous tiptoeing up the drive, like a bleeding lovesick teenager with a Dear John note. I slip the note through the letter box and leg it back to the cab.

Dad drives me across town and lets me off outside New Street Station. Never ones to show each other much emotion, we shake hands.

"All the best then, son. Stay in touch. For your mother's sake, y'know."

"Yeah. I will. I'll give you a call when I get to Bordeaux. Well, tarra then Dad. And ... thanks."

I pick up my hold-all and guitar case and walk into the station. I don't look back. The message in the note I've just put through the boss's door runs a tape loop mantra in my head ... "Fuck this, gone to New York ... ... Fuck this, gone to New York ... ... Fuck this, gone to New York ... (to the tune of *Message In A Bottle*) ... Fuck this, gone to New York ...... eee oh eee oh ... Fuck this, gone to New York ...... eee oh eee oh ... Fuck this, gone to New York ..."

Chapter Two
Halfway Up The Stairway

Huh! I come awake, my chin on my chest. Neck pain. Eyes throbbing pain. Drooly shirt front. Bladder full.

"I need to piss!"

"No time big boy." Miki says swerving us across three lanes of downtown traffic, "We're almost there."

"We're late, Luke." Annette adds.

Fucking managers. "We'll be wet Luke if I don't have a slash soon."

"Shut up."

The truck lurches, stops, doors swing open and spit me out onto the asphalt. Staggering for balance, ice cold night air knifing my lungs, head clearing but then I'm shoved toward and swallowed by the stage door mouth. Down narrow gloomy corridors, through a door bearing a tarnished star on flaking paint. The dressing womb. Toilet stall in the corner, thank fuck. Pissing in almost orgasmic relief, I lean one hand against the wall in front of me. Back in the room I find a speckled mirror, framed by light bulbs, only three of which work, and a cold, metal, folding chair. Starting to focus, make-up ritual, deep breathing. Enough of that, fuck all that yoga shite Sting does, get a cigarette lit, suck some blessed relief. Fag balanced on the burn-decorated table edge. Foundation, eye-liner, eye shadow, blusher, hair gel, spiked ... perfect.

"Any chance of a beer?" I ask the room.

"No." Annette says.

"Two minutes." someone yells through the door.

"Whaddya mean two minutes? What about the sound check?" Dik demands.

"Have to do it in the first number." Mulligan says.

"Shit."

"Are the guitars and bass in tune with my synth?"
Mulligan asks.

"Give 'em here." I say.

Practice amp dead, my ear pressed to bass guitar like
fucking Beethoven trying to guess the bugger into tune. Have
to do, close enough, I think. I hope. Back out into another birth
canal corridor, low ceiling, naked bulbs barely above the top of
my head, wading from pool of light to pool of light, feeling the
floor rise beneath my Docs. Rumble of crowd growing. Doors slam
open, blinding lights, red, green, searing gold, silver, blue. Lights
die, I'm plunged mid-step into an abyss. Tap-dancing across
snakes nests of cables, a starter roar from the crowd. Fumble
guitar lead into pedal, then into a strange amp set to fuck knows
what, drag pedal next to mike stand, cable into pedal, cable into
guitar, eyes adjusting to the gloom, back to amp and flick standby
by switch. Twist volume knob up full, middle all tone controls.
Menacing tidal wave of feedback pulsing as I swagger back to
the microphone.

"Good evening!"

Blam – lights up, full chaos, searing heat, blindness.

"We are Fashion." Dik's voice booming all Bog-like, bam,
bam, thud, as he does a quick check of his snare and bass drum.

"Meeeep ... warble!" Mulligan's synth up and running.
"Boom-boom ... boom-boom ... boom-boom-boooom" bass line
intro to *Red Green and Gold* and we're away. Oceans of light,
then drowning in darkness, coming up gasping, sweat building
already, guitar neck slippery, finger positions and song structure
now rooted deep in muscle memory, automatic pilot engaged,
adrenaline thrill sparking like high voltage through tired wiring,
head aflame with pulsing beat, guitar slicing magnesium chops
through the back beat. Huge breath, mouth to mike to find it, pull
back a couple of inches, and:

*"Red, green and gold – let this be the color for all .. no more
black and whi-yite game – together we can overcome all!"*

This next one must be *Burning Down*, teeth gritted
throttle that fucking guitar neck, smash the chords' face in,
sweat flaying in arcs through the lights as I dip and whirl, psycho
carousel of thunder, rising like Poseidon to the mike:

"Can I borrow your lighter – 'cos my forehead's getting tighter – and I gotta go gotta go – bu-urn some-um-thing da-own".

And even before there's a chance, the smallest gap into which might creep a whisper of applause, we're into the third number:

"Die in the west and you're halfway to heaven, heaven, heaven!" bawled over bratty chords, thunderous bass and drum avalanches.

There's a gasp of breath after the last looping vocal note and into the sudden ear-roaring silence the applause wells and breaks over the lip of the stage. Take that and I'm straddled, balls to the crowd, and don't you all just wish *you* could be me! A dip to the bottle of water a roadie has magicked at my feet, seared throat soothed with ice-cold water shock.

"This is our new single. It's called *Citinite*. You probably won't like it!"

And we're off into Mulligan's hurdi-gurdi carousel, drowned Ferry, acid vocals with Andalusian guitar slicing the face from the windshield. Slamming into *Sodium Pentathol Negative*, my throat is raw, notes totter on the brink of discord, breath is now furnace hot with every landed fish mouthful seeming to deliver minimum oxygen to starved muscles. One more song segment to go – I think –into *Big John* and then *Hanoi Annoys Me*, both of which Dik sings, before I have to sing *The Innocent*. Move off the mike and dance this beautiful fucking guitar around the moonscape stage. Mulligan and Dik's faces rising occasionally through the lightshow bombardment like satellites lost in a cosmic stew. Teeth and grins and nods and snarls slamming in strobe. Back to the front of the stage to strafe them with the opening chords to *Hanoi Annoys Me*. Light spilling back off the stage giving occasional glimpses of upturned faces, arms snaking above a mass of writhing bodies. Then back to the mike to boast:

"We are innocent, it's not our fault, if we don't stop moving, we won't ever come to a halt."

And then we've nailed the set's carcass to the back wall and we run for the wings, a passing *"thank you very much"* tossed at the mic.

Panting side-stage like dogs, sweat drenched, grinning at the growing roar for more.

"Not too long, now – let's go, before they change their fucking minds."

Back out into the land we now own, a roaring wave of applause washing up over me. Mea culpa, absolved, and adored. No messing, smack them with the *Fàshiön* anthem and then dive back off down the rabbit tunnel to the dressing womb.

Sweat everywhere, gasping, drowned as rats, towels lobbed over heads, Annette bobbing and gushing, the words "fucking brilliant" buzzing through the air like honey-stoned bees. A drink, a drink, my condom for a drink. A soothing stream of some cheap lager, ice cold pinning me in my seat, a babble of voices, the room filling. I can hardly breath, somebody gets me a cigarette. A line, then two of white powder appear on the table at my elbow. No need to even roll my own note these days, kapow, brain floodlit, mouth buzzsawing words into easier to understand pieces, delivered with accelerating blood pulse. Limbs, smooth arms, slim shoulders, silky hair, long legs of mini-skirted slinkers, ruby mouths, proffered breast fruit, juicy arses, a joint here, another line, a shot, then outside, into a cab, I'm suddenly in orbit around a club dance floor or two, then a hotel lobby, the room, the bed, the faceless orgasm, the exhausted slump sideways into tomorrow. The door is being pounded. It's time to get up and do it again.

Chapter Three
Where Do I Plug In?

"Hello luv."

"'Lo."

Mascara tarantulas wave at me from around baby blue eyes. I'm standing at the dole counter talking to a young, dole office dolly clerk.

"Done any work since yow last signed on?" she asks, and yawns without covering her mouth.

"No." I say, "Course not." If the DHSS find out you're in a band, they stop your dole.

"Saw yower gig at the Barrel Organ." she says and pushes my giro through the gap beneath the everything-proof glass.

"Really? Hope you enjoyed it."

"You were crap!"

Out on the street, I meet up with Mulligan. We have a bit of a cough at the traffic then head for the post office to cash our giros. The queue is out of the door and halfway down the road.

Jonathan Salvador Mulligan has something of a reputation as style-maven and photorealistic painter. I've run into him occasionally at various Moseley Village parties, where he sports his own versions of the new punk look, currently dragging its safety pin-stuck carcass up the motorway from London. There is a certain, self-generated mystique about this androgynous, elfin, leather boy.

"I hear you left your band." he says,

"Yeah. Something like that"

At a Rudi and the Rationals rehearsal a few days earlier, the cheeky fuckers only fired me from my own band!

"So are you looking to put another band together?" he asks.

"Dunno. Might just go solo again. See what happens."

I kick a fag packet just to make sure it's empty. It is.

"Only I've got this bass and I was wondering if you had time to show me how to play it a bit. I'm trying to impress this bird." he says, "Be some spliff in it for you."

Unbeknownst to me, there is another reason behind Mulligan's desire to become the next Sid Vicious. He'd also been at the Rudi and the Rationals, lunchtime gig at the Barrel Organ. Now, Rudi and the Rationals were such a cacophonous conflict of egos, that not even a drunk with a faulty ear trumpet would have called us good band. Nevertheless, I apparently struck an imposing, visual figure at the front of the band. I'm close to seven-feet-tall, and was sporting my newly-acquired, studded dog collar (thank you very much Fido) and razor-slashed, black tee shirt. Having decided (but not actually mentioned to me) that I was to be the front man of his new band, Mulligan left The Barrel Organ content in the knowledge that all he had to do now was take care of a few minor details – like learning how to play an instrument, finding a drummer, writing some songs, getting a record deal, and conquering the world. Now, what could be simpler?

▶▶▶▶

So, when Mulligan shows up for his first bass lesson he has a rolled-up poster under his arm.

"Before we get started," he says, "I wanna show you this."

He unrolls the poster to reveal a black and white print of a 1960's Vogue model in a wide-brimmed hat and the word "Fashion" slashed across the top.

"Very nice," I say, while he fumbles a beat-up Kay bass out of its black bin liner carrying case, "what's it for?"

"That's our band!" He grins, "That's what that is."

"Who else is in this band of yours then?" I ask, completely missing the "our" part of his statement.

"Well, so far … just me and you. I was up at three this morning plastering town with those." he nods at the poster, "Getting the name out there, like. You can have that one, if you like. I'll even autograph it for you. Have you got a cable I can use? Where do I plug in?"

When Mulligan answers his front door I think for a second that he's gone all geisha, white-face in his latest attempt to look different, but then I realize it's just the effect of the UV light bulb in his hallway. He's decked out in a zebra stripe shirt, black leather trousers, and Docs, his hair is a platinum firework. He's shaved his eyebrows off again. Me and my fluorescent white teeth, fingernails, and dandruff step into Fàshiön HQ.

In the living room, I see he's added a fourth TV set to the stack of tellies balanced precariously against the back wall.

"You want to try getting a toaster and vacuum cleaner up there as well, John. Dead multi-media that'd be."

Drummer Dik Davis looks quite dapper with backcombed, jet black rats nest hair, sporting a new mid-blue suit, dotted here and there with primary-color geometric shapes, and Docs. His eyebrows are drawn a good two inches above the ones he's shaved off. He's chopping out tiny lines of white powder on the chipped glass coffee table.

"Tut tut. Who's a naughty boy then." I chide.

"To each his own big nose." Dik grins.

"Been out being a hippie again this afternoon have you?" Mulligan asks.

"You want to try something a bit faster than all them joints you smoke." Dik says.

"What, like your moped?"

A cloud darkens Dik's face.

"Alright, alright. There's no need to take on so." I say,

holding up a hand. "How is your motorbike anyway?"

Dik has an old Triumph 250cc, while Mulligan has a 150cc Suzuki dirt bike . From time to time, these two bike boys make the trip down to London's Kensington market to flog Woolworth's razor-slashed tee-shirts to West London punks who have more dosh than brain cells.

"Somebody nicked it." Dik says.

"Oh. Sorry."

"Why? You didn't nick it did you?" he asks.

"No, no. Just a bit of a bummer that's all. Here, any news on getting us a manager then?" I ask Mulligan, eager to change the subject.

Mulligan walks over and changes two of the TV channels. He pops a dub cassette into his boom box and floods the room with ire yoot, to accompany *The Magic Roundabout* and *Midlands Today.*

"There's this girl I know." Mulligan says. There usually is.

"And?"

"Well, she's our new manager."

"Great. Who is she? Has she got good connections?" I ask.

"She's got decent tits." Dik says.

"Oh well thank fuck for that." I say. "Main thing, that."

"Her name's Annette," Mulligan says. "She lives over Kings Norton. She's got a phone."

"Yes, I can see where that would come in handy. When did this happen?"

"Er, well I started handing her number out a couple of weeks ago. She must be getting some calls by now." Mulligan says and shrugs. A light bulb goes off over my head.

"She doesn't know does she? You haven't soddin' told her have you."

"Oh, I will." Mulligan says, as innocent as a chemistry teacher with something nasty in the cellar at home.

"Well, when?"

"Soon. Don't worry."

"But what if she says no?" I ask.

"She never has yet." Dik says snorting up half the contents of the coffee table. "At least not to me!"

He grins, then lets loose an enormous sneeze and blows Mulligan's line of speed into the carpet.

I finally manage to stop laughing. This has been made all the more difficult by the way Mulligan is eying the carpet, like some sort of lovesick vacuum cleaner.

"Here," I say, wiping my eyes with the back of my sleeve and wincing as the studs gouge my forehead, "there's something else. We need to find someone to do sound."

"What?" Dik asks. "Why?"

"Yes," Mulligan says, "Good point Skyscraper."

"What are you pair of tarts on about?" Dik wants to know.

"Well there's not much point us rehearsing until we're all barking, if when we play all the crowd hears is a garbled wall of noise. Is there?" Mulligan says.

I can all but hear the cogs turning as he scans the universe for the right mug. But there's no need. I already have just the chap lined up. And what's more I'll have the common decency to let him know what's happening well in advance of the first show. Unlike certain manager recruiters.

"Well, walls of garbled noise have always worked for you in the past." Dik says and grins, "Least from everything I ever heard. What were they called … *Corky and the Cuntholes*, wasn't it?" he asks, referring to my last band.

"That was mostly because we didn't have Miki Cottrell doing sound. He's also a dab hand at getting great deals on PA and van rentals. He's also got a driving licence."

"Sounds like a real renaissance man." Mulligan says.

"Oh he is John, he is." I say, and turn to Dik, "And we were called *Rudy and the Rationals*, you cheeky cunt."

"Well you were still rubbish, whatever you were called."

"Couldn't agree more." I agree.

I'm really excited about inviting Miki to our next rehearsal. I think I finally have something for him to get his teeth into.

▶▶▶▶

An hour or so later, I'm trying to materialize a mention of Fàshiön into that week's *NME*. Dik is playing paradiddles against the edge of the coffee table. Mulligan has given up trying to gather his line of speed from the carpet and is sulking over his mascara. Suddenly the door bell rings.

Mulligan comes back in with two thin, white dukes in trench coats. They have long hair and a dab or two of make-up about them.

"This is Nick and John." he says. "They're in a band as well."

"Duran Duran." the Nick one says, and sniffs.

"Do-what, do-who?" I ask.

"We've got a new demo." John says.

"Well, let's hear it then." Dik slips his drum sticks out of his back pocket.

Nick hands Mulligan a cassette.

"The first track's called *Girls on Film*." he says.

"Girls on what?" Dik asks, as the opening guitar riff fills the room.

"Very nice John." Dik says, "Oy Nick, put the kettle on would you and make us some tea. I'm gasping here."

"Nine sugars in mine," I say.

Chapter Four
The First Gigs

We refuse to do cover songs, so it takes me, Dik, and Mulligan a month to come up with our first five songs. This is Birmingham, 1978 and we decide that only old hippies do cover songs. We're the future of no future we are, mate.

We rehearse in this derelict hotel halfway up Moseley Road hill. A six-inch nail jammed into the fuse box gets us the power back on. We stack old mattresses against the windows to give us a bit of soundproofing, and to also keep any nosy coppers from noticing the Belleview Hotel suddenly has guests again.

As we come up with our songs we write the lyrics directly onto the walls with in big, black marker pens, always careful to add the copyright symbol and the legend "no unauthorized wallpapering!"

It's as if the music has been lying dormant in me for many years, like seeds under soil, waiting. I suppose that makes Dik and Mulligan the fertilizer then. The air in that crumbling room doesn't smell of mold and mildew, it smells of promise, of the future, it crackles with excitement. Dik lays down rock-solid, yet shifting beats, segueing easily between punk, dance, and reggae. Over these drum segments I sing snatches of verse and chorus, play riffs and chord sequences. In between learning bass patterns, Mulligan devils up great, sweeping, whooshing, stately, industrial noises from his black and yellow plastic WASP synth. In a frantic rush of creativity we grow our songs, we become the swaggering, cutting-edge band of our dreams, and bollocks to anyone who thinks otherwise. The real world grows daily more insubstantial, as we immerse ourselves ever deeper in the thrilling exhilaration of the future. We assemble the scenery, we write the soundtrack.

Late one dark and freezing Summer's afternoon, I go round to Mulligan's flat. Dik is already there. Mulligan's place is rough but dead arty. There are lots of pictures on the walls that you can't quite tell what they're supposed to be, plus he has the tidiest piles of rubbish you ever saw. A couple of weeks earlier, he made this sculpture thing out of the bog, so I'm never quite sure where to piss, not that it matters. He also has this two-way mirror stuff stuck all over his front windows, so you can see out but no one can see in.

Dik waves me over to the window. I peer out and see that Mulligan has dug his cat up again. Mulligan's cat, Sid, had died about a week ago (we never did find that bag of speed) and we buried Sid in the back garden with full punk honors. Since then Dik must have reburied Sid at least five times, because Mulligan keeps digging him up again, insisting Sid isn't dead, just a bit under the weather. So, there's Sid's kitty corpse, propped up on the front porch, and here comes the bloke from the DHSS to interview Mulligan about why he still doesn't have a job in this crumbling, jobless wreck of a country of ours. The shiny-shoed bastard finds Mulligan's bell and rings it - no superglue this time, I note. After a bit, he rings the bell again. Then he notices Sid. Now, any undertaker in town would have been proud of the job Mulligan has done, Sid almost looks alive. Mr. DHSS leans down to stroke the nice pussy cat. The look of horror that spreads across his face as he strokes dead kitty has us falling away from the window, laughing fit to bust a bollock. Funny, but he never comes back, does old Mr. DHSS, the cat fancier.

I plop down onto Mulligan's settee, which if anything feels a bit more alive than his cat.

"So what's all this about us playing with The Mekons?" I ask, innocent as sperm in the Vatican.

Dik is trying to scratch his bollocks through his leather trousers. I make a mental note to buy him a knitting needle for Christmas. Mulligan has shaved one of his eyebrows off again, but other than that it's business as usual. He's wearing a kimono, black leather trousers, with black Docs, and has bits of what look like transistor radio braided into his platinum hair. He's doing his best not to poke his eye out with a mascara brush.

"Yeah well, they don't actually *know* we're playing with them, do they." he says, "But don't you worry about that. I'll have a bit of a chat with 'em and everything'll be alright."

In certain quarters Mulligan is legendary for having a bit of a chat with people and "everything being alright". The gift of the gab and a set of bollocks to match, that's Mulligan.

The Mekons gig is at the Bournbrook Hotel, down in the Bierkeller, a ratty, low-ceilinged horror of a place, full on Birmingham/Bavarian stylee. We slap on a bit more make-up, and jump on the number sixty-two bus over to Selly Oak.

Down into the bierkeller dungeon we go. Mulligan goes off to have his chat with The Mekons, who are setting up their gear. Me and Dik sit over in the corner and suck down a couple of pints. We have a bit of a look round. It's early yet but clocking the other punters, I see my "Elvis IS Fucking Dead" tee-shirt and fake fur coat are definitely the dog's bollocks. Dik sits fidgeting and radiating menace, all black leather everything, including the fingernails.

"Oy!"

Mulligan waves us over. "We're on first. Five songs."

"So, where's your gear then?" a Mekon wants to know.

Me and Mulligan pull curly red guitar leads out of our pockets and Dik twirls drumsticks out of nowhere.

"Er, we were wondering if we could borrow yours?" Mulligan says, and grins.

Ten minutes before we're due to go on, Dik and I have to piss, big time. Not so much a question of nerves or anything, just those pints of gnat's piss Brew XI for the men of the soddin' Midlands we've sucked down. So, upstairs we go to the gents, which is stinking up the corridor outside the saloon bar. The saloon bar is full of British Leyland track workers, swilling it down and setting fire to their fingers to prove how hard they are. Me and Dik are standing in the ammonia, puke stench, taking a leisurely piss, when we hear a voice behind us, slurred and thick with menace.

"What the fuck am that doin' in the gents?"

"'Ey girls, the ladies is downstairs," booms a second voice.

"Oh very fuckin' funny, you cunt." Dik says.

"Ha-soddin'-ha tossers." I add.

"What do yow say, yow bleedin' queer?"

Dik turns from the tile, smiling, "Your missus doesn't think I was very bleedin' queer last night."

I don't have time to even laugh, much less brace myself or zip up. My face is slammed into the tiles and everything goes to fuck. I get hit, I try to hit back, I get kicked, I try to kick back, but there are fists and boots everywhere. It doesn't last long, it's over really quickly, which is probably just as well. As suddenly as it started, it stops and they're gone. The lads from the bar are already back in the saloon bar, laughing over a fresh pint of slop about the fun they had with the queers in the bog.

I'm down on my knees, my cheek against the tiles. I struggle up from piss-stained knees, wobbling, waiting to see how badly I am hurt. I can taste blood and my lips feel like old inner tubes. I see a pair of black leather legs sticking out of a stall. Dik's lying on his back, head propped against a crusty, brown toilet bowl. One of his eyes is already starting to close and his nose is streaming blood.

"Yow alright?" I ask him. My mouth feels broken. He's grinning up at me.

"'Ello darlin'," he says, "Come here often do you?"

Limping like beaten dogs, we stagger from the gents back down into the Bierkeller.

"Where the bleedin' 'ell have you been?" Mulligan asks, "We're on in – " He notices the damage.

"Nowhere." Dik says. He grins and winces, "We were just upstairs in the gents. Putting some make up on like."

"Yeah," I point to my ruined mouth, "Lipstick and that."

We play our five songs – one of them twice as an encore – and fourteen minutes later we're out of the door, up the stairs and gone, with the applause still ringing behind us.

"Better leg it, in case them prats from the saloon bar fancy another couple of rounds." Mulligan says.

We run down onto the Bristol Road and hop on a bus. Upstairs we go for a smoke, sprawled across the back seat. Dik magicks a bottle of vodka out of his jacket. He takes a swig, winces, and hands me the bottle.

"I thought it went quite well really," he says, ever the sodding optimist.

▶▶▶▶

The first Fàshiön gig proper is at The Golden Eagle in the middle of Birmingham, on May 20th 1978. A couple of hundred people show up to check out this new band, Fàshiön music. Mulligan, Dik, and I have wallpapered what feels like the whole city center with our posters. There isn't a blind man in town doesn't at least know the band name.

"Fuck my old boots." Miki says, "But them stairs are a bit steep then."

His voice emanates from behind a massive bass bin. The bin totters over to the edge of the stage and crashes down, raising dust. Mulligan swans in with his tiny black and yellow, plastic WASP synth tucked under his arm.

"Are they?" he says, "can't say as I noticed."

Miki is now officially Fàshiön's sound engineer, first-class, unpaid. Indeed, he's been my sound engineer for the last nine years, and my best friend since we were eleven-years-old. Miki is now effectively the fourth member of the band.

"Alors, les mecs."

And then Symiane walks in and my mind (although definitely not my trouser department) goes blank. Symiane is my new girlfriend, a well-tasty, eighteen-year-old French girl I met a few weeks back at a Steel Pulse gig. She has long black hair, smoldering dark eyes, pouting red lips, golden complexion, a body to die for, to kill for ...

"Anyone get a mop?" Dik asks, "Only it looks like lanky here is in danger of drowning in his own drool."

Having sound checked, we drive back across town to The Old Moseley Arms, an old, gas-lit Irish pub, and settle into the Victorian splendor of the snug, nursing half pints and fragile nerves.

"Do you think we sounded alright?" I ask Symiane. "In the sound check, like."

She gives me a lingering, languid look while I struggle to remember my name.

"Boff," she finally says, "what does eet mattere? You are not playing ze Beethoven."

"Right," says Dik, "but I tell you what love. If we were, we'd win. Five nil I reckon."

"Vot is zis fife nul?"

We arrive back at The Golden Eagle about half an hour before we're due on. We swan in through the double doors and stop dead, caught short and gob-smacked.

"What the sweet creeping Jesus ...?" Miki eventually manages to croak.

To say that the support band have rubbished the room doesn't even begin to describe what they've done. The audience, our audience, look as if they've gathered shivering in the back half of the room for their own protection. The air is filled with the stench of burned plastic. A river of oil, sand, paint, and bog knows what else runs moat-like across the floor in front of the stage. Everything, walls floor ceiling – our gear!!! – has been generously decorated with what looks like shaving foam. At least, I hope it's only shaving cream. Dik wheels around, eyes blazing.

"Where are they?" he demands of the room.

But of the support band there is no sign, which is just as well for them. I step gingerly across the floor, trying not to trail the turn-ups of my new shocking pink Oxford bags in the muck, and see my amp lying on it's side next to my stack. When I pick it up it rattles ominously. Sure enough my amp is dead. Twenty minutes to the show. I look at Miki, shocked as a hurricane survivor.

"What am I going to do?" I ask him.

"Er. Just a minute. I'll be right back."

"But what about the show?"

"I dunno. Stall them." And he's gone, skidding out through the door, like Chaplin on speed.

"When I find them ..." Dik growls.

But Mulligan is already on the mic. Thank Costello the PA still works.

"Have everything ready as quick as we can. Meantime, I'm going to spin you some sounds."

He jumps up into the DJ booth and soon has the room dancing, everyone weaving in and out of mops and buckets, like some punk version of the Sorcerer's Apprentice.

Twenty minutes later, a smoking trail of red traffic lights and speed limits behind him, Miki appears hauling a new amp in through the door.

"Where'd you get that so quick?" I ask, grinning. "Back of a lorry job?"

"No sunshine," he says, "someone over Moseley way owed me a favor. At least, unless they wanted me telling their wife about the snogging I saw going on in the Fighting Cocks last Saturday night, they did."

By the end of the third number, *Bike Boys*, I have worked up such a sweat I have to take off my leather jacket. Stage clothes is something I'm still working on – it has to look wonderful but not reduce you to a blob of grease before the set is over. The breeze blowing up my billowing, pink Oxford bags is a definite plus.

Our half hour set is note-perfect, the applause builds song by song, we look divine, or at least weird, we'll settle for either, preferably both. We do one encore to thunderous demand and are gone. Leaving everyone asking:

"Say, who was that mascaraed band?"

I have a feeling they'll be back to find out.

Chapter Five
Steady Eddie Steady

By the end of August 1978 we've played ten gigs, including the LSD Club in Handsworth, the Bournbrook Hotel (sold-out show in the upstairs room), and Lark In The Park, an open-air festival at Birmingham's Hexagon Theater with The Specials and Steel Pulse. After the promoter at Barbarellas (God rot him!) pulls our support spot to The Clash (for fucks sake!), we play a hastily organized show at the Cannon Hill Art Center, with an early version of Duran Duran opening the show for us. But of course everyone's at Barbs to see The Clash.

One day Mulligan comes to rehearsal and announces that he's managed to come up with the five hundred quid needed to record and press a thousand seven-inch records.

"I've managed to come up with the five hundred quid needed to record and press a thousand seven-inch records." he says. Say no more, we think, so we don't.

We decide to record at Outlaw Studios, the same eight-track where we did our demo tape. Outlaw is tucked away in a tiny, cobbled courtyard at the back of one of Birmingham's many derelict factories.

Once we're set-up and in tune Mulligan holds up a little plastic baggie with a couple of inches of white powder in the bottom.

"Let's get a bit of this up us then."

"Not me." I say. "I need to concentrate. Make sure I get things right like."

"Well, this'll help." Dik says.

"Yeah," Mulligan agrees, "Give you a bit more energy that's all. It's only speed."

"I know what it is and I don't want any. And before you start banging on about hippies, I don't need to smoke anything either. Christ, I didn't even have a drink last night!"

Mulligan and Dik go off to the toilet together, conspiratorial as a couple of Satan's schoolgirls, while I check my tuning for the umpteenth time and run through the intro riff to *"I Don't Take Drugs, I Don't Tell Lies"*. That hit of the engineer's joint I'd snuck earlier has leveled my hangover nicely and I actually feel pretty good, ready to record the future. Dik and Mulligan buzz back into the room like a couple of gigantic, black leather bluebottles.

Two hours later we find ourselves still on that first track. At one point we leave the studio, absolutely nothing useable recorded, and walk round the corner in the chill drizzle to a greasy spoon cafe. In through the door, we find a tiny, fag smoke, and fried fat haven. A couple of blue-overalled factory escapees look up as we bundle in through the door. They do the obligatory double-take, and take to nudging each other in the ribs and scowling at us.

"Chins up ladies." Miki says as we settle ourselves round the sacred cuppas and sausage rolls.

"We sound the way we look." Mulligan says, his smeared mascara framed by drowned rat tail dreadlocks.

"Well I definitely sound the way I feel." I say gloomily.

"Well I don't know what's wrong with you pair of drama queens." Dik says, "'Cos I sound fucking great. Most likely 'cos I am!"

"How nice for you." I say.

"And it's a good job for you I am." Dik says, his tone uncharacteristically serious. "Look, we're the dog's bollocks. I know it, you know it. Fuck me, even he knows it," pointing at me, "It's just a question of giving everyone else in the world a chance to hear that. Right?"

Spoons tinkle, sausage rolls are nibbled, fags are lit.

"Right?" Dik insists. "You remember - the rest of the world? As in, us against them. Fuck my old boots, we can knock these songs out in our sleep. So let's wake ourselves up and get on with it, eh."

▶▶▶▶

"So, if I've got this right, it seems I've been appointed your manager." Annette says.

"Er, yes." Mulligan says, and grins like a cartoon dog.

"Well, okay then, let me show you your schedule."

"You what?" I ask.

"You didn't think I was just going to be answering the phone, did you? There's more to being a manager than that. A lot more!"

"Right. Have you, er, done this before then?" I ask.

"Of course not, wonder boy. But that's not the point, is it. The point is I'm doing it now. Now then ..."

And doing it she is, for two weeks later we learn she's got us a spot playing one song, live on a BBC TV show,.

►►►►

The traffic roars and grinds its way up Moseley Road Hill. Dik and I stand outside the dole office in the early afternoon murk. Conspiratorial biros wag across our UB40 dole cards. "Professional musician" we each write on the line that begs a description of our new job titles.

"Well lanky," Dik says, "I mean we can hardly risk being on the dole if our mugs are gonna be on telly can we?"

"Too right, my son."

We fill out our dole sign-off cards, and dance a ceremonial jig of glee as we shove them through the dole office's post slot.

"Let's go and see if we can blag some drugs from off of Jane." I suggest.

We might officially now be professional musicians but that doesn't mean we aren't skint. Off up the hill we charge. Dik has a red plastic transistor radio pressed to his ear. Suddenly he stops dead in his tracks.

"Fuck my old boots!" he says twisting up the volume, "Listen to this!"

"Steady Eddie steady is this the only way out, Eddie hold the gun steady ..." is warbling out into the monoxide air, vying with the traffic's thunder. The demo of our first single is being played by Robin Valk on BRMB Radio. We're definitely on our way up the sodding hill.

►►►►

We choose *Steady Eddie Steady* for the A-side and *Killing Time* for the B-side of the first single. We spend hours sticking the labels on the records, and folding and gluing the outer picture sleeves. A month later, the record is ready to go. All the record shops in town take copies, and they start to sell. We keep a hundred aside for radio stations and to use as ammunition on our first foray to attack the London Biz.

About halfway way down the M1, the conversation turns to sales of *Steady Eddie Steady*. We've had a few good reviews, a couple in *NME* and *Sounds*. Annnette tells us that we've sold all but the fifty or so we've with us that we're going to use to do the rounds of London record companies.

"Bit of a relief really," Mulligan says with a grin, "I mean it could have turned out quite nasty."

"What could?"

"Well, the people I borrowed that five hundred quid from. They only let us have it for a month." he says.

"What do you mean?" I ask.

"Just that if we hadn't sold the record and paid them back -- which I did day before yesterday - there could have been some ... er, broken fingers ... sort of thing."

"Yeah," beams Dik, "or even arms and legs. You don't fuck around with those *(name deleted for safety of genitals)* Brothers, do you? Not and get away with it."

"You borrowed the money for *Steady Eddie Steady* from the *(name deleted for safety of knee caps)* Brothers?" Miki asks, "Are you fucking mental?"

"Yeah, well it is a song about suicide, innit." I chuckle, trying desperately, but not quite managing, to see the funny side.

▶▶▶▶

As we guessed, down in London our single is greeted with less than what you might call wild enthusiasm. A few people express interest but we're down to our last couple of stops when we pull into Blenheim Crescent, just off Ladbroke Grove, looking for the mews office of Faulty Products/Illegal Records. We exit the van and trot up the rickety wooden fire escape to the first floor reception of Faulty Products. Posters of bands both massive and unknown dare us to state our business. This we do, in no uncertain terms, to the receptionist, whose eyes are fixed, or rather glued on the front of Dik's leather trousers.

"'Spose her mid-life crisis must be to do with drummers then." I mutter.

"Not a bad looking old boot though," Dick grins as we follow her derriere from reception through the main office area, down a corridor to an oaken door.

The door is studded with triangular metal rivets and a copperplate script sign boasts "Miles A. Copeland III"

"Blimey, this bloke must think he's Henry the soddin' VIII," Miki says, as we're ushered into an office that gives weight to his judgment.

On a low platform stands a massive desk behind which sits a burly, sandy-haired man on a golden throne. The throne has carved lions for arms. He watches us approach his throne, snake eyes behind oversized spectacles. It's a bit like being on acid and looking at John Denver.

"Guys! I heard your record. Steady Eric, and I gotta say I like what I hear."

"Eddie." I say, "It's called *Steady Eddie Steady*."

"What? Oh yeah, whatever. I like it. I like it a lot. Now lemme tell you what I'd like to do ..."

▶▶▶▶

We sit out in the empty 77 Club in Nuneaton. It's our twenty-second gig and we're opening for a new band from Scotland called The Skids. The dressing room is a cupboard so small we have to keep our drum and guitar cases out in the van. The bar is just opening, sound checks are done, the doors are supposed to be opening in half an hour. Annette is off somewhere doing managerial-type things. Opposite us sit The Skids. All we know is that they're Scottish and have just signed a deal with Virgin Records. We just sit and glower at each other, the blood of our respective ancestors coursing through our veins. I'm thinking this could be sodding Colluden Field all over again. And where do I stand if it is? My granny was Scottish, so I'm Scottish from the knees down. If a ruck breaks out, am I supposed to attack myself, beat myself around the knees. They probably think we're just a bunch of Sassanach poufters on account of the make-up. I'm a bit worried Dik will explode – he has a tendency to do that if stared at wrong. The Skids are a bit arty-looking as well though, still they are Scottish and we're just ignorant and prejudiced enough to be wary of them. One of them gets up and comes over. Here we go.

"Hawah ya bassa, name's Jobson. What are ya drinkin'?" Jobson asks.

"Ta very much, mate. Mine's a pint." I say

It's the beginning of a friendship that will long outlast our respective bands. As we chat, I learn that their deal with Virgin gained them a twenty thousand pound advance. Quite a tidy sum for an unknown band in 1978. I further learn that recording the first album and the tour to promote it has cost nineteen thousand pounds. It should, but this teaches me nothing about the music business

"So me and Stuart (Adamson) bought a couple of guitars with what was left." Jobson says, "That's mine over there."
He points to beautiful shiny, black Strat leaning against the wall.

Later, with our shows played and the club well and truly rocked to the bollocks, we take Annette back to meet The Skids in their cupboard-sized dressing room. We time it to perfection, two of The Skids are in their skivvies and the other two are stark, bollock naked, toweling themselves down as we shove her ahead of us into the room.

▶▶▶▶

I'm pushing my speaker cabinet past a row of gigantic Botticellis, or some such. Loads of fat, naked people writhing about in bits of gauze – bit like that dream I had last night come to think. I'm deep inside the Birmingham Art Gallery looking for the auditorium where the gig is scheduled. It's ten o'clock in the morning for fuck's sake, and as I haven't been up all night, I ought to be asleep! Plus I'm gasping for a fag, even something to eat would be alright. But there are old gallery guards posted under no smoking signs every twenty yards or so, and to add injury to insult, as I round a corner I see the café is closed. How the fuck Annette has dug us up this gig is beyond me. But then most of what Annette does is beyond me. My job is to write songs, play guitar, sing, and look as extraterrestrial as possible. The auditorium is big, with a good-sized stage, lighting towers and footlights, and faces row upon row of metal, folding chairs. The dizzily high, white ceiling makes me feel a bit like I'm inside a gigantic wedding cake.

A sudden tidal wave of white noise followed by a series of beeps and squeaks blasts into the room, signaling that Mulligan might be close to having his sometimes self-firing WASP synth set up. His head looks like it's framed by a peroxide atomic blast.

"Oy! Mics." Miki commands from the back of the auditorium.

And so I'm into another round of one-twos and peter piper picked a peck of pickled ganja.

"Miki, is there any way we might move this piano?" Mulligan asks, pointing at a gargantuan Steinway parked on his side of the stage.

"Well, you might," Miki says, "I'm not. I'm busy." And he bends over his mixing desk, tweaking nipple switches.

"You could always try learning to play it." Dik says.

Mulligan sniffs, purses his lips and plays an approximation of the opening riff to *Product Perfect* on his WASP.

The sound check goes quickly enough – by now we more or less know what we're doing and the room, while a bit more acoustically designed to house old Ludwig, Mozart, and Bach and the like, is fairly good. Now if we can all avoid getting Brahms at lunchtime, we'll be fine. Actually that is proving less of a problem the more we gig. No one drinks, snorts or smokes anything (other than fags) before shows. Of course, afterwards is an entirely different kettle of spanners.

"So what are we gonna do now?" I ask, putting my beloved custom John Birch guitar carefully back in its case.

"I'm going to look at some of the paintings." Mulligan says.

"Thrilling." Dik says, "Here, lanky, fancy finding a kaff and getting some scoff down us?"

"Yeah alright. Miki? You up for a spot of the old double egg and chips?"

"One of these days," Mulligan says, "It'll be my paintings hanging in here."

"Listen Gauguin," Dik says, "if we don't play well this afternoon, it'll most likely be *us* hanging up in here."

It's still light outside. Our intro music, some esoteric piece of obscurity that Mulligan has dug out, is fading into whooshes, whoops, and what sounds like whales with bad colds as we take the stage. Covering the back windows is a huge blackout curtain that has been left slightly open to reveal a slice of incongruously blue sky. The afternoon is turning out to be well surreal, and getting more surreal by the second.

"Good afternoon ladies and gentlemen," I say in my best BBC announcer voice, "We are Fàshiön Music and we have the perfect product."

As we wheel into the intro to *Product Perfect* I squint down through the footlights at the front row and see ... a line of grannies clutching their handbags, interspersed by the occasional knot of giggling schoolgirls. Like I say, stranger and stranger.

But the show goes smooth as smooth can be, no major fluffs, and bags of swank. As we are coming off after the second encore, Dik grins a huge mouthful of teeth at me.

"Better than sex!" he announces, sweat-spangled.

Well I wouldn't go quite that far, but the sight of grannies skank-dancing with schoolgirls down in front of the stage while we play *Red Green and Gold* is not something you could have paid me any amount of money to miss.

►►►►

"I hate the countryside." Dik says.

"Yeah," Mulligan agrees, "It's just so ... so, quiet."

"And dirty and smelly," I add.

"And miles from anywhere. And empty." Dik concludes

"Where are we Miki?" Annette asks.

"Just driving past another field full of cows," Miki says, quite cheerfully.

"Only it'll be getting dark soon." she says, sounding a little nervous.

"We are all ... going to die." Mulligan intones.

"Try turning left at that haystack," I suggest, "then if you come to a main road about two miles on-"

"It'll be a bloody miracle." Miki says. "Put that map away and stop pretending you know where we are."

Half an hour later, we stand, shivering in a haute couture knot beside the van and stare from the car park at a huge wooden shed. Once night had fallen, Miki's radar kicked-in.

"Says Fàshiön on that poster over there." Miki points out.

"But it looks like a fucking sheep shearing shed." Dik says in disgust.

"Well, we are in Wales." I say.

"That poster's probably just for a knitwear parade put on by the Women's Institute." Mulligan says.

"Well if it is," Annette says, "they'll need a band won't they. So get the gear in."

Sound check over and the doors open a good twenty minutes earlier, I peer round the stage curtain at the room. There look to be over a hundred bodies – everything from punks to tractor jockeys. Who knows where these people come from.

Halfway through the first set, I see Mulligan has two teenage punkettes standing staring up at him. Flattered by their attentions, he smirks and starts skanking, whipping his bass and dreadlocks back and forth. His smirk grows into a lecherous grin, interspersed with the odd bout of pouting. I catch Dik's eye, nod at Mulligan, and roll my eyes. Dik blows me a kiss between cymbal crashes, and I mouthe "fuck off." Pretty much business as usual then.

We're toweling down in the dressing room after the first set.

"We get *what*?" Dik asks.

"A bowl of stew." Annette replies.

"A bowl of stewed what?" Mulligan asks.

"Look I don't know. That's the backstage rider, two twelve packs of lager and a bowl of stew each." Annette says, fighting hard not to smirk.

"Stew?" Miki asks, coming into the room in his own personal cloud of B&H smoke, "Stewed what?"

"The last band that played here probably." Annette says, and points at a battered aluminium cauldron sitting next to a small stack of polystyrene bowls.

"Well I'll have a go." I volunteer. "I am a bit peckish as it goes."

"Pig bin", Miki grins through owl glasses. He tugs at a lager ring pull.

"You what?" Dik says.

"That's what they used to call him when he was little. Pig Bin."

"He was never little." Mulligan says

"On account of he'd eat anything left over." Miki says.

"Bollocks!" I say through a mouthful of stew. "Here this isn't too bad. Once you get over the initial shock." I sit down and poke through the brown goo in search of something identifiable. "Open that door would you. Its like a broom cupboard in here."

"It *is* a broom cupboard in here, Luke." Annette says, pointing at a clutch of mops and buckets over in the corner.

Dik opens the door and I see a corridor outside. He sticks his head out.

"The bogs." he announces.

"Well at least the dressing room's not actually in the bogs. For a change." Miki says.

"Yes," Mulligan sighs, "a definite step up this is."

"Goin' for a slash." Dik says.

"Thanks for sharing," I say through a mouthful of stew.

"And try not to get beaten up." Annette yells at Dik.

A couple of minutes later there is a ruckus out in the corridor and suddenly Dik appears, backpedaling and swinging punches at what turn out to be three skinheads. Mulligan, all seven stone (ninety eight pounds) of him, leaps into the corridor and joins the fray. I shift my chair slightly so I can see better. I swear I nearly choke when Mulligan swings at a skinhead who ducks and his fist slams into the wall. Security in the shape of a couple of tractor mechanics with fists like ham hocks arrive and soon restore peace. As the Fàshiön rhythm section come back into the dressing room, Mulligan is wagging his injured hand back and forth.

"Does anything feel broken?" Annette asks.

"Dunno." He's pouting like a bruised five-year-old. I swear he's blinking back crocodile tears. "It hurts like fuck though."

"Diddums." Dik says to Mulligan. Then to me, "Here, the bass playing might pick up a bit in the second set then."

"Couldn't make it any worse." I agree.

We start the second set with *Burning Down* and then wheel into the hurdy gurdy of *Citinite*. This is Mulligan's only vocal, so while he holds onto his synth for dear life and croons the vocal through semi-clenched teeth, I have a chance to step back and stand next to Dik's drums. I'm chugging out the chords to the second verse when I see Mulligan's two little punky girl admirers. They stand side by side, gazing directly up at him. They're each holding almost full pints of beer. Mulligan is really hamming it up now, shooting them little pouts between lines. Suddenly they look at each other, nod, and ... throw their beer up at the stage and all over him. The look of total shock, followed by the sight of drenched rat tail dreadlocks are too much for me and I lose it. Dik and I finish the number with a good deal of unamplified hyena howling.

Chapter Six
Hello, My Name's Sting

It has snowed for a week, then frozen the slush into huge banks and swirls of steel grey ice. A bitter wind howls through Mulligan's platinum dreadlocks as we unload the van.

"Well ... this is ... nice." I hiss steam through clenched teeth, skittering to keep my end of Mulligan's bass cabinet from flattening me.

"Cold enough for polar bears." Mulligan says.

We're loading into Mr. Sam's, a Saturday night gig at the Imperial Hotel in the middle of Birmingham. We've decided to be all socialist, give our road crew the night off, and hump the gear ourselves. So Miki's inside, having a pint with my brother Roy. Roy is a stalwart of the band, selling tee-shirts, badges, and records at gigs, lugging gear, often pretending to our Dad that he is out driving their cab on nights but secretly talking us to gigs for free, and generally being wonderful and indispensable.

This is our thirty-first gig and a big deal to us because Miles Copeland is supposedly coming up from London to check out our live show.

"Alright girls!" The bearded, yeti-like Sid appears, Miki's brother, a Brummie biker.

Sid has written off half a dozen motorbikes and broken most of the bones in his body, except his head which he's presumably saving for last. Sid is security. He's also already drunk and clearly none too secure.

"Any chance of a hand here?" Dik asks.

Sid gives a slow hand clap, missing his hands a couple of times.

"You had to ask." I say, "And you can keep him away from my gear." I then tell Sid, "I'm quite capable of destroying that myself thanks all the same."

"Bleedin' charmin'." Sid says, and goes off in a huff.

"Well, I don't fancy your chances later if a gang of skinheads decide to play kick the singer." Mulligan says.

"With Sid in that state, I wouldn't fancy my chances if a gang of schoolgirls decided to have a go at me ..."

And all three of us suddenly get far away looks on our faces.

Our dressing room is one of the hotel rooms and therefore easily the best dressing room we've had so far. We're a little disappointed to find there's no TV set in the room, so we mime throwing one out of the window. After the sound check, Dik prowls the corridors looking for a maid.

"I love those French maid uniforms. Well kinky, innit."

"Good luck finding one to fit." I say. "A uniform or a maid."

I'm enjoying the luxury of a big, well-lighted bathroom mirror, and concentrating on the application of the old warpaint when in strolls dear old Dad. He's taking a break from pushing his black cab around town. He stands behind me and shakes his head slightly.

"Hello Dad. Don't worry, I haven't gone peculiar or anything. It's just show biz as usual."

"Hello, son. Heard tonight was a big one, so I thought I'd drop by and wish you luck."

"Thanks."

"How you feeling? Nervous?"

"Naw. To be honest I'm more like ... shitting myself. Miles bleeding Copeland is supposed to be coming up from the Smoke to check us out live. Might be important."

"Well there's bloody hundreds of people down there. And more outside trying to get in."

"Thanks Dad. That's calmed me right down that has!"

I stand up, strap on my guitar and have a quick squint at myself in the mirror. I'm clad in an oversized black dinner suit, trousers hiked up with bright red bracers to reveal sparkling black 24 hole Doc Martens, a black see-through shirt and neon red pencil thin-tie, with a short but wayward mop of dyed red hair atop the face of a bleedin' angel.

"Lovely," I say, "Bloody marvelous really."

"Well at least you've never been short of self-confidence. You big headed bugger."

"Come on Dad, it was you always me to never be backwards in coming forward. I just took it a step or two further, that's all."

Like some nightmarish jack-in-the-box, Mulligan springs into the room.

"The Yank's here." he exclaims, as if Santa Claus has just materialized and granted him his wish for an additional penis.

The gig goes like a dream. Four hundred or so sweating bodies are crammed into the club, while outside the line of people trying to get in stretches round the block. The PA is halfway decent, Miki's brother Sid sobers up a bit and does security with his biker gang. Quite impressive that is, sort of like a grubby imperial guard. We play a near perfect forty minute set, followed by delirious cries for encores. Blimey, Miles even helps load the gear into the truck before his driver takes him and Nick back down the M1 to The Smoke. Standing in the freezing alley, the van doors gaping like a still-hungry mouth, Miles shakes his head,

"Goddamn," he exclaims, "I have seen more great bands in the last six months than I can believe."

"Yeah. Good innit." I say, voicing my agreement at the phenomenon.

"And you guys are definitely up there. You are going to go places my friend."

"All right then. When?"

"Soon. Soon."

▶▶▶▶

A week later, following a phone call from Faulty Products, Annette calls a band meeting round at her architect boyfriend's house.

"This is definitely a bit of alright." I say, eying the luxurious, split-level living room.

For about three seconds, I sort of miss the squalor of Mulligan's arty slum.

"Will you please stop bouncing on the settee Luke." Annette says, "You'll have the springs through. We didn't have it shipped all the way from Stockholm for you to use it as a trampoline."

"Not exactly comfy anyway." I say.

"We'll hold the meeting in the kitchen then." Annette says.

"Good. I am a bit peckish, as it goes." Mulligan says.

"And keep out of our fridge."

Their kitchen is quite a bit bigger than my flat.

"Er, I don't want to worry you," Miki says, "But a small horse appears to have just strolled in."

"What? Oh that's Holly. Our great Dane."

"You should have called her Hamlet then." Mulligan says. "Hur hur."

"Why would you name a dog after a cigar?" Dik asks.

"Any chance of a ride later?" I ask Annette. "On the dog I mean. Er, I'm just making this worse, aren't I. Can I have a glass of water please?"

I walk towards the sink, duck right past it into the fridge, and emerge with a long necked green bottle of Canadian beer.

"Thanks." I say smacking my lips. "Now, what's up?"

"I've got you a gig." Annette says.

Dik is languidly buttering a piece of cold toast left over from Annette and Kevin's breakfast. "Oh yeah. Where?" he asks.

"Kings College."

"Where? Not bloody Oxford?" I say "I'm not keen on playing Oxford?"

"Why not?" Mulligan asks. "What's wrong with Oxford?"

"They wouldn't let him into the University." Miki says.

"To use the toilet." Dik says through a mouthful of toast.

"Very funny. No, the whole town is full of children of the rich. All learning how to bugger each other in Latin. I'm not providing them with entertainment."

"No you're not." Annette says.

"They can bloody well go and listen to someone else. King Crimson or Yes or one of those—"

"Kings College, London." Annette says.

"London, eh?" I ask.

"Yes Luke, London. Anyone there you object to playing to? No? Good. We're playing with two other bands." She zips open her black leather file-o-fax and consults some notes. "Resistance. And The Police."

"Here, that's that band. Mulligan played us their single. Roxette or something." I say.

"Roxanne." Mulligan says. "They're on A&M. Miles Copeland manages them."

"They're not bad as I recall." Miki says. "Nice touch of white boy reggae, right?"

▶▶▶▶

King's College, London

"But I'm hungry." I say for the fifteenth time in ten minutes.

"There will be food when we get there." Annette says with something approaching infinite patience.

"You always say that and there never is. Anyway I'm here." I insist, "not there. Where the food supposedly is."

"Dangling participle." Miki observes.

"What?"

"Talking of danglers, I could use a slash." Dik says.

"You should have gone before we left." Annette says.

"Any chance of stopping for a game of Space Invaders." Mulligan asks.

"I'm not even going to grace that with an answer." she answers.

"Nurse Ratched." I say petulantly, "I want my cigarettes. Now!"

"Miki, what are you doing?" Annette yells, as Miki swerves across three lanes of traffic and bounces onto a service station ramp.

"You lot may well be hungry space invaders who want a piss," he says, "But this van needs petrol."

We're out of the doors and haring across the forecourt in different directions before the truck has even stopped.

The hall at Kings College is a dusty barn of a place that smells of school disinfectant. As is often the lot of the support band, we aren't allowed to set up Dick's drums on the riser. But we are allowed the luxury of a sound check, a whole fifteen minutes. There are plenty of times when sound checks are conducted in the course of the first number of the set. We even have a dressing room with, as Annette promised, sandwiches and a few drinks. These are luxuries student gigs tend to provide, as opposed to the club circuit where you are lucky to get a dry floor in the toilet, or anywhere else for that matter. One advantage we have though, as far as dressing rooms go, is that we walk around all day sporting what we wear onstage. The only time we actually change is *after* the show, when we're sweat-drenched and need to change into cleaner versions of what has become habitual dress. I'm wearing my black dinner suit and Doc Martens, Dick has black leather trousers and a blue jacket decorated with red and yellow geometric patterns, and Mulligan with feather-decorated peroxide braids, is wearing his jet pilot's underwear cooling suit.

"Sounds good lads." Miki says as I dive bomb out the last note of *Don't Touch Me.*

"Thanks Miki. Now can I get something to fucking eat?" I ask Annette as I hop off the front of the stage.

The corridor that leads to the dressing rooms is straight out of my junior school – what is going on here? It's more like doing a gig at Kings Norton Juniors, not exactly the glamorous first gig in The Smoke I'd envisioned. There are heavy double doors with wire-reinforced glass, tiny swivel windows high enough up the wall to warrant a window pole, that bloody awful smell of dust and disinfectant. I wouldn't have been surprised to find great cauldrons of cabbage boiling in the dressing room. Annette leads us to a small room, some kind of elongated cupboard, into which barely fit a small table and two tubular steel folding chairs with wooden seats. There is a small, cracked sink with a tap slowly leaking cold water in the corner, a toilet stall with no door, and a tarnished square of mirror with only three bulbs that work.

"At least we get our own piece of paper on the door." I say.

"Yeah, nice bit of magic marker work that." Miki says.

"When did we change the band name to Fishion?" Dik wants to know.

"Nobody tells me anything." Mulligan grumbles. He slumps into one of the chairs and eyes the small plate of curly sandwiches and three sad cans of lager. "This is the life, eh."

"Oh yes," I say swooping on one of the sandwiches. "Nothing but champagne and caviar from now on." I chew and pull a face. "Make that Red Barrel. And Marmite and sawdust."

"All you lot ever do is complain." Annette complains. "There's going to be a bloke from the *NME* here tonight."

"That's something to look forward to then." I say. "Wonder if it'll be same prat they sent to the Nashville Rooms gig."

"I doubt it." Mulligan says, then to Annette, "But in any case, could you please try to keep him away from the press, boss."

"Hey, I've get a perfect right to—"

"You got a perfect right to shut the fuck up and just sing and play guitar." Dik says. "We need some good press."

"Bunch of crawlers. Alright, alright, pardon me for having a brain in my head."

"Just as soon as we find one, we will." Annette says. "Now come on you miserable bastards. Aren't you even a bit excited? Big show tonight. Next step on the ladder you know."

"Right. Whatever you say." Dik says. "Here, let's see what's going on with Copeland and his coppers."

The Police's dressing room is much bigger, but it still looks like a schoolroom from the 1900's, tiny high windows, beige gloss enamel painted walls. There's a fair old crowd in there, people drift around, circling like wreckage going down the drain. The first thing we notice are several women, punkily and scantily-clad.

"'Allo darlin'," Dik says to a pouting lovely with Siouxsie make-up and hair, "Why don't I let you take me away from all this?"

She spirals away unimpressed.

"We're playing here tonight you know." I tell a slightly chubby girl I'm randy enough to consider. Well, Symiane is back in France and I haven't had it in a couple of days. I am, after all, basically a set of genitals and an ego, loosely camouflaged as a git with a guitar.

"You're playing here? Really?" she says "Me too. With any luck." She yawns with exaggerated boredom, and drifts off toward the middle of the room.

I see Mulligan has speared some girl to the wall with his blag and is waving expansively at the plastic tube coils on his suit.

I approach the Police hub. Annette is on the edge of the circle, a drink in her hand. Where did she get that? I glance around and see a table loaded with lager and wine. I splash myself a red plastic cup full of Chateau Pissoire and sidle up to the group. Annette grabs my arm and propels me in front of her, yelling: "This is Luke" like I'm some sort of entrance sacrifice. Hardly the kind of proclamation to inspire awe, I think. But Stewart Copeland wheels round and peers at me. At least he's a decent height so I don't feel too much like a craggy peak.

"From Fàshiön." Annette adds.

Stewart's face splits into a big homeland grin.

"Hi Luke." He says, "My brother tells me you guys are really weird."

He's wearing a schoolboy jacket with a hundred dollar bill sticking out the top pocket, like a posh hankie.

"Right." I say, "Well if old Miles reckons we're weird, then I suppose we must be, eh. Seems like the sort of geezer who knows weird when he sees it." I chug some wine and grimace, "Here, I like your record. Roxanne, innit?"

I notice I'm now standing next to Andy Summers, all five-foot-nothing of him. Now I *do* feel like a rocky crag, or in my case more like a factory chimney. The way he seems to have his nose permanently in the air doesn't help. I feel like he's peering up at me.

"Alright mate?" I yell down at him. "You the guitarist? What do you play?"

"Brilliantly." He says and turns his back.

Okay. Suddenly, a bloke with leopard skin spots dyed into his dyed blonde hair bobs in front of me and holds out his hand. He's wearing what looks like a pilot's gray flight suit.

"Hi," he says, "My name's Sting."

"Of course it is," I shake his hand. "Pleased to meet you Stig. Here," I say, eyeing his flight suit, "you should go and have a word with our bass player. I think he's got your underwear."

"Alright you fuckers! Everyone except the band out. I'm in charge here and we're clearing this dressing room." The slight, but demented-looking, gap-toothed figure of Kim Turner, the Police sound man and road manager, has spoken.

▶▶▶▶

I'm standing with Dik and Mulligan at the side of the stage while Miles is ranting something into the mic about *"making a fashion statement."* He loves to intro his bands does Miles – may the force be with you indeed!

I'm finding the stage bigger than I'm used to. It's not so much a case of tripping over the usually vipers nest of cables and blundering into my amp, as actually having to walk to the bugger. Dik is settled behind his drums like a mad gunner in a bomber. Mulligan is tweaking knobs in the dark, teasing the first test meeps and swooshes out of the synth. I plug my guitar in, looping the cable through my guitar strap to prevent accidentally unplugging it during my gyrations. I reach to flip the amp's standby switch and flip the wrong switch. My amp dies. Bugger! I switch everything back on and hear that satisfying gut-rumble hum that signals cheap cables that have done too many gigs plugged into ungrounded amps that are hooked up to dodgy Victorian wiring systems. Then I hear the frantic four count clack of Dik's drum sticks and we're off into *Burnin' Down.*

"Can I borrow your lighter?" I'm belting out, *"'Cos my forehead's getting tighter and I gotta go, gotta go bu-ur-urn something dooooooown!"*

Sheer bloody poetry innit. There are more stage lights than I'm used to and they seem closer. It's getting bloody hot and we're only halfway through the first number. Sweat is running down my legs into my Docs. I slam into the middle eight chords and execute a tightly-controlled spin designed to not clart Mulligan in the bonce with the head of my guitar. This is a danger born of height differences and tiny stages. In the early days of the band (about six months ago!) I'd quite enjoyed occasionally clipping the little git in the side of the head but I'm much more mature these days. Besides, he's a good thirty feet away on the other side of the stage, skank-dancing behind imaginary bass lines. On certain numbers Miki will sometimes have bass coming off the stage amp and the monitors only, cutting it out of the mix coming through the main PA speakers – ("Well, he's crap innee." Miki says and sniffs, "Besides I just mix Dik's bass drum all the way up and no one notices.") This means that only Mulligan and possibly the front row of the audience can actually hear his attempts to play the notes of which he has yet to learn the names. He plays by memorizing patterns on the fretboard, or so he claims.

I throttle the shit out of my guitar neck, face screwed into an orgasmic mask, then strut stiff-legged and pop-eyed around

the stage. Probably looks quite impressive, right up to the point
where I fail to get back to the mic for the start of the last chorus.
Still, I'm almost certainly the only one who notices. The first
number slams to a halt and a small wave of semi-interested
applause washes up over the front of the stage. No time to waste,
work on that and build it, a quick "thank you" and Mulligan
booms into the opening bass notes of our reggae danceathon *Red
Green & Gold*. Miki has switched the bass through the main PA
speakers and it's thundering out fit to rumble everybody's guts
("He's not so bad on the repetitive reggae lines, is he." is Miki's
wise judgment.)

   *"Red Green and Gold, let these be the colors for all, no more
black and white game, together let us overcome all."*

   Thank you and goodnight MLK Jnr. A few of the more
drunken bits of the audience are now up and dancing about
down the front. So during Dik's plastic banana harmonica solo
(later replaced with a Hohner blues harp) I hop off the front of
the stage to join in. It's not much of a drop and I'm hoping my
guitar cable is long enough to not bring my amp stack smashing
down onto the stage. Nothing like living dangerously, especially
in these early days of horrendously expensive radio guitars that
tend to pick up passing taxi broadcasts, when they work at all
that is. But the cable is long enough to allow me a quick skank-
dance with a couple of skanks before attempting a somewhat
undignified scramble back up on stage . This has me deciding to
scratch any future "Luke, guitarist of the people" stunts. Besides,
I'm sure Mulligan and Dik will give me a bollocking later for not
being all aloof and that, the elitist little sods.

   The applause after *Red Green & Gold* is decent so we
immediately swerve into *Citinite*, our current single, a piece of
uncommercial vinyl suicide, five minutes long, so no radio play,
no hook, so no hit, so fuckin' what? When you're the future of no
future who gives a toss about doing it like everyone else? Hurdy
gurdy synth and burbling flanged guitar get the whole unlikely
thing off the ground, and then to add the cherry atop the whole
messy pie Mulligan, who can't hold a tune to save his life, starts
singing into a mic that Miki has routed through enough phasers,

flangers, and reverb units to render Mulligan the Martian
Frank Sinatra.

"Heeeeee's a taaaalll mon inside a smaaaaall mon ..."

I get a rare break from the mic, a chance to fully
concentrate on and enjoy what I'm playing as opposed to running
on muscle memory, so of course I immediately play a G minor
instead of a G Major 7. But in the sick wheeling carousel of
the song I'm the only one who notices. I mean, it's not bleedin'
Beethoven or anything is it, and even if it was I wonder just how
many of those cultured gits would notice the odd major seventh
chords as opposed to old Ludwig's intended thirteenth flattened ninth.

I drop the palm of my right hand fractionally to damp the
chords of the pseudo-Flamenco section and stroll over to say
hello to Dik.

"Fuck off lanky," he mouths, and grins insanely, driving
his drum kit like some unlikely, clockwork, mountain-
climbing machine.

"I love you too." And I blow him a kiss. Mulligan has
started chanting *"oh citinite"* like some terminally depressed
neon monk, so I dodge up to the microphone for the responses.
I wonder vaguely if even Dik and Mulligan, who wrote the lyrics
for this epic piece of nonsense, really know why after each
chanted "Citinite" we respond *"holo-gramuh"* and *"rear li-ite"* and
"calculate", ending predictably enough on *"terminate!"*. Still it's
only a pop song for fuck's sake. There's a huge wash of synth
white noise to mark the end of the song and baffled applause is
rippling up off the audience. A lot of them are not quite sure what
they just heard or if they liked it, which is precisely why I put
Sodium Pentathol Negative next when I wrote out the set lists. I
grab a quick swig of tepid, flat lager. Nothing too brain straining
about Sod Pen Neg, some pretty flanged chords and linking riffs
as an intro that then gets bludgeoned to death by a falling-down-
stairs fit of three-chord punk. Over which I wail a bit about how
bored I am, ask why if paradise is so perfect I have to leave,
and promise that if I was a crow I'd rip out your eyes. All good,
wholesome stuff that has me spraying the front of the crowd with
sweat and saliva as they slam dance and pogo around a bit, in
that semi-polite way that half-drunken students go berserk. Still,

it's way better than being ignored and as we slam into the brick
wall at the end of the song, a primal burst of real applause blows
some of the sweat off my brow.

I grab a slug of water, wishing it was vodka and we
monkey-dance into the unlikely Egyptian rhythms of *Product
Perfect.* By now I am completely drenched in sweat, from hair dye
to Docs. A slick, manic-eyed, New Wave ad man promising I will
make everyone's life complete. I just have time to towel sweat out
of my eyes as the applause at the end of *Product Perfect* competes
with Dik and Mulligan's drum 'n' synth intro to the *Big John/
Hanoi Annoys Me/ The Innocent* trilogy. It's going to be a hot and
heavy lunge for the finish line and I'm starting to feel my throat
rasp and tighten, my breathing is heavy and less controlled. So
I sit back and take a guitar-strangling break while Dik yodels on
about Keith (Richards) being at the clinic, Sidney (Vicious) always
having too much rope, and Big John (Lennon) living in the Big
Apple raising cows cows cows cows...

By the time we're into the ringing guitar harmonics that
intersperse the power chords of *Hanoi Annoys Me* I've got my
second wind, and before I know it I'm screaming about how
innocent we are. We dead stop at the end of *The Innocent* and
after a stunned second of silence the show's first barrage of
truly delirious applause bursts from the audience. It washes
over me like an ecstasy shower, runs up my arse like a cocaine
enema, tingles my balls, and lights up my face with a grin of epic
proportions.

I suddenly have not the least shred of doubt as to why
I put up with all the bollocks and boredom that lead to this
moment. Okay so the booze, drugs, laughs, risks, and sex help
pass the time as well, but this right here, this mindless adoration,
this is what I really want. Brainless approval – you can't beat it!

A last mad dash through the last chorus of *Die In The
West* and I feel as if my lungs are going to collapse, I'm blinded
by light, heat, and rivers of sweat, my guitar feels as slick as a
gigantic eel (paging Dr. Freud!) and my throat is sand-papered,
bleeding red raw. And I feel fucking unstoppable, riding a
runaway jumbo jet towards the crash landing at the end of the set.

"We are Fashion music. Thank you. Goodnight!"

I'm stumbling, blind and exhausted, buffeted by Dik and Mulligan, blundering into the small knot of people standing in the wings.

"Fucking brilliant!"

No way can that be Annette.

"You guys were amazing. Now get out there and do another one!"

Yes, that would be Annette. Herded like giggling sheep, we duly stumble back onstage before the applause dies and leaves us stranded and embarrassed.

"Thanks a lot!" Dik says to crowd.

"What do you want to do?" I mouth at Dik.

"Tecnofascist!" Dik announces into the mic and we're off into the theme tune for one of George Orwell's toasted cheese nightmares.

We tumble through the dressing room door, grinning and babbling like loons, a quick towel-down, a touch up of the old war paint, a dab of Rive Gauche under the uxsters, and off to The Police dressing room we go, a-foraging. Which Kim Turner has very sensibly locked. The untrusting bastard. By the time we get back to side stage, The Police's roadies have dragged Dik's drums and our amps off stage and dumped them in an unceremonious pile. While Mulligan and I wheel our amps back to the dressing room, Dik starts disassembling the 3-D jigsaw of his kit.

"Nothing like a little something up the nose and a quick blow job after a show, eh?" Mulligan says.

One of the casters on my cab has locked and I'm grunting as I drag the bloody thing down the corridor.

"Yeah. And this ... is nothing like .... either one." I say.

"Personally I'd settle for a nice cup of tea." Mulligan says.

"Bet ... there's no milk." I say and slam my cab into a fire extinguisher that falls off the wall and gouts foam all over my feet.

Chapter Seven
It's A Toilet, Man

Nick Jones looks up from his desk as I saunter unannounced and uninvited into his office. Iggy Pop looks down from a god-like poster on the wall behind Nick's desk. Nick rolls his eyes and speaks into the phone with infinite patience.

"Look Ron, I know the gig's a fuckin' toilet man. But then the band *are* shit, aren't they."

He grins at me, baring nicotine-stained tombstones. Nick, is a dark-haired, specky bloke in his early thirties, who looks fifty. He's dressed like a refugee from one of those espresso, beatnik b-movies. I always think he ought to have bongo drums under one arm and a reefer behind each ear. He runs Faulty Products for Miles Copeland.

"Yeah, right. Nice one. Look I gotta go. You won't believe this, man, but someone with talent just walked in." He puts the phone down. "Hi man. Hey, where are the others?"

If I didn't know better I'd almost believe he was pleased to see me.

"Going through the drawers in Miles's desk. Can you lend me a fiver Nick?"

He spread his hands.

"I'd love to but ... y'know."

"But you're not going to."

"Right. I got you a gig though. With The Cure."

The Cure's first single, *Killing an Arab,* is at that time the darling of certain *NME* and *Sounds* hacks.

▶▶▶▶

"It's mobbed out there." Miki says as he sidles into the backstage corridor that is the Marquee Club dressing room. The narrow space is cluttered with instrument cases and jostling bits of The Cure. I suppose that must make us The Disease then, eh?

"I wouldn't bother mate," I tell Robert Smith. He's sitting next to me daubing lipstick around his gob. His hair alone takes up half the dressing room.

"I mean I used to use the old lipstick as well. But I was just leaving it on the microphone. End of the first number and I wasn't wearing any, was I. Waste of time and money."

"You mean you actually let the microphone touch your mouth?" he asks.

"You see, I told you it was me taking all the risks up there." I tell Dik, who's sitting on the other side of me, losing a hair teasing competition with Smith. "And he's killed an Arab, and all, so I bet he knows whereof he speaks."

We play a blinding set, perched on the edge of a stage that towers above a boiling pit of punks, and get two encores; but the DJ only let us play one before he bangs on a record. Luckily, the old spitting as a sign of approval is dying down a bit – but at the Marquee we are so far above the crowd most of them probably couldn't have reached us anyway. I've had enough of coming off stage covered in lung butter. Every now and then some cunt actually managed to spit right down my throat as I opened my gob to deliver a particularly venomous line.

▶▶▶▶

"So what exactly is it that Fashion are trying to do?"

I stare at the nerdy little git in the shabby overcoat. He scratches his stubble with his biro and shifts the dog-eared steno pad on his knee. I'm backstage at The Nashville Rooms, drenched in sweat, make-up smeared, an encore-punctuated second set lying dead and steaming behind me. Outside, the DJ is strafing the crowd with *Holiday In The Sun*. I stare at the graffiti directly to the left of the journalists head. This is the *NME* I remind myself. Annette has already warned me not to piss them off. Apparently, we need the publicity.

"Well," I say "let me answer your question with a question of my own. What exactly is it that *you* are trying to do?"

He looks puzzled then does something with his face that might have indicated thought.

"Um … trying to find out what it's that *you* are trying to do."he says.

"So we're both trying to find out what each other
are doing?" I ask.

"Er, yes I suppose so. Look, given the current climate of
unemployment, do you think it's socially relevant to dress the
way you do?"

"Well, I know what *I* am doing. But other than trying to
find out what I am doing, it's not clear to me what *you* are doing."
I say ignoring his question. "Or why."

I bury my face in a towel."But I'm from the *NME!*" he
blurts petulantly.

"That's nice. And I'm from Birmingham. You ever been
there? Course you haven't. I'm trying to never have to go back
there. Now if you'll excuse me I have some fans to talk to. Y'know
important people. People who forked out part of their dole to get
in tonight."

"But we're going to do an interview."

Mulligan hustles over to the little sod, his mouth already
working. So runs my hate/hate relationship with the press.

▶▶▶▶

There's a great flapping tarpaulin where the main entrance
of and part of the wall should be. As we're sound checking I
can occasionally glimpse a red dinosaur bus lumbering through
the high street gloom. The skinheads have petrol bombed the
Nashville Rooms again. Not that I care. We've got another gig
opening for The Police, who are fresh back from their second trip
to America, and their re-released single *Roxanne* is in the Top
Twenty, so we're in for a mobbed night. They're only playing the
Nashville Rooms because the gig was booked prior to their single
charting, and to their credit they've decided to go ahead and play
what for them is now a small London venue

"Have you seen the new graffiti in the ladies toilets?"
Mulligan asks.

"Disgusting." Dik says. I can tell he's more than a
little jealous.

"Look at that." I say, pointing to the stage where Andy
Summers is setting up his guitar pedal board. "How come he's got
a box full of pedals and only have one poxy flanger?"

"Because he's got a hit record and you're a git." Miki says, "Anyway, that flanger of yours is an important part of the Fàshiön sound innit."

"Flattery, thy name is Cottrell." I say.

Annette arrives, smiling and brandishing a large cocktail.

"And there's no need for you to look so sodding cheerful." I tell her, "Oh, and by the way, I want a word with you. I was sure I'd pulled at the Marquee last week. It was only when her dog of a friend came up and told me that she'd blow me even though, according to you, I was queer that the penny dropped."

"Well someone's get to look after you." Annette says. "Besides we had to get you back in the van and get going."

"I would have only been a couple of minutes." I grumble.

"Yes. So I've heard." Annette says.

"That long, eh?" says Dik. "That can of Stallion delay spray we got you for your birthday coming in handy then, is it?"

▶▶▶▶

I'd heard about the legendary Hope and Anchor. Everyone has played there, from the Pistols to Steel Pulse, Elvis Costello to Dire Straits. There are a couple of compilation albums out of bands that have played there. So it comes as something of a shock to discover this legendary gig is just part of a cellar under a pub. The load-in is through a trap door in the pavement. Whereas in times gone by they had lowered foamy tuns of beer from draft horse wagons, we now lowered Peavey 4x12 cabs and Premier bass drum cases. The room itself has a ceiling that is just fractions of an inch above my head. The brick walls and cement floor are painted fire engine red.

"It's like playing inside someone's mouth." I say.

"Well, you'd know." Annette says. "And do you ever do anything other than complain?" she asks.

"Not to you I don't. And that's all you're getting from me thank you very much all the same. And you can count yourself lucky. Here, I wonder what's in there?"

I walk over to a bricked up doorway that boasts a large sign that says "PRIVATE".

There isn't exactly a big crowd for the gig, there isn't exactly room. I sit in the tiny dressing room hole with our Roy. How the hell Steel Pulse had fit on the postage stamp-sized stage, much less into the dressing room is a mystery of Dr. Who proportions. We're listening to Manchester United on the radio, playing Liverpool in the replay of the semi-final of the FA Cup. Four days earlier United had drawn, but now here's Greenhoff scoring the decisive goal in extra-time at the Goodison Park replay.

"Goal!!" Roy and I yell, and we both jump up and whack our heads against the brick ceiling.

With a slight headache, we aim the set as instructed by Annette at the journalist from Record Mirror, a punky young lady with pierced things. We get an encore, a good review, and Mulligan later claims he shags the journalist. Even so, somehow we still get a good review!

▶▶▶▶

Lafayette Club, Wolverhampton

"The Pistols played here you know." Dik says.

"That's nice." I mumble, holding Mulligan's bass against the side of my face, trying to guess whether it's in tune by the vibrations. Talk about sodding Beethoven!

"Yeah. There's balconies up there that run the length of the club. Apparently they were chucking tables and chairs off. Aiming them at the stage, they were." Dik enthuses.

"Oh good." I say, wondering just when this quest for global stardom is going to stretch to a tune-up amp or a couple of guitar tuners that actually work. I swear the last one I had tuned my guitar to a bleedin' balalaika and occasionally picked up Radio Luxemburg.

"Good crowd out there." Miki says, swirling into the dressing room barely ahead of a wave of smoke and noise.

"Good, as in …?" Mulligan asks.

"Well, there's no fighting going on. Not any more anyway. Good bouncers, at least." Miki tugs a tiny can of Harp lager free of its plastic restraint.

"So there's a crowd then." I say. "At least."

"Shut up Luke."

"Yes boss. Here, when am I going to get a sodding tune-up amp? Ever tried tuning a bass without an amp?" I ask Annette. "Ever tried tuning a bass?" I ask Mulligan.

"Why do you think we keep you in the band?" Mulligan says and grins.

"Orright men?"

I look up as the mass of muscle known as Jimmy The Con squeezes himself in through the door.

"Hello Jimmy!" we all chorus enthusiastically, as you do if you know what's good for you whenever Jimmy is doing security.

We first met Jimmy when we played JBs in Dudley, to a mob of bikers who just stood there and stared at us, giving no indication as to whether they were going to applaud, or kill and eat us until the last note of the last song died away. They applauded, we bolted for the dressing room.

"Yow see this is how yow handle someone without there being a fight." Jimmy tells me as I'm touching up my make-up. "Yow tek this," he holds up a muscle-bound index finger, "and yow shove it right up the fucker's nose. As far as it'll goo." He chuckles. "Believe me, he'm gonna follow yow wherever yow goo. So yow lead him around a bit like and then steer him into this." He smacks his index finger up against his fist, which is the size of small table. "No trouble then." he says and grins.

He later tells us that, whereas our set has gone down well and we are cool, we are to let him know if anyone tries to fuck with us.

"Ain't no one fucks with *my* bands."

We can well believe it. Earlier that night when Annette's boyfriend Kevin walked in through the main door a punter sails over his head, perfectly vertical to land face first on the frozen car park outside. And Kevin's well over six feet tall. Some throw that Jimmy.

▶▶▶▶

Earlier in what is now, like it or not, her career Annette managed to wangle us the opening spot for Squeeze at Birmingham University union. The gig, back in what already seems the mists of time, went well. I remember Jules Holland telling the crowd they were sorry they'd taken so long coming back out for their encore, only they'd all been in the dressing room wanking off to the applause. And who can blame them?

So now, as Squeeze are also shackled to the Copeland wheel, Annette is able to persuade him to give Fàshiön the opening spot on some of the *Cool For Cats* tour. Squeeze are due to set out on a tour of bigger university and college gigs, as well as a few mid-sized concert halls. Their song *Cool For Cats* is sitting at number two in the Top Twenty.

It's now really starting to occur to me that this pop star thing might become a reality. After all, here I am on tour with gits who have hit records. My band's records are distributed by a geezer who manages The Police, who are becoming increasingly famous in both America and the jolly old UK. A chap might be forgiven for thinking that he too is in imminent danger of becoming a famous git, especially when he's surrounded by people who are forever telling him just that.

At the Squeeze gig at St Albans Town Hall we're engaged in a relatively new dressing room procedure - rehearsal. It has occurred to me that now that we're going out on our second tour, and playing a lot more gigs between tours, we're spending practically no time in rehearsal. Generally speaking, I come up with a basic structure for a new song, chords, lyrics, melody starting points and we kick those around in rehearsal until we have a new Fàshiön song.

A year or so before, we had only been playing one show every few weeks, making each one a special local event in order to build our reputation and following, the rest of the time we were in rehearsal. A lot of bands spend a year or more writing and polishing their first album. They then go on the road to promote that album, during which time they write practically no new material. Then lo, comes the day when the record company is demanding delivery of the second album. What usually happens is the hasty assembly and recording of a bunch of sub-standard material that results in a second album that all but guarantees the band are consigned to oblivion. Well not us mate, we're determined that our second album will be far superior to our first.

So now that we find ourselves in reasonably spacious dressing rooms, we set up a couple of practice amps and half of Dik's drum kit, and work on new material.

So there we are bashing away at the bare bones of a new song called *Artificial Eyes,* when Glenn Tillbrook sticks his head round the dressing room door and listens for a minute or two. When we grind to a halt he says,

"That looks like a good idea. Mind if I jam with you?"

"Er, alright then. Yeah." I say.

It should be noted that whereas I have been in a couple of bands before and have been playing guitar of one sort or another since I was sixteen, I've never really learned any of the standards that other musicians seem to use as frames of reference and starting points when jamming. Basically, I have little experience of jamming, Mulligan has none whatsoever, his musical knowledge and ability is strictly limited to Fàshiön songs. So when Tillbrook comes back armed with a black Rickenbaker twelve-string and asks us what we want to play, there is a moment's embarrassed silence before I say:

"Er, this ...," and I carry on where we've left off with *Artificial Eyes.*

I try yelling out the chords but after about ten long minutes the resultant racket is obviously going nowhere, and we grind to an embarrassed halt.

"You wanna play a blues?" Tillbrook asks.

"Er, not really." says Mulligan, who couldn't if his life depended on it.

"Sorry mate." chirps Dik.

"Thanks anyway." I say.

As he reaches the door Tillbrook turns and grins,

"Well, thanks for the try out. Sorry I didn't get the gig. You lot *are* weird, you know that."

There we are with that weird stuff again.

"I thought he was supposed to be some great songwriter guitarist." Mulligan says after Tillbrook has left.

"Oh he is, Jon, believe me, he is!" I say, "it's just that we're ... how can I put this without causing offence or denting any egos ... crap."

"You what?!"

"Well all we can play is our stuff, so as far as being a musician and like communicating with other musicians is concerned, we're crap."

"Well fuck 'em then." Dik says, scowling.

"Yeah." agrees Mulligan.

"Oh good," I say , "Fuck everybody."

But they've already gone back to strangling the life out of some reggae.

▶▶▶▶

Coatham Bowl, Redcar, sits like a concrete boil on the gentle grassy slopes that lie above the flatiron steel of the North Sea. Redcar is typical of the miserable seaside resorts I was occasionally dragged to when I was a kid. There's a main promenade full of amusement arcades and gift shops teeming with fat sea cows with corned beef legs, hordes of screaming snotty-nosed kids, and red-faced, beer bellied factory workers with knotted hankies on their heads, trousers rolled up to just below the knee. I used to feel out of place back when I was a gangling five foot eight inch, twelve-year-old, so imagine how weird it feels now, pushing through that same throng as a gangling six foot nine, black-clad punk rocker, in the company of assorted punk weirdoes and Squeeze wide boys. We get some fish and chips down our necks – the best fish and chips come from northern seaside resorts, loverly — and then it's back to burp through the soundcheck inside the Coatham Bowl.

Imagine a great dome originally designed to hold agricultural trade shows or livestock auctions and then build a ten foot high stage against one wall, and you have the gaping barn that is The Coatham Bowl. As Squeeze have a hit single, the place is sold out. I'm noticing that in the smaller towns and more remote cities the crowd tend to lump the support band together with the main act into one show which they then proceed to go barmy enjoying. Which if you ask me gives them a whole lot more common sense than those posturing, jaded buggers that swarm through the London clubs like lice in a punk's underpants.

▶▶▶▶

Back in Brum a week later, we're taking a breather with a round of coffin nails when, red-faced, Annette burst into the room.

"You'll ... never ... guess ... what ..." she gasps.

"You just can't stand being away from us a second longer?" I ask, and blow her a kiss.

"Shut up Luke." She glowers at me, then lets the corner of her mouth to twitch ever so slightly upwards.

"Yes boss. So what's up?"

"Squeeze are going to be recording *Top of The Pops* tomorrow." She says.

"Very nice for them, I'm sure. So what?"

"So if we can get ourselves down to Southampton by half-past-two tomorrow afternoon we can open in their place. For The Tubes at the Gaumont."

▶▶▶▶

We're about an hour outside of Southampton. It's a fiercely sunny day and even through my darkest night wraparound shades the glare is adding considerable pain to my hangover. I roll down the window, stick my head out, and yell,

"Oy, come on Dad. Can't you for fuck's sake turn the light down. I'm bleedin' suffering down here aren't I. Wasn't that enough for you last time? All that getting nailed up?"

"What's he doing? Luke, shut the window. It's blowing a gale back here." Annette shouts.

I turn around and repeat the gist of my rant at God. Almost immediately the sun slides behind a bank of cloud.

"Thanks Dad," I mutter.

Annette, who has probably been brought up a nice, guilt-ridden, Catholic girl, tells me to stop fucking taking the fucking Lord's name in fucking vain and enough already with being so soddding blasphemous.

"The fuck I will." I say.

The sky grows darker and darker. Daylight drains entirely from the sky. Just as Miki turns on the headlights, the first fat dollops of rain splatter onto the windscreen.

"Er, Luke." he chides.

"Oh don't be so fucking ridiculous." I say, but all the same I am beginning to feel a bit nervous.

The rain, when it comes, is nothing short of a full, biblical deluge, the kind of thing that must have had Mrs. Noah scrambling to get the washing in off the line. Miki slows to a crawl as visibility drops to practically nil. A drum solo to rival Dick at his most frantic is hammering the van roof. A few minutes later the engine sputters, dies, catches, dies again and we roll slowly to a halt. Miki grinds the starter motor but the engine is having none of it.

"Too much bleeding water in through the grill," he yells above the din on the roof, "We're stuck."

"Luke," Annette has to almost scream against the rain's roar, "You get your head out that window and apologize to God this instant."

"Fuck off. It's tipping it down out there. I'll ruin me hair. Me make-up will run."

"Luke," she commands in a voice that is not to be disobeyed, "Do it! Now!"

Face up into the downpour, snorting breath in through my nose, trying not to drown, I yell: "Alright, alright already, you old bastard, I'm sorry. I didn't mean it. Okay?"

Sitting dripping, I scowl out at the undersea world of Jacques fucking Cousteau. And lo, in the space of no more than two minutes the rain eases up, then stops altogether. The sun has the effrontery to come blazing out again. Miki turns the ignition and the truck starts right up. No problem.

"That's the trouble with these bleeding omnipotent beings." I mutter, "No sodding sense of humor!"

"What was that?" Annette snaps.

"Nothing Mom."

I ride the rest of the way to Southampton with a towel over my head, sulking.

▶▶▶▶

"Bonjour Trieste!" I yell across the stage at Mulligan. "Can you hear me?"

"Hear you?" Mulligan yells back "I can hardly bloody see you."

We've tried setting our stage positions as we normally do with me stage left and front, Mulligan far stage right and Dik center stage and back. It's obvious we'll be needing binoculars and semaphore flags to communicate during numbers. We've so many switches of style and rhythm within our songs that a bit of nodding and grimacing at each other is essential.

So we move everything closer together, but then Miki says we look like a bunch of castaways perched on a tiny traffic island center stage. So we compromise and move to somewhere in-between. This is something we'll have to get used to. Concert halls are not small clubs or rooms over pubs.

Behind us on the stage looms the mountainous stage set used by The Tubes. A gigantic portrait of a baby in a stroller, a TV screen with a nipple instead of a volume control. Great image.

Almost before I know it, a booming voice is announcing that, due to them recording Top of The Pops for the jolly old BBC, Squeeze weren't playing tonight but that the last minute stand-ins are a fantastic band all the from Birmingham ... *Fàshiøn*!!

There is a rumble of discontent, a few boos and then we're out under the heat and glare of the lights. I've never been under a lighting rig like that before either. The temperature onstage is already feels in the hundreds and I haven't even started flailing around yet. I walk up the microphone and suddenly decide to forgo all that humble, great-to-be-here bollocks.

"So, a big thank you to *Squeeze* for not being able to make it. We're *Fàshiøn*. And if you don't like it, I'll see you all out in the car park afterwards. Alright? This is called *Die In The West*."

And we're away. The set works. How well we're playing I can't honestly tell - I'm too busy doing it - but the end of our set-ending anthem *Fàshiön* brings us a reasonably thunderous encore.

The dressing room is an ocean of sweat, smeared mascara, and mile-wide grins. Annette announces that she's so proud of us that she feels like crying. So we tell her to fuck off. About twenty minutes later, the steam is starting to clear and suddenly there's a knock on the door and in walk Fey Waybill and Prairie Prince, his Robert Mitchum look-alike drummer.

"You guys," he says, "Are fuckin' weird. Great set, but fuckin' weird."

He's telling us *we're* weird. Well alright then, ta very much and I'll take that as a nice, fat compliment.

Out in the car park there's a crowd of people standing around our van.

"Go on then mouthy," Dik grins, "You're the one called 'em out for a punch-up at the start of the set."

"Yeah," Mulligan chips in, "So go on then and get stuck in. We'll be over here, watching."

Thanks a bunch. But the small crowd are more interested in getting autographs than kicking my head in. It's the first time I'd ever had an actual crowd of people wanting autographs and telling us we were better than *Squeeze* anyway (as if!). And only a liar would say that it felt anything other than fucking wonderful.

Chapter Eight
Product Perfect, JCC, Cool For Cats, and Rock Lobsters

"Bit bigger than Outlaw this then, innit." Miki eyes the mixing desk. He licks his lips and starts rolling up his sleeves.

"Here, have you seen out there?" Mulligan bustles into the control room.

"Brilliant studio." Dik adds, coming in behind him.

"This is John," Annette says, introducing us to the engineer and studio owner.

"Hello John!" we say, like a line of kids greeting Santa.

"Hello ... " John scans his clipboard, "... Fashion. Well, we've never actually recorded a pop group before."

"Oh-kay. So what have you recorded?" I ask.

A prim-looking lady with her hair in a bun comes into the control booth carrying a tea tray.

"I thought you might like a nice cup of tea before you start." She says. Her accent is every bit as posh as John's. They sound like a couple of BBC newsreaders circa 1940.

"This is my wife, Anne." John says, "Thanks awfully old gal."

Anne sets the tea tray down. John and Anne seem to have inadvertently taken a wrong turn somewhere along the road to their rose-framed cottage in the country, and ended up in Handsworth. Fate can be a right bastard sometimes. I decide John is a retired Spitfire pilot, one of The Few, and a thoroughly decent chap, still endowed with an innocence that the rest of England has long since surrendered.

"Well to answer your question chaps," John says, "we've mainly recorded classical music ensembles. The occasional choir. A brass band or two."

"Don't forget that reggae band." Anne says, "They were all

such decent chaps. I brought them a tea tray just like yours."

We sit and nibble arrowroots like the good little choirboys we've suddenly become.

"Now I can see that most of you smoke, and John enjoys a good rum-soaked, perrique-filled meersham now and again. But these reggae chaps were all smoking large herbal cigarettes. I expect they're better for you than the normal ones. Anyway, the air was quite thick with their smoke and it was the strangest thing but after I left the booth, do you know, I felt as happy as a lark."

"Yeah," I grin, "well reggae is likely to make you feel a bit happy, innit."

"Oh yes," Mulligan says, "especially if it's played well."

Having shared dressing rooms with a couple of reggae bands, I know exactly what she means. Jah rasta contact high mon!

The recording of the album takes two weeks and is our first taste of "real" recording. The twelve songs we record are *Product Perfect, Die In The West, Red Green and Gold, Burning Down, Big John, Hanoi Annoys Me, The Innocent, Citinite, Don't Touch Me, Bike Boys, Fashion, and Technofascist* .

▶▶▶▶

At the end of two weeks of sweat and swagger we're sitting around in exhausted clumps on the main studio floor.

"Well what time is he supposed to be here?" I ask Annette.

"I don't know. About two I think."

"What time is it now?" I ask.

"You've got a watch. I'm not your Mom." She says

I suddenly throw myself into Annette lap bawling "Mommy, mommy, I want my mommy!"

Annette disengages herself with a swift karate chop to the throat and everyone has a good laugh while I crawl around on all fours gasping like landed fish.

"Well I think he still works for the CIA." Mulligan announces.

"Who?" Dik wants to know.

"Who? Kevin Keegan. Who do you think?" Mulligan asks.

"Well, his Dad was acting head of the CIA when Miles was a lad." Miki adds.

"Who, Kevin Keegan?"

"Shut up Luke!"

"Hard to imagine Miles as a kid though innit." I say.

"Well I still say he's here to undermine the government. Just using this record company, band manager thing as a cover isn't he." Mulligan insists.

It isn't the first, or the last time, that this theory is posited about Miles Copeland.

"Look dopey," Dik says, "In the first place, America are our allies. Secondly, last time I looked outside we weren't exactly a Third World banana republic. Well no bananas anyway. And thirdly, the government are doing a fine job of undermining themselves, thanks all the same."

"Do you know," I tell Annette, "I think that's the most words I've ever heard him string together at one time that didn't have anything to do with tits."

Miki strolls in wreathed in B&H smoke.

"Oy, ladies. He's here."

Miles Copeland and Nick Jones, Fagin trailing Bill Sikes, make their entrance. Miles takes a quick look around at the studio he's paid for us to live in for the last couple of weeks. There are two chairs in the middle of the floor, facing gigantic studio monitors. Miles and Nick seat themselves, while Miki scurries off to the control booth. As the opening riff to *Product Perfect* thunders out, Dik, Mulligan and I slink outside. We crouch shivering round our Galoises.

"What if he doesn't like it?"

"'Course he'll like it."

"He doesn't have to release it you know."

"Well fuck him then. If he doesn't like it, he has no class."

"No taste."

"No vision."

We look at each other.

"We could be in trouble here." I say.

Back inside the studio they are over halfway through listening to the *Big John/Hanoi Annoys Me/ The Innocent* trilogy that we planned to use to close side one of the album. Dik has finished singing about John Lennon living in the Big Apple raising cows, and has moved on to ranting about being sick of hearing about the Vietnam war and is screeching: *"what about the Catholics, the Commies and the Jews, what about the fascists, the Moslems and Hindus, what about the Irish, the Poles and the Blacks, What about the Russians, the Aussies and the Japs … Hanoi annoys me, … Hanoy-oy-oy-oy-oy-"*

I'll finish it all off by singing about how nothing is our fault. The track ends. Miles stands up and walks about, looking thoughtful.

"Yeah," Miles drawls, most of his forebrain most likely occupied with shaved percentages, fine print, promotional budgets, and expected returns,

"Well it ain't great," he says. "I don't hear a single."

"Now come on Miles," grins Mulligan, "don't beat about the bush, hiding behind hyperbole, just come right out and tell us what you really think."

"But it is good," Miles continues, completely missing the sarcasm, "We can work with this. Get 'em a tour Nick."

And they leave, scurrying back to London without even listening to the tracks for side two.

▶▶▶▶

Our first tour proper is announced by Annette with a degree of cautious triumph that immediately has me suspicious.

"We've got the opening spot on the upcoming John Cooper Clarke tour." she says, smiling too much.

We all speak at once.

"Who?" Dik asks.

"What am I gonna wear?" Mulligan wants to know.

"I s'pose this means a lot more bloody driving, then." Miki says.

"Okay boss, so what's the catch?" I ask.

"Well," Annette yells into the general hubbub, "there *is* a *sort* of a catch but I want you to bear in mind that this is a national tour. A tour that includes some of the best clubs in the country."

With every word I feel the catch grow.

"And then lots of support bands have to pay to tour these days and we're guaranteed to be paid at least fifty pounds a night."

"Will you, for God's sake, just spit it out woman," Dik says.

"He says that to all the girls." Mulligan says.

"We have to provide the lighting rig ourselves." Annette says.

"Oh is that all?" I say.

"And we have to carry it and set it up and break it down each night." she adds.

▶▶▶▶

The lighting rig is ancient, all cast iron, painted camouflage green, folding tripods and old arc lamps. We find it at the Birmingham Arts Lab in Aston, and rent it for three weeks for a song. Carrying the pre-historic thing out to the truck is a nightmare glimpse of things to come, not only does each stand weigh a ton, it's also a tangle of finger-crushing, folding metal.

The first gig is in Portsmouth. The club is an upstairs venue, up steep narrow flights of wooden stairs that would have daunted the average alpine gymnast. By the time we get there the PA is already in the club and set up, which is a blessing, on account of it is, of course, massive. And it still means we'll have to lug it down though at the end of the night and load it into the PA truck.

"Looks like old JCC must be a right big head then." Dik says, peering up at the bass bins that flanked the stage.

"Perhaps he's just get a quiet voice." Annette says.

We give her the band stare and she shuts up.

The door opens and a stick insect version of Bob Dylan enters. He's wearing oversized shades and clutching two plastic carrier bags.

"Alright lads." he says, "You the band, then?"

"No mate, we're the cleaners. This is just a very trendy club." I say.

"Take no notice of him." Annette says "No one else does. Hi I'm Annette, I'm Fashion's manager."

"Pleased to meetcha darlin'. What's that like then? Managing this lot, I mean?" JCC asks. He sits down and starts rifling through one of his carrier bags.

"Oh, never a dull moment." Annette says.

"Sorry I'm a bit late. Fuckin' Mini broke down again. Don't

mind me." And he unclips his earring, dips it briefly into a small glass vial and snorts hard. He sits back and shivers.

"Eeee. But that's a bit more like it."

He digs in the bag again and pulls out a half full bottle of vodka. He chugs a couple of mouthfuls, grimaces, and then turns to the other bag.

"Right that's me ready. Now then, what the fuck am I going to read tonight?"

"You're a braver man than me Gunga Din." Dik says. "Dik Davies, drums. That lanky git smearing his face with foundation is Luke, guitar vocals. That's Mulligan, bass and synth. And that's Miki, our sound genius." Wotchas and alrights are exchanged.

"They're not as bad as you think. That lot out there. The audience." JCC says. "I get glassed every now and then, but then who doesn't, eh? It's you lot I feel sorry for having to go on first."

"Fuckin' hell, thanks." I say.

"Settle down, Lukey baby. It'll be alright." JCC says.

A second figure skulks in through the door, riding a brief silence between DJ tracks like a man in a revolving door. He's a fresh-faced bloke, who looks a bit like somebody's best friend from school, wearing jeans and a sports jacket.

"This is Martin. Me manager and driver. What you got?"

A small lump of silver paper changes hands and vanishes into one of the carrier bags.

"I have to unwind afterwards like. I get dead wound up I do. Out there I mean. Nice little smoke after, that's the ticket."

He shuffles a sheaf of papers into order and stands up.

"Stressful this can be you know. Course I only do it for the money. Fuck Art, eh lads."

"Given how much money I made this week," I tell Annette, "that must make me an artist then, right?"

"A piss artist." Dik says.

▶▶▶▶

I'm standing at the back of the student union hall at Essex University, enjoying the start of JCC's set. There's a good, solid crowd, who are anywhere from half-drunk to rat-arsed, and they are already chanting along as JCC pops the cones on the PA:

"...the pest pulled up, propped his pushbike at a pillar box, pulled his 'peen, paused at a post and pissed!"

Brilliant. How does he do it? Last night at that club in Leeds I'd watched from the stage as several patches of slam-dancing boiled over into real punch-ups, head butts, split lips and noses. There was blood in the saliva and sweat spray washing up from the pit to splash over my flanger pedal and Doc Martens. But when JCC went on the crowd were suddenly punk pussy cats, cheering and chanting and loving this beanpole, madman poet.

►►►►

We arrive at the last gig on the tour, Manchester Free Trade Hall, on a rainy afternoon. In the lobby I notice that Joy Division have been added to the bill.

"What all this about Joy Division, boss?" I ask Annette. She is sorting through boxes of tee-shirts.

"They're all small." She says.

"Well right, come to think on it they didn't look too tall in that picture in *NME* last week. But then who is, compared to moi, eh?"

"What?" she looks up. "No, the tee-shirts. There are no mediums, larges, or extra-larges. Just smalls."

"What's going on in here, then?" Mulligan asks.

"Just Annette going through her smalls." I say.

"And a fair few have done that." Dik says, and ducks as she hefts an empty lager bottle at his head.

"They're going on before Cooper Clarke." She says answering my initial question.

"No, no." Dik says ,"*We* go on before JCC."

"Fuckin' hell yeah boss." I say, "*We're* the support band. *We're* the ones humped the PA and the lighting rig on every gig. Not them."

"Definitely. Why are they even on the bill anyway?" Mulligan asks.

"Manchester's their home town. Plus, they know Cooper Clarke." Annette says.

"Listen, I don't care if their home town is fuckin' Mars and they know the Queen – we've done all the graft as support on this tour and we're going on before JCC!" Dik says.

"Where are they anyway?" I ask. "The Misery Mob."

"I don't know. Maybe they're on stage." She looks at her watch, "It is about time for sound check."

Miki bustles into the room.

"What the bleedin' hell is going on. I've got some bunch of miserable buggers in overcoats all over the stage and some cunt has elbowed me off the mixing desk."

We boil down the corridor to the stage like a runaway train, with Annette tugging on disconnected brakes. Dik is first through the door, closely followed by me and Mulligan. Miki steams up barely ahead of Annette, dragon wreathed in B&H smoke and spitting sparks. We barrel up to a tight-knit clump of overcoat-laden misery.

"Listen," Dik says, "We're the support band on this tour. We play before JCC."

"Hi," Annette says, "I'm Fashion's manager. I was wondering if we could have a quick meeting about the running order tonight."

"Fuck that." I say, "We don't need a meeting. We're the ones who've lugged the PA and lights on this tour."

"Yeah. Fàshiön go on before Copper Clarke, and that's all there is to it." Miki growls.

"Oooh. Angry Brummies." An overcoat says.

"You what?" Dik asks. "What did yow fuckin' say?"

"Angry Brummies with make-up who want us to go on before them." Another miserable git sneers.

"Why not let them go on *after* Johnny." says the one who later turns out to be their manager. "That way they can play to the cleaners."

There is a short stutter of laughter.

"The fucking cleaners?" cut short by Dik throwing himself at Joy Division's manager.

The punch-up is short and vicious and over almost as quickly as it starts. All these choreographed Hollywood fights are just so much bollocks, a real punch up is just fast chaos. Annette and Mulligan manage to drag Dik off a couple of the Joy Division mob, and after a bit of a scuffle on the stage floor, I roll off the front of the stage. At least I'll know how far down it will be if I fall off the stage later.

In the end we play first, to a half-empty hall, and then all the way back to Brum we have to listen to Annette moaning on and on about how we'd almost gotten thrown off the tour.

"What fucking tour?" I ask, "That was the last gig."

To add insult to injury, for that particular gig we get no more mention in the press beyond something like: *"spare a thought for support band Fàshiön who's short first set was all but drowned out by the noise of ring-pulls as the hall filled up."* Bollocks! We'll run into Joy Division again though, and even if it does take the lords of karma a long time to to get their act together, when we do revenge will be sweet and cold.

▶▶▶▶

By the time we learn we have the opening spot on the B52's first tour of the UK, we're taking ourselves far too seriously. The following review of our second single is from *Sounds* dated June 16, 1979 and it does nothing to lessen that tendency.

> **FASHION: 'Citinite'** (Fashion Music). *Umlauts all over the place which will be a Brummie laugh on reviewers who don't read the enclosed blurb and think they're Krautrockers. Bloody excellent single. I feel I ought to say something more aesthetic as there are so many electronic tricks involved in producing the sound that this could well be Art. On the other hand it's also pop. A glorious warm texture of burbling, purring synthi-guitar and - bass. Plus a tune and discreet vocal. Discover them on tour right now.*

The B52's tour starts at The Lyceum in London on July 8, 1979. Starting the tour in London is exactly backwards from the way most tours are set up, but I for one certainly have no problem starting the tour at the sold-out Lyceum. There has been a considerable buzz in the press for a month or so about this new B52's mob, as well as some vicious record company in-fighting for who will get to sign them. The word around the Illegal Records office is that Miles Copeland is more than a little miffed that he has failed to sign them to A&M Records, with whom he has placed both The Police and Squeeze.

The Lyceum show is our most public appearance to date and we are dressed for the occasion. Mulligan, who has flirted of late with black leather/vinyl/latex bondage-type outfits, goes back to the good old jet pilots water-cooled underwear suit, plaits his peroxide locks into mini-dreads and decorates the ends of them with tiny multi-colored feathers. Dik wears his blue, geometric pattern-decorated suit with the usual explosion of big black hair. I don a snow-white boiler suit and shave my dyed-red hair down to peach fuzz.

The Lyceum is a great barn of a place, an old Victorian theater with the stalls ripped out to make a dance floor, but it still has the Zeus, satyr, and nymph-decorated balconies, all red and gold, plush splendor, looking down on a decadent society gone not so quietly stark-staring bonkers.

Nervous would be a fair word to describe us backstage, in our very own cavernous dressing room. But then Dik is leaping across the room, drumsticks beating out tattoos on any available surface, including the top of my head, inciting us to remember just who the fuck we are and how we've gotten the fuck where we are right now on account of we're the most original band in this or any other land and that it's our duty as complete and utter bastards to go out there and piss all over the B52's firework by playing the best damn show thus far in our short but increasingly illustrious career. Well there's no arguing with that, is there?

Also, it isn't as if we're going on cold, as Leeds band Delta 5 has gone out first and rattled a few champagne glasses with their crunchy boy girl punk funk. So then out we go and give our all. We earn our encore and threaten a second before being bundled from the wings by an irate stage manager, who is evidently not used to upstart support bands threatening to steal the show. And naturally when the excellent B52's hit the stage everyone and his mom (except us of course) completely forgets about Fàshiön and goes duly apeshit over the hotshot Yanks.

Later that week, there appear two reviews of the show, one in *Sounds* and the other in *NME*. I clip and carry these reviews in a vain attempt to remind myself that the whole media circus is just a load of old bollocks. *Sounds* then, proclaims that on that night's showing Fàshiön are the true hope for the future of pop music, while the B52's are a bunch of lame, squawking ducks. Our songs and musical abilities, our stage show, vocals, and style are praised to the heavens... *"Luke stepping around the stage like a vacant giraffe crooning some of the finest vocals this side of Nat King Cole ..."*

NME, on the other hand, who's stance is to loudly disagree with anything *Sounds* says, laudsthe mighty B52's and lays waste to Fàshiön's performance, calling us shallow and contrived, ... *"these jesters probably think that theirs is the future of music."*

Well all subjective bullshit aside Nick Kunt, yes we do actually. Or is it going to be yours? What's that? You don't play an instrument? You can't sing? You haven't written any songs? You're not in a band? Well, not to worry, yow marmy fucker, your ego's obviously big enough to take you right to the top sans talent. What a load of dick!

After the first show we set out to thunder up and down the jolly old motorways, zigzagging this way and that, just one big happy family, crammed together into a rental truck with our gear. At least we're not required to provide the lighting rig or help haul the PA system. What's more we get to stay in cheap hotels and whatever bed-and-breakfast places Annette can convince we aren't really a nasty band of crazed punk rockers. One bed-and-breakfast place up on the northeast cost is run by a dotty, old dear who waltzes around ankle-deep in Pekingese dogs and has, among others, Fischer Z and Squeeze posters up on the wall of the dining room.

"All as I asks," she informed us, "is that you don't cook in the rooms. Or piss the beds."

Right you are missus, I reckon we can manage that, now could you please get this fucking Pekingese's teeth out of my ankle.

▶▶▶▶

I shepherd two punkettes toward the van and suddenly see Dik sitting in the front. Bugger. He hasn't pulled, or if he has she's with him. Maybe a fivesome? Sounds complicated. But as I pull the front door open, one of the punkettes leaps inside, drags Dik into the back of the van and pins him against his bass drum case with her face. I climb in and help the other young lady up on to my lap.

"So are we dropping these ladies off somewhere?" Annette wants to know.

"Yes." I say, "My room."

"You heard what the bloke on the desk said about visitors in the room." Annette says

But I'm already engrossed in a bit of pre-hotel snogging.

"Don't come running to me if they throw you out and you end up sleeping in the van," Annette says.

"Mmmpffff." I reply.

There's no sign of Mulligan. Annette is cursing the fact that now she'll have to round him up in the morning, and Miki is cursing the fact that he has a room to himself for once and no one to share it with. But Dik and I are busy trying to come up with a scheme to get the girls up to the room. We pull into the hotel car park.

"Right. I've just got to take care of something, alright." Dik tells the girls. "Be right back. Don't go anywhere."

He climbs out of the van and scurries round the back of the hotel. He emerges a couple of minutes later and goes into the hotel. Just as he comes back out with the old bastard from reception desk, I see a whiff of smoke curl round the corner. Nice one. He's only nipped round the back and set fire to something.

"Okay, that looks like our cue girls. Shake a leg."

We hop out of the van, run into the hotel, through the lobby, and up the stairs. I slump down on one of the beds. The room is small, very small, just two single beds with about four or

five feet between them. One punkette goes down the hall to the
loo, the other one tugs half a bottle of vodka out of her purse,
takes a swig and hands me the bottle. A few minutes later Dik
comes into the room his arms loaded with bottles.

"Stopped by the bar while old misery guts was putting that
dustbin fire out." he says, grinning immensely.

Half an hour later, I'm pinned on my back by one of the
punkettes. Dik is on the other bed with the other girl. He appears
to be snoring.

"Here. Has he passed out?" Dik's girl asks.

There's a litter of empty bottles on the floor between the
two beds. My girl starts bouncing up and down on me again. I
groan. I'm knackered. I've just played a gig, I'm half drunk, a
bit stoned, and I wouldn't have minded going to sleep myself. I
reckon Dik has the right idea.

"Well can't you wake him up?" the girl whines.

With some difficulty, I reach down and retrieve my drink
from the floor. After a soothing shot of vin very ordinaire, I noticed
that Dik has passed out with his arm sticking over the edge of the
bed, palm up. Gingerly I place my half empty (full?) glass on the
palm of his hand. There, the prefect bedside beverage holder, a
comatose drummer.

"Look, is he going to wake up or what?"

My punkette is getting a bit carried away, I feel like one of
those artificial bulls cowboys are always getting thrown off.

"Dunno ... love ... oof ... ask him ... uh ... yourself." I manage.

I worry vaguely that her friend will expect me to service
her as well now that Dik is snoring. I seriously doubt I'm up for
it. I'm just about to suggest she go down the hall and knock on
Miki's door when she says,

"Right. Well I'm going to sleep. Try and keep the fuckin'
noise down over there."

I feel a bit of a tired spasm and realize I must have come.
Thank fuck for that. Now perhaps I can get a bit of kip.

"Oh no you don't," my punkette says, "I haven't finished
with you yet."

Oh bog! As she slides down the bed intent on reviving the
dead, I reflect that fantasies realized are nowhere near as great as

you think they're going to be. I mean, two girls in a hotel room, for bog's sake. It looks as if it's going to be a long night. A second set of snores join Dik's from the other bed. Great being in a band innit, I think, and grit my teeth.

▶▶▶▶

Groggy and sore, soggy and raw, fair descriptions of how I feel at the crack of nine in the morning with Annette pounding on the door. I slit-peer a cautious eyeball and apart from a faint tangy whiff to the air there's no sign of the punky sisters. Or of our drummer for that matter. The door bursts open and in saunters Dik, looking freshly powdered and painted.

"Morning Sky." He says, "See you finally managed to scare off the gruesome twosome then."

I prop myself up on one elbow and feel about on the floor for my fags.

"Got a cigarette?" I ask him. To his credit he proffers a lighted Gaulloise in two shakes of a punk's tail.

"Ta." I pause for a bit of a wake-up cough. "You were a bit out of it last night." I finally wheeze.

"Not really, dopey. I just didn't fancy catching anything." he says

"Charming. Thanks a lot."

"Generous to a fault, that's me. If there is anything catching afoot I reckon you could get a double dose."

"It's not me feet I'm worried about." I drop my dog end into an empty wine bottle.

"I'd have it steam cleaned if I was you." he says. "Come on. Let's see if the boss will spring for breakfast. Then back home to Brum."

"Oh good. I can hardly wait."

After Annette has shown us some out of focus photograph of some bacon and eggs on a Wimpy Bar menu and told us that's what our breakfast would have looked like, if she hadn't had to pay an arm and leg to restock the hotel bar and pay for double occupancy in one of the rooms, we are herded to the van. We drive through town, which looked shut, but then that's probably Cheltenham for you, until we come to the music shop where we have to return the echo unit hired for the John Cooper Clark tour. We all file into the shop and peel off to look at instruments we can't afford. I'm eying a Les Paul gold top deluxe that has seen better days, when this kid comes from behind the counter.

"'Ere," he says in that charming local accent that makes you think he's either going to offer to mend your tractor or ask if he can marry one of your sheep, "you wanna try 'er?"

"What? Oh no thanks mate. Just looking. We'll be off in a tick anyway."

"'Ere, you want some strings, do you?"

"No thanks mate. I think we're set." I say. I squint down at him. He looks about seventeen-years-old and a bit oily.

"You're in a real band, intcha?" he asks.

"Yes." I say, "Or so I imagine."

"Funny that," he says "Real. Imagine."

Perhaps he's not as dense as I think. Either that, or perhaps I am.

"You wouldn't have to pay for 'em." he says, "These strings. They're not in sets. Old stock. We'll most likely throw 'em out, can't really sell 'em."

"Free, eh?" I say, "Well, alright let's have a look. What gauges you got?" I ask, as I follow him back to the counter.

"Dunno really. Bit of everything."

He stoops and comes up from behind the counter his arms loaded with single-string packets. They look alright and they're free, so I start stuffing them into my pockets, which as I'm wearing a leather jacket and bondage trousers are numerous.

Back at the van, I proudly spill string packets onto the death seat.

"Look at what I scored!" I announce.

My smugness is short-lived.

"Me too." Mulligan says and adds more packets to the pile.

"And me!" Dik says, cascading a veritable avalanche of guitar string packets down onto the already sizeable heap.

"Alright, where did you get the money for those?" Annette wants to know.

"Money?" I ask.

"Don't tell me you nicked them!"

"No Mom," Mulligan says, "that little git in the shop gave

them to me for free. Honest."

"Me too." I add, "said he was going to dump 'em and they were going spare.

"Told me the same thing." Dik says.

"When you lot have quite finished playing mystery shopper," Miki says, "Could we please get going."

With some difficulty, I stuff the armfuls of strings into the glove compartment and kick it shut. Miki revs us up and we're on our way. At least as far as the car park exit we are, whereupon two cars swerve out of nowhere to block our exit. Blokes are jumping out of the car, waving ID badges in the air and yelling something about Sting's band.

Miki winds the window down and finds a police ID shoved under his nose.

"This your vehicule sir?" the copper asks.

"No occifer. It's rented." Miki says.

"That's as may be, but a vehicle matching this description was involved in a bank robbery in the town center yesterday."

"Oh, right mate." I say, "That was us. We robbed the bank, then waited till the next day to make our getaway."

The copper peers past Miki.

"You." he says. "What's your name?"

"Luke Skyscraper." I answer.

"Right. Out of the vehicle. Now!" he barks, and one of his fellow plods tugs the passenger-side door open.

Plod number one returns his attention to Miki. "License and registration." he says.

Without thinking, Miki leans over and pulls at the glove compartment door. It pops open and an avalanche of guitar string packets deluges out all over the floor. For a second the plod is a little taken aback, then he asks.

"Oh dear, what have we here then?"

He most likely thinks the paper packets are full of white powder. We should be so lucky. And so rich.

"And where did you get that little lot, then?" he asks.

Simultaneously, I say "Liverpool",

Miki says "Birmingham",

Dik says "Sheffield",
Mulligan says "Manchester."
"Right." says the plod, with a nasty smile, "You're nicked."

▶▶▶▶

I sit on the fold-down bed and read the cell graffiti for
the thousandth time. It doesn't get any better, or any more
imaginative. I peer up at a grime-crusted window that frames a
tiny rectangle of grey sky

I'm waiting and wondering just how much longer it's
going to be before British justice comes barging through the door
and wallops the shit out of me. Suddenly the little spy flap in the
cell door grates open to show a plod face. Here we go, I think and
try to suck my balls back up into my body cavity.

"'Ere." The plod says, in an accent as wide as a ploughed
field, "would you like a chicken salad?"

It's some sort of trap, a euphemism for would I like a good
kicking. Is that what they call the old rubber hose in Cheltenham,
a chicken salad?

I gawp at him, mouth open.

"You can 'ave a cuppa tea an' orl if you loike." he says and
disappears.

That's it, I'm fucking cracking up, hallucinating, and I
don't mean in that nice "oooh, look at all the breasts coming out
the wallpaper" way either.

A couple of minutes later the cell door scree-screes open
and in comes this plod who looks all of nineteen-years-old. He's
wearing a uniform two sizes too big for him, and bearing a plastic
tray upon which sits a plastic plate, plastic knives and forks, a
plastic cup, and presumably a plastic chicken salad.

"There you go then." he says, setting the tray down beside
me. "Plastic cutlery." he adds knowingly.

Oh yes, presumably for the same reason they've taken my
belt away and the laces out of my Docs. We wouldn't want the
international stolen guitar string czar escaping justice by doing
himself in would we?

So I munch my salad and sip the lukewarm, grey
approximation of tea, and ten minutes later the plod returns
for the tray.

"Won't be long now, I expect" he says.

"Till what?" I blurt out, 'The rest of your mates get back from the pub and come down for a quick game of kick the punk rocker round the cell. Or until the sodium pentathol you doused that salad with kicks in and I start confessing to murdering me granny."

He looks startled."I don't know nothin' 'bout that." he says, "I meant till they lets you out."

And true to his word an hour or so later, I'm hussled out of the cell and back upstairs.

"No charges, sir." The desk sergeant says, almost pleasantly. "Mind how you go."

Miki, Annette and Mulligan are sitting on a wooden bench by the main door.

"You took your bleedin' time, lanky." Dik says.

"What did they do to you lot?" I ask.

"What?" says Annette, "Nothing. You were the only one they locked up. They took statements from us. And we've been sitting here for hours while they interviewed everyone from the music shop."

"What?!"

"They've arrested the kid from the shop." Miki says.

"This bench has been murder on my arse." Mulligan complains.

"You mean they didn't threaten any of you with a chicken salad, then?" I ask.

Annette sighs, rolls her eyes and says "Come on let's get back to Brum.

►►►►

"What would you say," Annette asks, "if I told you you're going to America. To tour."

And for a good five minutes (a band record) no one has anything to say, we're all too busy smiling our way through lust-filled invasion fantasies.

"Oh, alright then," I eventually say, "I suppose so. If we have to."

Back at Faulty Products we settle ourselves around Miles's

office while he sits himself on his lion throne and calls for our attention.

"Now I know you guys are gonna be huge in the States and I'm sure you're real excited about getting to tour over there."

Mutterings of assent.

"You'll be doing some dates with The Police and I'm hoping to hook you up with gigs with The Cramps, The Ramones. John Cale's a possible, and whoever else we can find as we go. There's one thing though that I have to warn you about."

Uh-oh.

"I know you guys are creative artists and shit like that. I know you live in the wonderful world of rock 'n' roll. But one thing I absolutely will not have is any drug use by my touring acts. You guys get busted for even one joint while you're out there, one pill, I don't care, you're all on the next banana boat back home. And I will personally see to it that you never work again. Is that clear?"

I can feel the speed that Dik, Mulligan, and I snorted in the toilet at the US Embassy is starting to wear off and through the buzz of Copeland's speech I find myself thinking that a nice hit of Moroccan or maybe even Afghani black would be just the ticket right about now. Just as soon as old lard arse finishes blithering we'd have to go and see what we can find. In the meantime a drink or three wouldn't go amiss.

"Yes Miles"

"No Miles"

"Of course Miles."

"Whatever you say Miles."

"See you later Miles."

As soon as he leaves the building, we go back into his office and start digging through the file cabinets and desk drawers, coming up with a half empty bottle of scotch and a battered video cassette that bears the legend "Deep Throat". We settle in front of the VCR, watching a cassette that has been watched so many times everyone looks bright yellow, and pass the scotch round. Annette is saying something about us being on the guest list at a Cramps show at the Music Machine that night, when Andy, the Faulty Products, van driver comes in toking on a conical spliff the size of my arm.

"It's alright," he gasps, desperately trying to carburet some air into the wreaths of smoke that seem to issue from his every orifice, "Elvis has left the fuckin' building. Who wants a go on this then?"

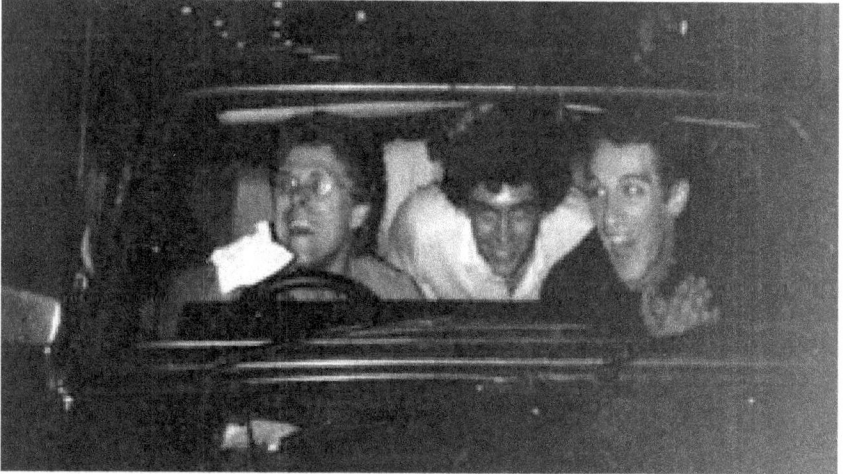

Chapter Nine
Turning Left At Greenland

As we stumble towards the baggage reclaim carousel, the terminal's air conditioning smells exotic to my poor, under-privileged Brummie nostrils.

The burgeoning Faulty Products/Illegal Records empire has only stretched to Laker Airlines flights and us bringing one bass, one guitar, and one bass drum as check-in luggage. Everything else is either secreted about our persons or will be "supplied" once we reached New York. I have visions of huge, volume-cranking, Yank amps and stacks of 4x12 cabs ... but then I often see things that aren't necessarily there.

"Look out!"

Mulligan's voice cuts through the baggage claim area like a clumsily aimed jumbo jet. Dik is standing staring at the gaping maw from whence he evidently thinks his luggage will issue. What he hasn't seen is that there is another maw at the other end of the conveyor belt, and it's from there flight 1952's luggage has starts to spew. The maw spits out a dribble of suitcases, then seems to hack, cough and hawk out Dik's bass drum case. The circular case, a giant's hatbox, bounces down the ramp, hits the carousel, slams up over the parapet and is off across the lounge headed for the automatic sliding doors before anyone can move. Scattering passengers in its wake and hotly pursued by a loudly cursing drummer, the errant drum case shoots through the exit doors and out into traffic.

"Now there's something you don't see everyday." I say and turn to snatch up my guitar case from the carousel.

I drag my suitcase and guitar out into edge of America and draw my very first lungful of raw American air, breathing deeply that fabled mixture of exhaust fumes and fried food. That I can smell food wherever I go on my travels through the States will impress me, that and the exotic smell and feel of air conditioning.

Air conditioning in London, I muse, pretty much consists of opening the window to check on the condition of the air. And nine out of ten doctors recommend closing the window immediately if you know what's good for what's left of your lungs. Well they don't call it The Smoke for nothing do they?

I sit on a bench with Miki, Mulligan and Dik while Miles and Annette play at being managers. A rusty, baby shit brown, Dodge Stagecoach pulls up at the kerb and a muscular, longhair wearing baseball cap, tee shirt, and jeans hops out of the van.

"This is Harry (pronounced hairy), "Miles introduces us, "He'll be taking care of you while you're in New York. Anything you need outside of guns and drugs, he'll get you. And maybe even the guns."

"Not exactly a limo then, is it." I say as it dawns on me that this is our ride.

"Well you ain't exactly a rock star, kid." Miles says.

"Yet." I mutter.

We climb aboard and Harry pulls us out into the first few yards of several thousand miles that lie ahead of us.

The light is just slipping from dusk into the edge of night when we come within sight of Manhattan. Suddenly all of the lip and banter dies and for probably the first and last time ever Fàshiön is collectively gob-smacked at the surreal, beautiful, sci-fi sight of Manhattan with her lights coming on. It's almost as impressive as the first time you get laid or stoned or score a goal in your dreams against Liverpool. Almost.

"Fuck me." Annette says, and for once even Dik is too stunned to react.

"Pretty cool, huh?" Miles says, smiling as if he is personally responsible for the sight.

Our coach sweeps down into the canyons, up W41st Street in a haze of exhaust fumes and deposits us outside a dilapidated hotel front, The Iroquois.

"Well this *is* nice." I say, once we're inside, eying the cage that holds a mummified-looking desk clerk.

The lighting is feeble, and everything seems to be either brown or dark orange.

"We've got a reservation." Miles tells the desk clerk.

"I've got several." Miki says, tugging a B&H out of his pocket and lighting up. Fags circulate and we all have a bit of a cough and a choke.

The lobby looks as if it's always been shabby, even back in the 1930's when it first opened. There's an air of transient defeat. Scattered here and there, on a deeply-stained carpet that defies color, are sad imitations of ugly Victorian furniture. The chairs and a single sofa are for the most part inhabited by equally sad imitations of ugly New Yorkers. Banks of stale cigar smoke drift here and there, whisping like poison gas around the orange light fittings. Behind the reception desk the mummified, bald Methuselah peers at us and then issues a gravel-throated,

"Mr. Copeland sir, good to see you again."

"Hello Joe. Got another band need rooms. Maybe a week."

Miles pumps bills onto the age-stained oak of the counter and a rattlesnake fast hand flashes through the grill to snatch them away.

"Hey, you!" the old desk clerk growls at a black bell boy, who if anything looks even older than his boss, "Get them bags up to the eleventh floor, and be quick about it ya monkey dick." He turns to simper toothless gums at the Great Wazoo, "This here's Mr. Copeland and one a-his groups."

Miles turns to us,

"Okay, you've got tonight off. But we're leaving for Boston early tomorrow. You guys best get some sleep. And remember what I said about the drug ban on this trip."

We stand and watch Miles disappear through the door.

"Sleep?" Dik says.

"Never heard of it." Miki says.

"Well I'm going to wash my hair." Annette announces.

"Me too." says Mulligan.

"What drug ban?" I ask.

Evidently, Miles regularly drops his new, incoming unknown bands at the Iroquois, and once we reach our rooms we understand why. The lobby has indeed been a fair indication of what we might expect of the place as a whole. We stalk along psycho-killer, brown-wallpapered corridors, past faceless doors only some of which are numbered. I wonder briefly what might be

going on behind these doors but then decide I really don't want
to know. Having reached a certain door, the bell boy collapses
beneath his burden, snatches at the dollar bill Miki offers him,
and is off down the corridor like a rat out of a trap.

Dik and Mulligan share a room, Miki and I share a room,
and Annette gets her own room. All of the rooms are the size of
small cupboards, and all command stunning views of the backs
of various ugly buildings. On the rooftop immediately below
my window, sickly yellow liquid bubbles in an open-topped air-
conditioning tank. But the noises of the city of New York thunder
around us and that is more than glamorous enough for these
gutter rats from Brum. The first thing I do is unpack my guitar
and retune it. Only then do I hop into the shower. As light brown
water spurts out and hits me squarely in the middle of the chest
I reflect that rarely, if ever, have I know such joy. Clean threads
and a new layer of war paint and we're more than ready to take
bites out of any apple you care to dangle in front of us.

►►►►

"It's tipping fuckical." I say.

"Whassat?" Miki slurs.

"Well, we've come three thousand odd miles –"

"There's only one odd Miles I know." Mulligan says.

"We're in New York. Admittedly, we're a bit knackered. But
we've got a night off, and where are we?" I ask.

"Is this a trick question," Annette asks and finishes off
her Becks.

"We're in the sodding bar next to the sodding hotel." I say,
shaking my head.

"Well, we went for a walk up 42nd Street earlier didn't we."
Mulligan says.

"Yeah, and what did we find?" I ask.

"Stuff we either couldn't afford or definitely didn't want."
Miki says, "Do you now someone actually offered me a –"

"Here," Dik interrupts. He arrives at the table flush-faced
as a battle messenger. "You'll never guess what?"

"Er, this is just an elaborate dream and it's time to wake
up and go to work at British Leyland?" Miki suggests.

"What? No, no, I was just talking to the barman. He owns this place. He's only from Acocks Green."

Mouths fall open.

"What in Birmingham?" Annette asks.

"Yeah. They've even got Watneys Red Barrel," Dik brandishes his pint. "Here, anyone for a game of arrows?"

"I think I'll go up to the eleventh floor now." I say getting up. "And jump off."

"What's the matter with him then? Dik asks.

"Must be his time of the month." Mulligan says, and Annette nods.

▶▶▶▶

The Rat Club, Boston

The load-in round the back of the Rat Club is a slope of Olympic ski-jump proportions. After dragging my amp and stack into the club, I come back out for air.

"It's like the inside of a fucking claustrophobic's nightmare in there." I say.

"That big, eh?" Dik says.

"Shut up. There's pipes running across the ceiling center stage. They have rags tied on them." I say.

"No excuse for concussed gigantic frontmen is there then." Miki says.

"And have you seen the PA bins?" Mulligan says.

"What are you lot moaning about now?" Annette asks, joining us at the van's back doors.

"They only have the words "Hell" stenciled on them. And they're upside down." Mulligan announces.

"Sounds like they might be on loan from an Australian hairdressers." Dik says.

Mulligan shakes his head and points at me.

"Sometimes you talk even more bollocks than he does." says, pointing to me.

"Thanks." Dik says and grins proudly.

▶▶▶▶

Halfway through *Burning Down* I get my first electric shock from the microphone.

"VZZZZZZZT!" I feel my eyeballs jerk crossed behind my eyelids.

I keep singing … *"there's nothing that feels quite the sa-ame, it's no ga-ame."*

"VZZZZZZZT!" "VZZZZZZZT!"

Actually, it's almost pleasant, this Yank hundred-and-ten volts. Not like the two-hundred-and-forty volts we have at home. I well remember that time I picked up a power sander in a leaky-roofed workshop in North London and woke up flat on my arse on the other side of my work bench. I sat at home feeling like shit for two days with sparks coming off my pubes every time a decent-looking woman came on the telly.

"Can I get a bit more vocals in the monitor and bit less electric shock from the mic please?" I ask through numb lips at the end of the song.

Burning Down? Burning Gob, more like! Although to his credit Miles does leap up and gaffer tape some lumps of foam rubber to the mike. Trouble is they not only block the electricity, they also block a good deal of the vocals, so halfway through the next song I'm forced to bite a lump out of one, chew it up and spit it at an appreciative audience.

Into the tiny dressing room we go, slathered in sweat and smeared make-up. Our first US gig and not too shabby, singed singer's gob aside. Dik is sitting on the edge of the table, sweating all over the sandwiches we're too excited to even think about eating, when our first US groupies shoe-horn their way into the dressing room. I'm crammed on the ever-present battered couch with Mulligan and Miki. Three trollops aux Etats Unis, wearing all the right gear, make-up, and hair, fill the air with a sort of routine sexual fervor and just a tinge of exhaustion and boredom that tells us they'd most likely been precisely in this room last night with last night's band.

"Hi! You guys were awesome! I'm Holly." One of them tells us.

"That's funny, our manager's got a dog called Holly." Dik says.

"Is he trying to be insulting?" Holly wants to know.

"Nah, darlin'. You'd know if he was." Miki says, smirking round wreathes of cigarette smoke.

"Oh. That's okay then." She says, and without so much as a by-your-leave, she leans over and unzips Dik's flies. She drops into a crouch and stuffs his dick into her mouth. He looks down at her bobbing head.

"That's disgusting. How can you *do* that?" he asks. "Don't stop!"

On the street outside the Rat Club a pitched battle is raging, bottles, cans and bricks arc up over the traffic from one sidewalk to the next and back. The disco opposite has just emptied out and the punks and disco kids are making it quite clear how they feel about each other.

"Disco sucks!

"Fuck you, punks!"

"Ah the gay banter! The thrust and parry of intellectual — "

Dik and I jump back into a doorway as a full can of Schlitz explodes on the pavement in front of us.

"You reckon this happens every night?" Dik asks.

"No Dik." Mulligan says dead-pan, "They knew you were in town so they organized it specially in your honor."

"Thought so." Dik says. "Still at least it got rid of old Fido, or whatever her name was."

Miki appears holding a trash can lid in front of him.

"Gear. Truck. Now." he says.

"I never get to have any fun." I whine.

"What's he whining about now?" Annette asks as we slouch up to the truck, "Look at him, face as long as a wet Monday afternoon."

"Some guys just have all the luck." Dik says, and pats his groin.

"Yeah well don't come running to us if you come down with a bad case of distemper." I say.

▶▶▶▶

Back in New York the next afternoon, we're perched in various configurations of vulture, scattered here and there on the lumpen chairs that litter the lobby of The Iroquois. Some of us are

smoking, others are extinguished. Miles comes out of the elevator
with Annette.

"Have a good shag then did you?" Dik asks.

"Sound check is in an hour." Miles says, ignoring Dik.
Then to his driver Harry, "Let's go.

"Sound check?" Miki asks.

"Yeah you know, that thing where we go one-two a lot."
Dik says helpfully. "And you twiddle with your knobs."

"Truck will be back." Miles calls over his shoulder,
"CBGB's. Patti Smith." And he's gone dragging Harry in his wake.

"Patti Smith?" Dik says. "Fuck me. Really?" he stares
at Annette.

"I was keeping it as a surprise." she says and smiles.

"Make-up, clothes, hair." Mulligan announces, and walks
off leaving his bass leaning against the elevator door. It's good to
see he's still get his priorities straight.

CBGBs ... The Ramones, Blondie, Talking Heads, New
York Dolls ... bands we'd only ever heard on record or seen in
the press. The inside of the van is quiet as a sweaty hearse. We
leave the neon bam-bam of Manhattan and thread our way into
the Bowery. The streets become darker, narrower, litter blows in
drifts, dogs limp, cars sit on blocks – we begin to feel a little
more at home.

At the end of the alley, right across from the stage door,
I can see a figure huddled on the ground. As I drew near, lugging
an amp head and my guitar case, I see he's sitting on a rotting
mattress. He has no shoes. His feet and shins are covered in
sores. Sweet fucking Jesus, the stench off this guy is so bad that
if I'd had any dinner, I would have lost it.

But inside CBGB's looks and smells a lot like my idea of
heaven, dank with stale booze, sweat and disinfectant, graffiti
sprayed across every available surface, a tiny stage facing the
length of the bar-lined room. Back out through the stage door, I
have a fag clamped firmly in my mouth to cover the stench. The
dosser has rolled over on his side and is moaning. Isn't anyone
going to do anything for this poor old sod? Well, I'm certainly not,
bastard that I am, I have a gig to play, an important gig. It's tough
shit, but they'll probably sweep him up along with all the other

bones in the morning. I can't save the homeless, I can't even save
myself, for fuck's sake.

We set up in front of Patti Smith's drums. I find myself
with the usual tiny patch of stage to run around in. We gaffer
tape everything to the floor, do a bit of one-two, one-twoing, Miki
moves a couple of drum mikes an inch to the left, and we blast
through *Die In The West*.

"How does it sound?" I ask Annette.

"What? Oh, alright I suppose."

"Alright you *suppose*? Here I am about to play New York
City for the first time. On the same bill as Patti Smith. At CBGBs,
in case you hadn't noticed, and all you can say is it sounded
alright you suppose?"

"It's very – nice. Alan."

"Thanks Mom." I say.

As to the gig, this is what a fraction of a second of it
looked like:

I'm dragging my amp off the edge of the stage – the set
has flown by and been enthusiastically received by a packed club
– when this cool blonde bird, wrapped in chic black walks up to me.

"Hi," she says, "What are you doing after the show?"

"I don't know. You with any luck." I say. Ever ready with the bon mot, that's me, oh yes.

We watch a bit of Patti Smith, then I wait until Annette is nowhere to be seen and suggest to Julie, for such is her name, that we slip out to a club or somewhere. The rest of the night is a bit of a blur – I think we're dancing at Hurrahs at some point, but at about 3AM I definitely find myself in a yellow cab on my way to Queens with Julie and some chick friend of hers we've met somewhere along the way. I'm relaxed, a bit drunk, and still buzzing a bit from a couple of lines of speed.

"You know you just did a very stupid thing." Julie's friend says.

"Oh yes?" I say, peering out the window at some bridge we're speeding over. "What's that then?"

"You just got into a cab in New York City with two women you don't know, and you have no idea where you're going."

"So?" I sniff. "If I was you I'd be a bit more worried about being in a cab with a seven foot English git you don't know."

"What is a git?" Julie asks.

"Don't worry, love. You'll find out." I say and give her my best lascivious leer.

I wake up with no idea where I am. There's someone sleeping next to me. But who? Then I remember, I'm in New York. The blonde stranger, who picked me up at CBGBs, is still a perfect stranger despite the fact that I've shagged her across the living room floor and back. I hear a dog bark and a distant siren wails. In the room's half light I can see the bedroom window slightly open. I worry vaguely about the real New York out there, not the TV version, although that's scary enough. But then I think about how far away Birmingham is, how far away from it I've managed to travel. The future is an endless road leading further and further away from Brum, dotted with milestone monuments to my growing fame. I turn over and fall happily asleep.

The next morning at breakfast she's all grins and carpet burn.

"I thought you British guys were supposed to be, you know, cold fish." she says.

"Yeah, well it depends on the bait darling doesn't it. Anyway, no matter how reserved we seem in public, all bets are off once the bedroom door's closed."

She touches her back and winces.

"Yeah, but we never made it as far as the bedroom."

"And there's exceptions to every rule, right?" I say and grin. "Here, where's your phone. I'd better check in with the powers-that-be. We're probably playing somewhere tonight or something."

Later, she comes out of the bedroom dressed in a smart business suit.

"Very nice." I say, gargling a little white wine around the first cigarette of the day.

"I work on Wall Street." she says.

We ride the subway back into downtown Manhattan. As we're getting up to leave the train, she says,

"Now when we get out of the subway, I'll walk you to 7th Avenue. You can find your way back to your hotel from there. But no public displays of affection, okay? We walk, we say goodbye. I'll call you."

"I knew you wouldn't respect me in the morning." I say. "So what, you don't want your fancy business friends to see you with a filthy punk rocker?"

"No," she says, "I er, have this boyfriend. He's Italian. He wouldn't understand."

Okaaay. Oh shit, have I just boffed some Mafioso soldier's chick?

"See you then." And I'm off down 7th Avenue (Fashion Avenue) faster than a greyhound with a bum full of chili peppers.

Back at the hotel I don't even have time for a nice shower in tepid, brown slurry before being herded into what is now considered "our" van. As we pull out onto W.44 Street I decide to investigate the glove compartment, you never know, I'm partial to a nice glove -- especially if someone has stashed drugs in it. But all I find is an almost empty bottle of antibiotics that bears the legend John Cale. We're dropped at the office and the van flits away like a baby shit brown bat headed for its car park bat cave.

"You guys have the night off *but* ..." ah, there is that "but" again, the one that's intended to stop us from having any fun damaging other people or ourselves. "... you have a radio interview tomorrow at KPIX at 2PM. So please make sure you're all at the hotel by noon."

"Yes Miles."

"And –"

"We know, we know. No drugs. No jail. No getting killed." I say.

"Yes. If you can just manage that for the next 24 hours we'd appreciate it." Annette says.

She's standing next to Miles like some surreal deputy headmistress.

"Yes Miss." I say.

Outside we go our various ways to sightsee. I hail a cab and elbow a couple of suits out of the way. See, I'm already getting the hang of this New York thing, I tell myself.

"Vere to buddsy?"

I clamber into the backseat cage.

"156 W 48th Street. Manny's Music." Fuck the Empire State building.

"Vere?"

"What do you mean ... vere?"

"Vot iss cross street?"

"I don't know." I peer at his license plate and see Vladimir Komokovski staring blurrily back at me.

"No haff English much." He says.

We still haven't moved and the meter is running.

"Or fucking geography." I mutter. "Look just drive over to W48th and drive up and down till we find it."

"Vot?"

"Jesus fucking Christ. Look, here." I tug a small tourist map out of my inside pocket and find W48th. I hold it up to the wire mesh. He glances at it for all of two seconds, and then floors it away from the kerb, throwing me back into the seat. What the fuck does it take to get a New York City taxi drivers license? Minimum requirements: an arm and a leg on each corner and the general ability to breathe in and out, it seems.

Manny's Music, the fabled walls covered with signed promo shots of everyone from Frank Sinatra to Jimi Hendrix to The Sex Pistols, is guitar heaven and hell all rolled into one. Heaven, because I can peer at, even play guitars I've only ever previously seen in magazines, at other band's gigs, or on TV shows. Hell, because I have precisely $57 in my pocket. In the world, come to that.

"Here mate," I ask a Manny's salesman, "How do I get our band's picture up on the wall?"

"What you wanna buy, kid?"

"Uh, some strings. Maybe some picks."

He chuckles, shakes his head, and walks away. I buy the strings anyway, vowing to come back with enough money to get us up there next to Jimi and Sid.

I walk back to the hotel, just enjoying moving through the bustle of Manhattan's avenues – when it comes to people trying to walk right through you as if you don't exist, they are certainly in a class of their own, at least compared to Brum's Corporation Street. Never mind Brum, I'm too excited about being on the loose, on tour, in New York, for fucks sake. I've spent far too much time being sick of home to feel homesick.

I find Dick on a bar stool in the Brummie bar next to the Iroquois lobby. He's staring morosely at a the dregs of a large gin.

"Evening darling." I say, sliding onto the stool next to him and whacking my knee against the bar. "Tough day at the office? What's for dinner?" I grimace and rub my kneecap. "I fucking hate the standardized world. You've no idea what a pain in the arse it can be being a giant."

He looks up at me, all bloodshot mascara.

"Shut up you lanky git."

"I love you too. A bottle of Becks and a double Jack on the rocks please, love." I tell the barmaid. "Why the long face?"

"I could be having more fun down the Barrel Organ. At least we'd have a gig."

"Yeah. I suppose. Still we are in New York though. I mean it's not exactly sodding Digbeth is it." I light a fag and look round the bar. An old bloke carrying a double bass case is struggling in through the door.

"Looks like they've get a band here tonight then." I note.

The old man disappears through a door into a back room.

"Thrilling." Dik says "Think they do any Pistols covers?"

"Well we can ask them. Might be a laugh."

I slug down my Jack, pick up my beer, and head for the back room.

Inside, I find a dingy lounge and an ancient drummer, keyboard player, and the stand-up bassist. They're all wearing Taho tuxes circa 1943. The audience consists of about twenty people who look as if they've also seen better days, and never mind they're wearing their best party frocks. Also there, are Sting and Stewart Copeland – who have days better than they can possibley imagine to look forward to, and more party frocks than Barbra Streisand (should they so choose!).

"Watcha lads." I say sitting down next to Sting. "What's going on?"

"It's the house band. A singer's night I think." Sting says. "This lot are all here to get up and do their party pieces."

"Sounds wonderful." I say, "Shall we do ours?"

One old dear in yards of taffeta has doddered to the mic and starts a crack-throated rendition of *When Somebody Loves You*. We listen to a few other relics strut their stuff, a couple of them quite tuneful as it goes, and then the keyboard player invites the Limey punk rockers up to see what they can do. So while Stewart hits the traps and brushes, Sting manhandles the bass, I nod at the keyboard player and lay down a decidedly dodgy Frank Sinatra impersonation in a surreal rendition of *Strangers In The Night*. I decide to add my stamp by singing every fifth note of the last chorus alternately sharp and flat.

"We'll let you know." Sting says to me afterwards.

"Not if I let you know first mate." I say, and stroll off back to the bar, where I'm treated to more scowling bloodshot mascara from Dik Davis. After five more minutes of silent sullen slurping Mulligan, Miki and Annette come to the rescue.

"What's up?" Miki asks.

"Drummer boy has got the right hump." I say.

"Well I'm going to dinner." Annette says, "With Miles."

"Okay, after you get him back to his hotel room and shag his brains out, I want you to get him to sign this blank contract." Mulligan says whipping a sheet of paper out of his flight case.

"Mulligan. It's only dinner. Business."

"Monkey business with any luck." Miki says.

"Will you lot shut up." she says, blushing like a schoolgirl.

"All we're saying," Dik says, "is think of us first."

"That's all you ever say." Annette replies, "I'm getting used to it."

She sticks her tongue out at us and sashays out of the bar.

"Well what are we going to do tonight?" Miki asks, "Strip clubs? Opium dens? Illicit scrabble parlors?"

"I've got something we can do." Mulligan says, "We could go and hang out with The Cramps if you like. I just talked to Bryan Gregory and he's in town. Staying at his roadie's place."

"They might have drugs." I say.

"Got to better than hanging around here." Dik says, swinging down off the bar stool.

We grab a cab to a dark, sleazy street somewhere on the East Side and are buzzed in through a security door that looks as if it has gone missing from Fort Knox. The Cramps roadie's name is Robert and his tiny apartment is crammed with Cramps gear and an immense collection of records. We squat on milk crate furniture beneath gigantic posters for various horror films and listen as Robert spins records, punctuating them with tales of his adolescence in Hong Kong. He truly has some of the weirdest Chinese rockabilly and surf music I've ever heard. Actually, the *only* Chinese rockabilly and surf music I've ever heard!

Later, we pick up Bryan Gregory, The Cramps goat-legged guitarist, and hit a variety of clubs, all of which seem exactly like clubs I've already been to in London. In spite of the company, I seem to be in danger of getting the Dik Davies blues, I definitely would rather have been playing a gig, no offence lads. Later, we're all jammed into the back of a cab, half-toasted on speed and booze. I turn to Robert who has the scariest, huge electric-blue eyes I've ever seen.

"You know," I say, "If I had eyes like yours, I could have been the Frank Sinatra of the blank generation.

"Instead of which," he replies coolly, "you're the blank of the Frank Sinatra generation."

At some ungodly hour of the morning Mulligan disappears with Bryan to score some more speed, Miki heads back to hotel to get some much needed sleep, and me and Dik find ourselves (don't ask how) in a dive bar somewhere near the East River. My head is buzzing like a faulty fluorescent tube. We sit at the bar and order Jack with Bud chasers. Well, we're still too new to this America place to know any better, aren't we. When the bartender gives us our drinks he also sets down two small glasses of dark green liquid and a plate with two heat lamp-curled burgers on it.

"Compliments of the house." he says.

We eye the green liquid and curly burgers. My stomach twists briefly in the grip of the departing speed high.

"That's alright, mate." Dik says, "We'll just stick with these, thanks all the same."

"I said," the barkeepers says, leaning forward and showing us his stubble and tattooed knuckles, "compliments of the house. Tonight only. Promo. Free burger and Bulgarian brandy with every drink. For everybody."

I look down the bar and see a couple of drunks nodding behind a barricade of little green glasses and burgers.

"Right." I say, firmly convinced that the drink is spiked and that I'll wake up in a gay brothel strapped face down on a buggering table.

As we chew miserably on our cardboard burgers, trying to wash away the taste with nips of green Bulgarian brandy that tastes as well as looks like hand cleaner, a middle-aged woman climbs up onto a tiny stage at the back of the room. The bartender punches the play button on a cassette player and rasping bump-and-grind music fills the bar. The woman starts a half-hearted shuffling dance, grinding her hips as if trying to free herself of a panty bunch. I realize with something akin to horror that she is a stripper.

"Oh my god." I say, "Look at that. Be more exciting if she started naked and slowly put her clothes back on."

"You mean put them back on quickly." Dik says through a mouthful of half-chewed burger, "Great being in a band innit."
▶▶▶▶

I peer round the edge of the hotel window shade and wince. Even through the fly-specked grime the sun is harsh enough to stab spikes through my eyeballs. Down on the roof opposite, the sickly yellow liquid bubbles eternally in the uncovered air conditioning tank. Around, through and beyond the cement spires and blocks, New York thunders its way through just another morning. Dik and I found our way back to The Iroquois just after sunrise. A couple of hours kip atop the bed is all I've had, nothing new there then. I need a slash, a shave, some make-up, a cigarette and a drink, in that order. From the bathroom I can hear Miki in the shower, singing *Steady Eddie Steady* in a comic falsetto – whatever would I do without that cheeky git to keep me going? And how lucky am I to be sharing my childhood dream with my best friend. The self-pity clouds lift for a moment and I actually feel excited. Later, I'm going to do an interview at KPIX radio, then I'm going to drive to our next gig, batter the crowd delirious with a mind-boggling set, and then shag some gorgeous Yank chick while inserting various drugs into my orifices. Loverly!

"BAM BAM BAM – Time to go! Let's GO!!!" the sweet piping of Annette's dulcet tones prove that you don't always need a PA system to make a godawful racket.

Mulligan calls an unofficial band meeting in the lobby and hands out water pistols. Things are looking up. I'm in a huddle with Dik, Mulligan, and Miki pouring vodka into the water pistols when Annette appears accompanied by a record company executive.

"Hello boss," I say, stalling for time, "Er, did you get your hair done? Looks ... er, nice"

That bring her up short. "Why yes Luke, I did."

"Thought so," says Mulligan, "Which one?"

"Hello Miles," Dik says to the exec. "Blimey, that diet's been working then. Lost some weight as well, eh?"

"And some height." I say. I see Mulligan now has the vodka guns safely stashed in his holdall.

"Very funny." Annette says, "This is Bob Laul. He's head of A&R for Miles here in New York."

"Poor bugger." I say. "Nice to meet you, mate."

"Oh I … I'm just killin' time, oh I I just want what's mi-hine …" Miki waltzes into the lobby now singing a falsetto version of our first b-side.

"Fuck me." Dik says, "It's Tiny Tim."

Reassured that our secret plans for the DJ at WPIX are still secret, I turn to look at this new bloke, Bob Laul. He looks alright, rugby shirt, jeans, hair and moustache, big tinted NY shades, doesn't look like too much of a style maven but then we can't all be me, can we.

"I'll be taking you over to the station." He says. "Let me know if you guys need anything."

Nice bloke.

"Anything?" I ask.

"Within reason." Bob says.

"What's that then?" Dik wants to know. "Reason, I mean."

"Nothing you'd recognize." Annette says, "Let's get going. And for god's sake behave. This is important."

We pile into the baby turd and Miki pulls away from the kerb. Bob leans forward and says,

"You wanna turn right on 5th Avenue. WPIX is on the East Side."

The East Side? Fucking hell, wasn't that The Bronx, or Brooklyn, or Harlem or something? You know, stop at a red light and they find the chassis of your car with your bones in it. I fumble the glove compartment open looking for a weapon. Maybe a knife, a can of mace, stone me, my granny always used to carry a hat pin and a box of black pepper every time she left the house in case she was attacked. Even though she weighed twenty one stone (three hundred pounds), and it would have taken a gang of four (sic) to bring her down. Thoughts of dear old Gran Turner pop and vanish as I realize we've stopped. I look up expecting to see something from Assault on Precinct 13, burned out cars on blocks, stray dog packs, hookers bawling abuse at the traffic, gangs squaring up to each other in the intersection …

"We're here." Bob says, "that's it over there."

We're on a street that if anything is posher than the one we'd been on three minutes earlier.

"I thought you said we were going to The East Side." I say.

"We are Luke. This is E42nd Street.' Bob says.

"But we only turned left and right a couple of times. I could have sodding walked. You had me all geared up to full survival mode."

Bob turns to Annette.

"What's he talking about? Is he okay?"

"Nothing. And, no not really." Annette says, "Shut up Luke and get out of the van.

"Yes, boss."

We spin round in the revolving door a few times eventually allowing ourselves to be catapulted into the building's shiny chrome and marble lobby, proclaiming undying love and spouting marriage proposals at leggy office chicks in chic business suits. On our way up in the elevator Mulligan waits until we've stopped to let a few more people on at the fifteenth floor before launching into, "Did you see that film last night. There were all these people in a lift and the cable snapped. So then--"

"You'd think they'd at least put up a "No Farting" sign." I say wrinkling my nose, then puffing out my cheeks, and exhaling loudly.

"Sometimes I think I've died, gone to Hell and been put in charge of Satan's kindergarten." Annette tells Bob.

"Yeah, and I'm driving the sodding school bus." Miki says, glowering at the No Smoking sign.

Dik turns to a middle-aged lawyer type bloke who's wearing the old, full-on suit and tie.

"Tell me," he asks with a tone of concern, "are you happy in your job?"

The lawyer type eyes him with sideways glances and clutches his briefcase a little tighter to his chest. Dik, all back-combed jet black rat's nest hair, lipstick, mascara and black leather everything, shuffles a little closer, grinning up at the guy.

"I mean, maybe you need a change. Have you ever considered doing what I do?"

The elevator doors open and Annette shoos us out into WPIX reception. Dik, Mulligan, Miki, and I bound over to a huge, black leather couch.We sit down in a row and cross our legs, one over each others. We sit bolt upright, arms folded, nodding and smiling. Annette and Bob go to talk to a rather startled-looking young lady at the reception desk.

"We're Fashion." she says, "Here for an interview. With Dan Neer."

The actual interview is a blur of vodka-filled water pistols, handcuffs, and random make-up application. At one point Mulligan and Dik handcuff me to my chair and conduct a mock interrogation. Every time I fail to answer a question correctly, vodka is squirted down my throat. It might not make great radio but I'm quite happy. I start out denying I know my own name. We manage to plug a few shows we're playing, and some we aren't. Even though our US single isn't out yet, we get Dan to play (and keep) a (signed) copy of *Steady Eddie Steady*.

After the interview he tell us that we've been the most fun band to interview since he interviewed The Beatles.

"Who?" Dik asks.

▶▶▶▶

We make a few forays out into the edges of America to play gigs on our own. All I can really remember about them (even the day after) are freeways, speeding past industrial wastelands and suburban templates, and playing anonymous, smallish clubs. I come down with a cold bad enough to necessitate a couple of bottles of chloraseptic a day so I can croak my way through a set. We stay in the world's smallest and cheapest motels. There's not enough booze, no drugs, and I don't get laid.

I do, however, remember the Hot Club, Philadelphia. As we drive through the outskirts of the city of brotherly love it becomes increasingly apparent that whereas there's no shortage of brothers (and, indeed, sisters) there does seem to be a bit of a shortage on the love front. We drive past crumbling apartment buildings, vacant lots, derelict stores, stripped cars up on bricks.

"Just like home." Dik quips, but no one is laughing much.

When emerge from some tunnel, like a turd out of sewer overflow, and into weak sunlight on rubbish-strewn streets. I peer at the map, turn it this way and that, barking out "next left" or "right here", and despite this Miki eventually finds the Hot Club.

Inside, the club is much the same toss-pot, piss-hole cave as any other, but the dressing room does hold a surprise. The first thing I see is the eternal, battered couch. I have a theory that the same couch is preceding us on tour, the mysterious couch truck arriving at each gig a couple of hours before us and offloading its festering cargo into the dressing room. But then there is also a moose head nailed to the wall.

"What the fuck is that?" Dik asks.

"That is Philadelphia Lil." I say, christening the beast. "Look she's even got lipstick." Someone has daubed the poor deceased beastie's mouth with half a tube of Revlon.

"Must have been going at a hell of speed when it hit that wall." Mulligan observes.

Dik stares at Mulligan and shakes his head. "Wit, charm, good looks, brains, they all run in his family you know." he says.

Mulligan puffs up what little chest he has and beams a smile.

"Yeah, took one look at him, and ran." Dik says.

We soundcheck, Miki doing his usual brilliant job of coaxing a clear mix out of PA speaker cones coated in mold and dried phlegm.

The club promoter, Bobby Startup, shows up, talking fifteen to the dozen, waving his arms about, and tells us that Gang of Four, who are booked to headline the two nights we're playing, have phoned and are broken down, stranded somewhere, so we'll be headlining the first night, but we aren't to worry because he'll dig up some local mob to open for us.

"Who was that?" Dik asks.

"No idea." Mulligan says.

"Talked a lot." I say.

"And fast as well." Miki says, clearly impressed.

"Wonder if he's got any spare drugs?" Dik asks.

Annette blusters into the room, red-faced, out of breath, swinging her fancy, new, aluminium flight case briefcase thing around, striding up and down the cramped dressing room, also talking fifteen, if not sixteen to the dozen.

"... so just make sure you're on top form tonight 'cos this radio DJ is from the biggest station in Philly." And without so much as glance at Philadelphia Lil she flies out of the door.

"Who was *that?*" Dik asks.

"No idea." Mulligan says.

Miki sniffs. "She said something about a first class dinner jacket and a horse at a large railway station, I think." he says.

"Yeah. That'd be it then." I say. "Here, I wonder where Gang of Four are right now. Only I think the doors have opened."

"Wonder if there'll be anyone important here tonight?" Mulligan asks.

"Like who?" Dik asks.

"The fucker that shot that." Mulligan says, "I'd like to meet him."

"Not on a dark night, I wouldn't." I say.

"I pity anyone who meets you on a dark night." Miki says. "Any of you."

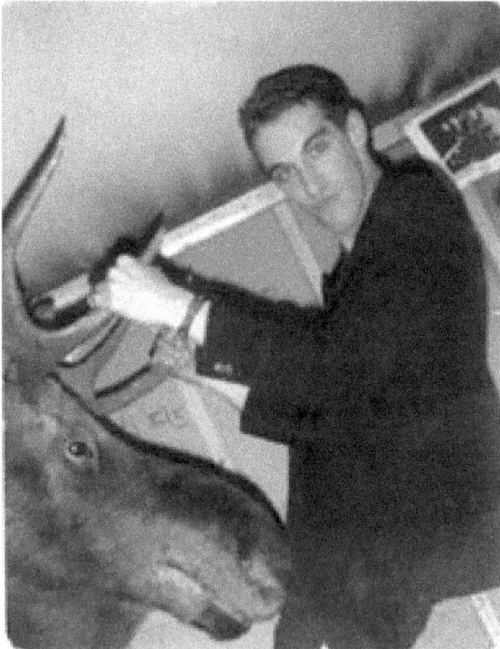

Back at The Iroquois, I'm taking a rare afternoon nap when the by now familiar thumping on the door rouses me. I sit up and blink at the sunlight streaming through the raggedy blinds. Miki is sitting on his bed pouring over a road atlas.

"That must be our wake up call, dear." I say.

"Hmmm?"

"Wonder what she wants now, the old trollop. Got any fags?"

Without looking up from the map Miki reaches over and grab his B&H from the bedside table. He tosses them in my general direction and I clamber down on all fours to retrieve them from the floor. Peering under the bed I see a cobweb-decorated chamber pot.

"Here," I say getting up digging through my pockets for a light, "you'll never guess what I just saw under the bed."

"A chamber pot. The very chamber pot used by Theodore Roosevelt on his visit to New York. Tuesday February 1, 1916." he says and sniffs.

"What?"

"He was here to visit crippled children at the New York Orthopaedic Dispensary and Hospital." Miki says. "You know, good PR, what with the Great War raging in Europe and everyone on his case about his foreign policy."

I get back down on the floor and fish the chamber pot out. I peer inside and see a small curl of fossilized turd sitting in the middle of the dusty porcelain.

"Worth a small fortune on the antique crap market if there's anything in there." Miki says absently. "Here, do you have *any* idea how fucking far it's from here to California? Road-wise, I mean."

He looks up just as I slip the fossilized turd into my jacket pocket. Well you never know, especially with Miki and his bleeding psychic powers and arcane knowledge, he might well be right. And after all, if the band do go belly and bollocks up, I might well have just secured a retirement I will never live to see.

"Oh, a long way, I imagine." I say and stub my fag out on the bedside table. "Let's go and see what the boss wants."

I'm sitting in the gloomy lobby trying to get comfortable in a horsehair-stuffed armchair that feels as if it still has the horse in it, when Annette swans in followed by Miles and his shadow,

Harry. I stare at Harry, marveling at the fact that every time I see him he looks bigger and hairier, more beard, more hair, more Harry. What does he do, wash down a couple of dozen monster-sized pizzas with a large bottle of hair restorer for breakfast every day?

"Okay! Listen up guys." Miles says in his official, megaphone, I'm-about-to-make-an-announcement-that-will-change-your-lives tone of voice.

"The Police have just hit number one back in the UK with *Message In A Bottle*. There's a two week promo tour starting in three days and you guys are opening. Get packed, Harry will drive you to the airport this afternoon."

"Don't we have any say in this?" I ask, after Miles has gone, more to break the stunned silence than anything else. "I was just starting to like it here.

"Luke." Annette says.

"Yes, I know. Shut up."

Chapter Ten
Loads of Bottle

In my head, I have been on the road for most of my life.
True, I've only been on this particular part of it for a little under
eighteen months, but that's still long enough for me to decide
that I don't need a place to live. Why have a flat and all the
associated financial burdens, when you can live in hotels and
have everything given to you? That's how I see my life from now
on, right up until I have enough dosh to start buying penthouse
suites dotted here and there about the globe. However, as there
is still a bit of a way to go on that front, I've persuaded Annette
to let me stay at her and Kevin's house, up in the spare attic
bedroom, until the *Message In A Bottle* tour is over and we go
back to the States. I haven't exactly gotten around to telling
her that Symiane's due to arrive in time for our first gig at the
Birmingham Odeon, but I'm sure that'll be alright. Have to keep
the frontman happy, right boss? And Symiane does do a rather
superb job of keeping my front happy!

As Brum is rarely more than a couple of hundred miles
away from anywhere, we're going to save hotel money by basing
ourselves in Brum. Dik will stay at his Mom and Dads place in
Acocks Green (on the off-chance he doesn't find some young
lady's bed to accommodate him.) What is it with drummers
and women? I mean, they sit at the back of the stage, you can't
actually see them most of the time, and yet they get more women
per square gig than the rest of the band put together. I have a pet
theory that it's their ability to do four different things at the same
time with their hands and feet that's attracting the girls, but then
no one's ever mistaken me for Desmond Morris, have they. And
no bad thing that. Mulligan still has his flat, as does Miki. Our
gear will travel on The Police's trucks with their road crew, so
no humping gear for us. We're free to travel to and from gigs in

a rented car. I know Miki will insist on something fast, and we'll insist on something black.

Looking at England's green and unpleasant land whizzing past the window as we drive back to Kings Norton, I realize that the old place looks different. We were only in the USA about ten days, zooming through siren-laced, artificial canyons, streaking along freeways seemingly wide enough to land several planes on side by side, blurring days into nights and out the other end, blasting eardrums and confounding senses of rhythm, but those ten days have changed me. England suddenly looks small, slow, still stylish I suppose but a little smug in it's thousand year sameness. America on the other hand is a gigantic blank canvas that positively roars at me, exhorts me to paint whatever I damn well please, and as big as I like.

▶▶▶▶

Not having quite adjusted to how much faster the rental car is compared to a van, we arrive well early at The Assembly Rooms, Derby for the first gig. We leave Miki outside dozing in the front seat of our hired Mark VI Cortina, dreaming his hundred mil an hour dreams. Inside the hall we find a kick-about going on. Across the huge polished wooden floor several roadies are being given dribbling lessons by the impossibly fit Sting. A nippy Andy Summers occasionally dashes in and out of play like a terrier stealing the ball. I light a cigarette.

"On me head Sting." I yell.

"Fuck me. It's Fashion." Sting says.

"No thanks." Dik says, "I've just had one."

"There's no way I can kick it that high, lanky." Sting says, and blasts the ball straight at me.

I sidestep neat as a pansy bullfighter and the ball rockets away into the darkness at the back of the hall. There is a clatter of things falling.

Andy Summers cups his hands around his mouth and yells, "Please mister. Can we have our ball back?"

Oh the joy! A sound check, a huge stage, a top-of-the-line PA system, and stage monitors that work. That means we can actually hear everything we're playing. Of course that does rather mean we have to play everything just right. Then again, I am planning on doing that anyway. After the sound check, Miki's wandering around with a look on his face like a dog that's just discovered it's grown another, er … tail.

"Got enough nipples to tweak back there then have you?" Dik asks him, referring to the mixing desk.

I wander about backstage, occasionally drifting out into the cavernous hall. I'm standing in the wings, looking out at the stage. Miki joins me.

"This is all a bit different then." I say.

"Tell me about it." He says, "My back certainly doesn't miss humping all that gear in and out of trucks."

"Comes of having a hit record." I say.

"Well get your finger out and have one yourself," he says, "Because I could get well-used to this."

Back in the dressing room, I sit and look around. It doesn't even vaguely resemble a toilet or a broom cupboard. I nibble a sandwich, sip some orange juice, and dab at my makeup, eying myself critically in a real dressing room mirror, light bulbs all round it there are. Our first steps as a band might well have been away from Birmingham, but they had only been as far as a bunch of small dodgy pubs and clubs. This, however, is the life, definitely. Only up, up, up from here on out.

I make a quick last minute tuning check that guitars, bass, synth, and make-up are all in tune. Miki makes sure everyone has set lists and water onstage. And then I'm ready to step out into the blaze of light that is my future.

▶▶▶▶

Birmingham Odeon.

About teatime, Miki drives us into town for our sound check. Despite the empty gin bottle now shoved down the back of Annette's Swedish designer sofa, we're all surprisingly sober. Our gear is already set-up on stage, right in front of The Police's back line. The sheer bloody luxury of not having to carry anything around except a couple of guitars is something I could very definitely get used to. A less stupid guitarist might have appreciated the situation a little more for as long as it lasted, but then I'm not a less stupid guitarist, am I. Indeed, I've already started to think of these cavernous auditoriums with stages big enough to land helicopters on as my right, not a luxury. Oh dear, not *another* sold out three thousand seater! Git!

The sound check over, we sit in the dressing room and stare at the floor.

"Well, this *is* fun." Dik says.

"Stone me, who died then?" Miki says auguring in his cloud of B&H smoke.

"Er, just a bit nervous that's all." I say.

"What? Not Luke Sky, scourge of the noo wave. Not the man who picks fights with entire auditoriums. Attacks coach loads of Milwall fans armed only with a Little Chef spoon?"

"Everyone and their Mom is out there, you know." I say.

"Bit better than the place being empty, then." Miki says, and snorts loudly, "Or would you like to go back to that?"

He is referring to the pulling power of pretty much any band you cared to name that I'd been in for the last nine years. Not that anyone could. Name any band I'd been in for the last nine years, that is. Gob nose I've managed to forget most of them.

"Here's what we need." Mulligan says, fishing a small placky bag out of his tights. "A quick snort of Billy Whizz and we'll be laughing."

"Gibbering more like." I say, but in the end I relent. I'd rather be a rampaging, drugged lunatic than go onstage armed with all the charisma of a nervous woodwork teacher.

And so it is that, in front of almost everyone we know in Brum, not to mention the national press, we bound on stage and wallop through a note perfect forty minute set ... in a little under twenty eight minutes.

"It was like the chipmunks on acid out there." Miki says, "I could barely keep up. Echo and reverb all over the wrong bits everywhere, there was."

"Sounded fucking great to me." I say from somewhere under an Odeon towel.

"Much as I hate to admit I agree with him," Annette says, "I agree with him. What happened?"

"Er, nothing." Mulligan says sheepishly.

"Sheer youthful, fucking exuberance boss." Dik says,
"I don't suppose there's any chance of a blow job is there? No?
Thought not. Anyone fancy seeing what message Sting's got in his
bottle tonight?"

"As long as it's via their dressing room." I say.

"Yeah I fancy a bit of the old foie gras and chips as well."
Mulligan says.

"Pint of gin with a pickled egg in it." Miki says.

"Since when did you start drinking cocktails?" I ask him.

▶▶▶▶

The next night we're back down to Southampton
Gaumont, and to be honest other than the fact that this time Dik
doesn't throw a wobbler and disappear, and I don't pick a fight
with the audience, all I remember is thinking that I now own this
venue – after all of two gigs there. Oh yeah, this is also the night
that Sting complains about us constantly getting encores. He
might have been joking ... but then again he might not. Anyway,
as I tell him, it isn't our fault we're brilliant and everyone loves
us, is it?

▶▶▶▶

We plough through Oxford's New Theater, leaving a
smoking pile of rubble in our wake and then on to Leicester
DeMontford Hall, another legendary gig I'd only ever seen on
bigger band's tour lists. A right big, Victorian, old bugger of
a hall it is too. The day dawns foul and grows fouler, as upon
arrival we discover that the Police's roadie's, bless them, have
left Mulligan's synthesizer case at The New Theater in Oxford.
And, further, no there isn't time to pick it up before that night's
show but they'll have it for the shows in Wales, night after
next. Mulligan is devastated, despite Annette's ranting at all
and sundry that this is disgraceful and what are her band, the
future of technopunkreggae, supposed to do with no synths, and
despite Dik and I telling Mulligan it doesn't matter because he
can't really play the synth anyway, the poor, little, dreadlocked
sod is disconsolate. So it's his turn to refuse to go on stage and
disappear. We hunt him down, and find him skulking in an office

in the bowels of the building. Somewhat incongruously, he's eating a plateful of sandwiches. He must be upset!

"There you are." I say, "At last. Gis' a sandwich."

"Fuck off."

"You can tell he's been at the poetry books again, can't you." I say to Dik.

"Look, we're sorry we said you don't know how to play. Of course you can play." Dik says.

"Yeah, come on." I add, "There'd be no Fàshiön if it wasn't for you. You put the whole idea together, the style, the look."

"You're as important a part of the sound as old mutant Julie Andrews here." Dik says. For a second Annette looks flattered, then angry, then embarrassed as she realizes Dik is talking about me.

Eventually Mulligan is persuaded not to bollocks the gig up and we don as much black leather as we can muster, have a desultory snort of what little sped is left over from the Brum gig and swagger out in front of over two thousand people. More front than Southend, more bottle than a pop factory, is all it takes for us to still get an encore. I can just picture Sting fuming in the wings.

"This one's for The Police. They'll be on a bit later." I announce and we launched into *Bike Boys*.

A while back, at The Nashville Rooms gig, Sting had laughed that he was dedicating *Can't Stand Losing You* to me as it has the line *"your brother's gonna kill me and he's six foot ten."*

I'd replied, "Well okay then, I'll dedicate *Bike Boys* to you lot then."

He probably thought I was referring to what big, bad, motorcycle boys they looked with those freebie motorbikes Yamaha had given them. As if! That night in Leicester, I have a bit of a grin off the mic after I deliver the line *"Police left standing, a road riot squad."* Number one record, be buggered, we still have our swagger, balls, and dreams.

▶▶▶▶

We're sitting in the dressing room of the Top Rank in Swansea when Annette bursts in.

"The album's out in the States!"

"That's not all that's out." I say, indicating Dik who is

standing stark bollock naked, holding his black leather trousers above his head.

"My, you look lovely tonight, boss." I say. "Almost as much of a glow to your cheeks as his."

Dik is now bent over, starting the laborious process of levering himself into his leather trousers.

►►►►

The next afternoon finds us in Cardiff – another top Rank. Stone me, I'd heard about this process whereby you are on the road so long that all cities starts to look the same, but this is ridiculous. So far I haven't succumbed to this jaded view of the world. I love driving into new cities, and find each one exciting in its own way. Blimey, I still feel a thrill staggering into service stations at two in the morning, intent on a plate of greasy fry-up. It's the fact that this is my life now, the life I've dreamed of for so long, to be on the road with a working band. That's still more important to me than wherever I happen to be. I suppose every Top Rank in the world is exactly the same inside and out, but even so that doesn't stop me being irritated all day by a nagging sense of deja vue. Until that is, a middle-aged man in a suit storms into our dressing room. He looks as if he's about to burst a blood vessel.

"Alright mate?" I ask, "Here, sit down before you fall over."

"Never mind that." He says in a broad Welsh accent that has me, Miki, Annette and Mulligan smirking with basic, low-level, English racism. "Do you know what just 'appened?"

"Sorry Dai. My crystal ball's in the pawn shop." Mulligan says.

Dik appears in the doorway. His hair is soaking wet.

"Raining out, is it?" I ask.

"No, I just had a shower." he says.

"A shower? A bloody shower is it?" says old Icy Steddford. He rounds on Annette. "It's bloody disgusting. I mean, I know about you bands and your drugs and rock and roll and such like, but this is too much. I 'ad some very important people in that board room. Some very important people."

"That's funny" I say, "'Cos I've has some very bored people in important rooms."

"Who is this tosser." Miki wants to know, "And what the fuck is he going on about?"

"Right in the middle of delicate negotiations concerning the Lord Mayor's banquest when I 'ear that the ensuite shower is bein' used. So I excuse myself and go to see who's in there. Well the bathroom door opens onto the boardroom doesn't it and when I open it I see this ... this ..."

"Drummer." I supply, ever helpful.

"And he has this young girl bent over the wash basin. Both of them stark naked and —"

"Okay, okay. Thank you, Spare us the grisly details please." Annette says. "And what have you get to say for yourself?" she ask Dik.

"Well, like I always say," Dik says, "I like to give 'em a bit of a scrub first. You never know where they've been, do you."

"Common sense that." Mulligan says.

"You'll never play 'ere again." Old Yackky Dai says.

"Oh, that's a shame." I say, "I really like it here as well. I hear the bathroom facilities are first class."

After the sound check, back in the dressing room we're variously employed in pre-gig pursuits. I'm reading The Stand by Stephen King for the umpteenth time, Dik is playing paradiddles on a Penthouse centerfold, and Mulligan is plucking his legs. Miki bursts into the room under cover of his B&H fog.

"Here, guess what?" he asks.

"Our album's gone straight to number one right around the world?" I say.

He eyes me with something akin to pity.

"Right. Since yesterday?" he asks.

"That's old lanky." Dik says, "Ever the unreasonable soddin' optimist."

"Does no harm," I sulk, "Could happen. Will do, one day."

"I found out why The Pollis are late getting here." He says. We wait.

"He's not going to tell us, is he?" Mulligan says, looking up from his shin.

"What's it worth?" Miki asks.

"Keeping your job?" Annette says.

"Job? Job? Oh yes, that's that thing you do and then get paid isn't it?" Miki says. "Never heard of it."

"You'll get paid tonight. After I do." She says.

"Me too?" I ask.

"Don't push your luck." Annette says.

"Right."

"Okay," Miki says, "They are late because they stopped at the motorway services."

"And couldn't find their way back onto the motorway?" Mulligan asks.

"Salmonella?" Dik asks.

"Kidnapped by aliens?" I venture.

"I know, Miles got them jobs at the Little Chef." Dik says.

"No, arsehole. Their rental car only went up in flames!"

We digest this in silence.

"Bloody hell! Not while they were inside it?" Annette asks.

"No. While they were in the Little Chef." Miki says.

"So we're not top of the bill tonight then?" I ask.

Everyone stares at me.

"No, Mr. Sensitivity," Annette says, "We are not."

"Car was a write-off. They had to wait for another one to pick them up." Miki says.

"Bet they checked under that one before they got in." Dik says.

"Still, you've get to laugh for fuck's sake." I say. Although no one is.

Later that night I take my by now usual photo of the sold-out crowd. One thing I love about Wales is the way the crowd shows up for both bands and have themselves a right old time. Intent on having a great night out they are, after all that damp wool and coal dust. As long as you aren't total rubbish, they give you a great reception. After I take their photo, I tell them they'd best behave because I'm writing a book about audiences and they are going to be in it. So of course they go totally barmy, an ocean of packed, heaving bodies, outstretched arms, with sporadic pockets of pogoing and slam-dancing. Enough to give anyone a messiah complex is that. We get a heartfelt encore. The Police go on half an hour later and do their usual, consummately

professional job of whipping the already warmed-up crowd into
a frenzy. But afterwards in the dressing room there is an almost
quiet air of introspection about Sting, Stewart, and Andy. That's
what being reminded of your mortality will do for you. No dressing
room antics that night, put the mockers on any party that sort
of thing will. So we leave early and drive back to Brum where I
have a hot Symiane waiting to drive all thoughts of death from my
heads, both large and small.

►►►►

What can be said about the Hammersmith Odeon? It's the
end of the tour circuit, the promised land. Lemmy and his mob
don't get any sleep until they get there and having met him, I'd be
surprised if they bothered even then. Seen from a hundred and
twenty miles down the M1 from Brum, it's the halls of Valhalla,
only with a better PA system.

We make Miki drive around the wheel of death that is
Hammersmith roundabout until we're well dizzy, just so we can
see our name up on the marquee a few times. And then we leave
the gently steaming rental car in the car park round the back
and rollick in through the stage door. We drag our tour bags
and guitar cases down narrow, beige gloss-painted brickwork
corridors, light bulbs glowing fitfully from wire mesh ceiling cages.
Anonymous doors fall behind us until, having successfully failed
to find the dressing rooms, we come to the stage. Out onto the
darkened, gaffer tape bedecked stage I go for a squint out at tiers
of dark red upholstered seats, thousands of them. Clinging to the
wedding cake-frosted walls high above the upper circle are the
posh boxes where restless ghosts shuffle fans and programmes,
rattle their jewelry, and peer through opera glasses at the three
Brummy gits down on the stage.

September 27, 1979 New Musical Express
Fashion
Hammersmith Odeon
*'Product Perfect' they called their album and the song of the same
name was in their set at the Odeon when they supported The
Police. But it worried them a little. Drummer Dik felt constrained to
tell us "This is tongue-in-cheek". The song informs every listener*

'You will buy it/you will like it/it will make your life complete/
it's divine/I'm not lyin'/it will sweep you off your feet'. That
can be taken as very arrogant and scournful. It can be taken
as distastefully in line with their chic/Art fancy-dan stuff, like
the punctuation and umlauts and accents graves on the sleeve.
Their album is ambiguous enough to be seen as cleverclogs elitist
garbage which would not be popular. But they're not like that at
all. Hence Dik's touch of self-conscious unease about appearances.

Though what they appeared to be when they rushed into
'Burning Down' was a fairly standard new wave band, brazen and
incoherent. Then they came looping out of that into their most oddly
identifiable piece to date, 'Citinite'. Bassist Mulligan switched to
synthesizer and began to crank out the distinctive rolling chords.
Luke's fattened up guitar sound wheeling along behind it, the vocal
a synthesized urban horror show. It's a strange kind of quivering
tango as seedy and jolly as a fairground hurdy-gurdy and cosmic
as a starry night sky. Pretty and silly and rich textured. Not like
anybody else at all.

That was very early on for what I was expecting to be the
highlight of their set, but in a way that made me more aware of
their material, because it wasn't a 'build-up' to anything. Some of
it was as plain as that first song, moderately enjoyable rock 'n' roll
but not over stimulating, no danger of lesions in the grey matter.
Not for long though. They'd swerve away into variants on the trio
format with synth ousting bass or Dik neglecting his snares and
cymbals to blow harp, unorthodox gaps in the sound no object.
The result was an erratic flow of personalized pleasures from the
spoofish gyrations of 'Hanoi Annoys Me', 'Product Perfect', 'Die In
The West' and 'Pale Face".

Powerful enigmas you might say – for instance, short of
asking them you could argue forever about exactly how serious
they are in their hymn to capitalist culture, which claims you're
halfway to heaven already if you can 'die in the West'.

Fashion use electronics and they use their brains. Don't
hold it against them though.

And if any of you have even a clue what that's about
- good luck. It's apparently what some of the press think. And

we don't have a song called *Pale Face*. Still, just as long as they spell our name right and put a picture of me (no matter how unflattering) at the bottom of the review. All I remember are two glorious nights of sweat, and noise, and exhilaration, and "almost better than sex", and encores, and laughter, and the realization of dreams. And the only thing better than the realization of dreams is the next day when you have new dreams to realize. So, it's back to America with a vengeance.

Chapter Eleven
Finishing Off America

The Diplomat Hotel sits on W.43rd Street like a gigantic brown hatbox. Inside, the main ballroom is approximately big enough to park a zeppelin, and no this has nothing to do with Robert Plant's ego, (the ballroom isn't that big!) The first thousand tickets for our show with The Police have sold out so quickly that another show the next night has been added. Suits me, a chance to play in front of 5,000 punters without having to travel further than a few blocks across Manhattan? Yes, please. On the other hand, unlike Miki, I'm fair chomping at the proverbial bit to get out into the heart and lites of America and see what I can find.

We meet the other support band, New York band The The, at the first afternoon's ten-minute. shared sound check. The Police want the rest of the afternoon to get things right as WPIX is broadcasting the show live and Sting wants to get his eee-oh-eee-ohs all in a row. The The are a fine upstanding bunch of ne'er do-wells from Brooklyn or The Bronx or Jersey or somewhere dangerously exotic. They can't believe we end our sound check with *Massage Up Your Booty* (our version of the UK's current number one record).

The next morning, hunched over breakfast and hangovers in a diner down the block from the Iroquois Hotel, we're picking over the bones of last night's opening show.

"You'd think that a nation that has its boot prints all over the moon, that gave us Jimi Hendrix, Hunter S. Thompson, and Scooby Doo would know how to boil water." I say.

I stare at the dodgy tea bag floating in its tepid bath.

"What's he moaning about now?" Annette asks.

"And ultimately, does it really matter?" Miki asks. He dogs his fag in a pool of bacon grease.

"What I want to know," Dik says, "Is what is it that Sting said we were?"

He's referring to something Sting said about us from the stage near the end of The Police' set.

"Which particular time?" Mulligan asks. He tweezers an eyebrow hair and screws up his face. "Fuckin' hell that hurts."

"Yeah," I say, "You never get used to it do you?"

"I still want to know what he said we were." Dik insists.

"Look it doesn't matter, does it. We know what he thinks *you* are." Annette says.

I look thoughtful. "He said something like... er, "on the guitar Andy Summers. On the drums Stewart Copeland. I would like to thank Fàshiön. Come on. Fàshiön is a flurlbledurf. And also something about The The. And the Diplomat Hotel."

"A what?" Dik asks darkly, "Is that what he said? A flurbledurf? What the fuck is that anyway? What did he tell the whole of New York we were?"

"This is just because it was on the radio, isn't it?" Annette says. "Look, you got an encore. Everyone loved you. Judging by the state of your neck, someone loved you quite a lot!"

"Flurbledurf?" I say, "It's Dutch, innit. For a band with a brilliant drummer."

I swear his little ravaged, mascaraed face lights up.

"Oh. Well that's alright then." he says.

"Hi Stewart. Andy." Annette say. Two of the annointed ones have deigned to join us for breakfast.

"How's the tea?" Andy wants to know.

I point at my cup. He peers into it.

"Oh dear," he says and sits down in the next booth.

"Great show last night, huh guys." Stewart says.

"Yeah." Mulligan says. "You lot weren't bad either."

We all smirk at that, even Andy, as half of New York is well aware of the fact that The Police had brought the house down with a brilliant show that had the mob howling for more. Something it would collectively be doing today, all the way to the record stores.

"Listen guys, I want to ask you something." Stewart says.

"Wait a minute, Sting's not fuckin' Dutch." Dik says.

"Huh?" Stewart asks, baffled.

"Sting." Dik says, "He's not Dutch, is he?"

"No Dik," Andy say, "He's from Newcastle. Which I've often thought is almost as bad."

Stewart shakes his head, as if to clear it.

"Listen, I'd like you guys to be in a movie I'm planning on shooting during the tour." he says. "Andy spent three grand on a guitar yesterday at Manny's so I had to spend more than that on something. So I went out and got me one of those Super Eight movie cameras and all the accessories."

I reflected on the approximately $17.54 I have in my wallet, concluding that it probably has something to do with the fact that our first US single is still propping up the very bottom of the Billboard Hot 1,000, if that. Yeah, that would be it. Well that was going to change. And soon.

"Is it a big part?" I ask.

"Might be a stretch." Stewart answers, and grins.

"Is Sting in it?" Mulligan asks.

"Hell no!" Stewart says, "That's the whole goddamned point. I'm sick of him playing the big movie star. Ever since Quandrophenia came out."

"We'll do it." I say "Where's the script?"

"Script?"

"Okay, what's it about?" Annette asks, "The band on tour documentary?"

"No. Nothing that corny. I want this to be a spoof thriller. Luke plays the mad scientist villain, Annette is the heroine, Mulligan and Dik are Luke's henchmen. Say, ex-patriot Russian ballet dancer, kung fu experts."

"Ex-patriot Russian ballet dancer, kung fu experts." Mulligan obliges.

"Any nudity in it?" Dik asks hopefully.

"What's going on?" Miki asks, bringing a bank of smoke back from the fag machine.

"Making a movie. Without Sting." Annette says.

"Sounds like a winner already." Miki agrees.

Out on the sidewalk the morning rush thundering across Manhattan is almost over. Still, the air claxons with horns, a steady rumble of rushing feet vibrate the ground, and the background roar is peppered with the occasional heartfelt "Oh yeah? Well, fuck you!"

"Right." Stewart yells. "For this shot, Andy I want you to come storming round the corner and run smack into Luke. Then slowly tip your head back and peer up at him. Okay?"

"There's a madness to his method." Mulligan says, and looks pleased with himself, although I'm sure no one knows why.

If I imagine our impromptu filming is going to attract the slightest attention from the good citizens of fair New York, I'm soon disappointed. Our amateur antics don't so much as raise a passing eyebrow. This is after all a city where a dead body in the middle of the sidewalk is considered a slightly inconvenient pedestrian obstruction.

The following night from the stage before *Born In The 50's* Sting holds forth:

"On the guitar Andy Summers. On the drums Stewart Copeland. I would like to thank WPIX 102. I would like to thank New York band The The and the Birmingham group Fàshiön. Hi Dik. I would like to thank you too. Thank you. Goodnight".

"There. You happy now?" I ask Dik. We're chewing our way through The Police's dressing room buffet while they are busy with their first encore.

"Why?" he asks, cheeks bulging hamster-like with illicit cold cuts.

"Well, he mentioned you by name. To the whole of New York." I say, spooning mayonnaise into my mouth from the jar. "Good, this is." I say, holding up the jar.

▶▶▶▶

My Father's Place in Roslyn on Long Island is this 1950's Americana-style, dive bar, all rectangular brickwork (I hate that circular brickwork) complete with awnings and a restaurant. Well, I say a restaurant, what there is are a load of restaurant tables set up that reach right to the edge of the stage. I eye them warily throughout the sound check.

"They're going to move those tables, aren't they?" I ask Annette. "Before we play I mean?"

"What?"

"The tables, the tables. They are going to move them so people can dance." I ask.

"What's up with old big nose now?" Dik asks.

"He doesn't like the furniture." Annette says, not looking up from the mysteries of the aluminium briefcase she has balanced on her knees.

"Yes, I know what he means," Mulligan agrees, "Those curtains will have to go as well. And have you seen the state of the carpets?"

"Yeah, I hope someone's going to have them shampooed before old Mozart here yodels his first riff." Dik says.

"And we need some potted plants." Miki says, "And a nice Welsh dresser."

"Fuck you lot." I say, "I'm off out to find a newsagents. Get this month's Better Homes."

But as it turns out my fears are well-founded because later that night we play our pulsating set of quirky dance beats to tables filled with people busily stuffing pizza down their throats and swilling cheap vino reddo. Sweat spangled and steaming, I sit in front of a backstage mirror, a towel on my head, and stare at the rivulets of mascara that snake down my ravaged features.

"Anyone got any drugs?" I ask, more out of habit (sic) than expectation.

But much to my surprise a bearded, heavy-set fellow in Bermuda shorts, Hawaiian shirt, and sports jacket appears suddenly at my elbow.

"Hi, Harry's the name."

"Nice to meet you hairy." I say, wondering why so many American's seemed to be named after their most obvious physical characteristic.

"You guys were awesome. Wanna do some blow?" he holds up a glass vial half full of white powder.

"Alright. Tell me some more about how awesome we are while you chop us out a line or five." I scan the room for stray Miles Copelands.

"Lines?" Harry say, "How quaint. Wanna try something a little different?"

"Naw mate, that's alright. I'm not into needles, am I."

"No needles. Make a fist." He says.

"You wanna fight me for a line of blow? Blimey mate, I ain't that desperate, am I."

"No, no, no fight. Make a fist. I'll show you." he says.

I hold out my fist and he reaches out and turns it sideways. Then he uncorks the vial and tips a pile of coke into the hollow between my thumb and index finger.

"Now hold that up in front of your mouth and open wide." he says.

Like a lamb to the kebab shop, I do as he bids me, wondering vaguely what the fuck is going on. But before I manage any more wondering, he leans forward and blows the pile of coke straight into my mouth, down my lungs, and directly into my blood stream, do not pass Go, do not collect your wits, Houston we have escape velocity, bon fucking voyage, heart rate maxed, eyes bulging, coughing and choking, mouth engaged, brain disconnected, I'm up out of my seat, the top of my head missing, a verbal machine gun hail of nonsense spraying before me, I head straight for a gaggle of loitering groupies.

►►►►

Massively hungover, I manage to stagger off my cot and kick the empty bourbon bottle across the floor. I spend the next couple of minutes hopping up and down, clutching my bruised foot, cursing Bog and my luck. I slit-peer a pickled onion eyeball through the blinds at the magnesium flare morning. At least my diatribe against the old Supreme Bean hasn't made it rain this time. Behind me Miki swerves his Thunderbird through the guardrail and out onto the canyon of wakefulness. Before his eyes are open he's groped a B&H into his mouth and lit up. He sits cross-legged, puffing away beneath his mushroom cloud like a fallen Lewis Carrol character.

"Morning Blithers." He croaks. Then, after a bit of a rattling lung-clear, adds, "Night on the tiles."

It's not clear to me whether this is a question or a statement. Miki's smoke reaches me and I begin to feel both queasy and my own need for a cigarette. I wave vaguely at my guitar and the empty bourbon bottle lying next to it on the floor on the other side of the room.

"Ah Dithers. Top of the morning to you. As you can see, his lordship did indeed grow a trifle frisky after dinner last night."

"Better that, than growing a frisky trifle." Miki says, "Did you call down to the village to have the duck pond dragged?"

"Yes. But all they turned up was the treasure of the Sierra Madre. Oh, and Lord Lucan's Sopwith."

"What, again?"

"Hmmm."

Blithers and Dithers are personae Miki and I occasionally assume. They are gentlemen's gentlemen, butlers, to competitively dissolute masters. These two servants, under the guise of the height of decorum and sang froid, regularly dabble in extra mural adventures. Their pursuit of a few extra guineas might have them traversing the Steppes in Fortnum and Mason peddle cars, or indulging in a spot of international gorilla smuggling. Dithers collection of medieval refrigerator door handles is unrivalled anywhere outside the British Museum. Our conversations often baffle us, much less anyone unfortunate enough to overhear them, then again that is also often the case when we're just being ourselves. I am never quite sure whether I'm Blithers or Dithers and, despite claims to the contrary, neither is Miki.

By the time Mulligan turns up, I have my face on, if not my entire head.

"Wrote an opus last night." I say.

"Not another one," Mulligan groans, "What's this one about?"

"It's about here. It's calls the Use of A."

"The what of what?" Miki asks.

"Y'know, the US of A. It's a damning commentary on this latest Roman empire."

"Bet it's a damning racket." Miki says, nudging the empty bourbon bottle with the toe of his cowboy boot.

"Here, where did you get those?" I ask, noticing his new boots for the first time.

"Won them in a poker game last night, didn't I." Miki says.

"Yeah right. The fuck you did." Mulligan says and snorts.

"Did you win new panties to go with them as well, Mr. Blockhead?" I ask.

"That's for me to know and you to not." Miki says. He raises his eyebrows.

The door opens and a punky girl staggers into the room. She has her arm around and is barely supporting an extremely haggard Dik Davies.

"Mornin' ladies." he croaks, with all the energy of the recently deceased.

"What the hell happened to you?" Mulligan asks.

"He took some drugs last night," the girl says, "Don't know exactly what they were. Damn, I didn't think he was gonna make it back."

"Yeah ... spent the night ... er, off somewhere ..." Dik says and slides sideways onto one of the beds.

As we pack our stuff Dik begins to snore. Miki loads him into the truck along with the last of the gear, and we head north into upper New York State.

Now you might think Upper State New York would be a forest of skyscrapers, I know I did, but as it turns out the further north we go, the more dangerously rural it becomes. Farmland gives way to great empty stretches of what to my Brummie eye looks uncannily like wilderness. It's one thing to get a bit lost on the Yorkshire Moors or scoot around bits of North Wales trying to read indecipherable road signs, but this is a far cry from anywhere that might have a petrol station or a chip shop. You could die out here and who the fuck would ever know? I'm convinced they have bears and wolves just itching to strip you to the bones. Not to mention hillbillies. Do they even have hillbillies this far north? (I thought I told you not to mention hillbillies!) I mean, if I'm getting this nervous in Upper State New York, how the hell am I going to handle following the wagon train trails across the Great Plains or navigating the Florida swamplands.

"Breaker, breaker!" Miki suddenly barks.

"What's up with old Mario Andretti?" Mulligan wants to know.

"Who's he talking to?" Annette asks.

Miki turns fully round in his seat, completely ignoring the

highway flashing at seventy mph beneath our bottoms, and holds up a microphone from which trails a long, black, curly lead.

"We got one of these here CB radios, innit." he says. "I only just found it." He waves at the dashboard.

"That's nice," I say, "What does it do?"

He sighs and shoots me a look of disgust. "We can talk to truckers. Find out where the cops are. Speed traps. What the traffic's like up ahead."

"Think they can tell us where we are?" I ask, eying the complete lack of buildings flashing past the window.

"I know exactly where we are." Miki announces.

"Yes, I know," I say sinking down in my seat for a bit of a doze. "Directly above the center of the earth."

"That's a big ten-four on that one, big boy."

▶▶▶▶

When we finally find the club, I take one look at it and decide Miles is definitely taking the piss this time.

"He's gone too far." I tell Annette.

"No, this is the place." Annette says.

"No, not Miki. Miles. He's taking the piss." I say.

"That's the biggest log cabin I ever saw." A somewhat recovered Dik croaks, crawling from his nest of coats to peer bleary-eyed through the window.

"The kraken wakes." Miki says.

"But it's a log cabin, not a sodding club." Mulligan insists. "Fair does, it is a *big* log cabin but it's still a sodding log cabin."

"This is worse than that fucking scout hut in Wales you booked us." I say.

"Shut up Luke." Annette says automatically.

So I sit in the van and sulk a bit, refusing to help unload the gear, and not even Annette's threats of no per deums will shift me.

"You can keep your fuckin' pocket money!" I say, "Sick of being treated like a fuckin' kid."

"Not as sick as we're of you behaving like one." she says.

"Bollocks!"

But eventually curiosity gets the better of me and I go

in through the side entrance, where I spy a steep, dark flight of stairs. I'm suddenly very glad I've had my sulk and not had to hump gear up that lot. Dik appears at the top of the stairs and tap dances down like an epileptic Fred Astaire.

"Hello," he says, "Dressing room's up there on the left. Can't miss it. Watch out for the leopard."

"Leopard? Yeah, right." He shoulders past me and hares off toward the van.

Up the wooden hill to Gigfordshire I go, into the dressing room, and of course the first thing I see is a fully grown leopard in the corner of the room. It stares at me with look-at-that-huge-kitty-snack eyes, and licks its chops. I note with relief that it's chained to the wall and try not to think about dry rot or termites. I set my guitar case and bag as far away from Tiddles as possible, trying to act nonchalant beneath the smirking gazes of Miki, Mulligan, and Annette.

"Bet Luke gets some pussy tonight." Miki says.

"Har fucking har. Just as long as pussy doesn't get any Luke tonight."

Stewart Copeland heralds the arrival of The Police.

"Hi guys. Holy cow! How cool is that?" and he points his Super Eight camera at the leopard.

A grizzly, bear-sized bloke sporting a grizzly beard, bib overalls, and work boots clumps into the room and without so much as a howdy throws a whole raw chicken at the leopard.

"Had her since she was two-days-old," he says. "She's still got her teeth" – the crunching of deceased chicken attests to such – "but we had her de-clawed."

"So at least I won't get disfigured while she's ripping my head off." I say.

"Huh? Oh, no. Chain's good and strong. You'll be okay."

Sarcasm and Americans, oil and water, you have to love it, an endless source of amusement. It's somewhat ironic that I haven't even tried irony out on them yet.

We have a couple of hours to kill after sound checks and, as we're stuck in the middle of nowhere, Stewart announces that he wants to work on some more of the film. This is Sting's cue to go off and have a sulk over a Nabakov novel.

"Now for this scene," Stewart says, eying the leopard, "I want Luke on the phone. Demanding the ransom for Annette."

"They'd be more likely to pay me to keep her." I mutter.

"You still got that leopard skin shirt?" Stewart asks me.

"Yeah. But if you seriously think for one second that I'm gonna –"

"Aw, c'mon! It'll look *great!* With the leopard in the background and all." Stewart says.

Gob, he is so bloody enthusiastic all the time, how can I refuse? So when I hit the stage that night my leopard skin shirt is already soaked through with sweat before I've even played a note. Still, at least it isn't soaked through with my blood

Just to show how unimpressed it is with monkey antics, the leopard falls asleep during the after gig party. Around 2AM Annette herds us back to the van. We have an overnight drive to Boston. The club's owners, the lumberjack brothers – who claim to have built the place from scratch themselves, by hand, and who am I to doubt it – come out to say goodbye. They're effusive about what a great night it has been.

"Great show tonight." One of them tells me.

"Er, yeah thanks. Great … er, leopard, man." I say.

"Yeah. Y'know she really took a shine to you." One or other of them tells me.

"Really?"

"Yup. Must have been that shirt a yours."

"Er, yeah," I say, "Must have been."

"That and the fact she's in heat right now."

For the next week or so my nightmares are unprintable.

▶▶▶▶

"Well then I'm not fucking doing the fucking gig!" Lux Interior is screaming from the stage of the Paradise Theater in Boston. He sounds not unlike a thee-year-old denied his favorite red truck.

"Lux, Lux, calm down." The Cramps soundman cooes, "You don't need the goddamn reverb, man. You have a great voice. Screw the fuckin' reverb!"

"Screw the reverb? Screw the *reverb?* Ya fuckin' retard.

The Cramps *are* fuckin' reverb. My voice ... is fuckin' reverb. Now you get me reverb or you find another fuckin' band! Go screw up their sound!"

And he storms off the stage in a mincing flash of black, skintight, vinyl trousers. We're back in Boston and this time several notches above the delights of the Rat Club, at least in terms of venue size and ranking. Although as I lounge at the back of the auditorium, stretched out across three uncomfortable red velvet upholstered seats, I find myself thinking of the Rat Club almost fondly. Okay so I'd electrocuted myself on the mic a few times, I'd suffered a mild concussion (that no one noticed) after slamming my head repeatedly into the steel ducts that decorated the low-slung stage ceiling, there has been that bottle fight outside the club, and drummer-slurping groupies in the phone box-sized dressing room, but we'd played a great set and connected with the audience at some deeply superficial level, like a good shag with a stranger you'll never see again.

There are four bands on the bill at the Paradise: The Police, John Cale, The Cramps, and us. The Paradise is a huge Victorian barn of a place, a bit like some of the bigger London gigs – The Music Machine, Astoria, Rainbow – and is the sort of hall we're only going to find in the bigger, older America cities. We do our ten minute soundcheck and barely have time to go and find something to eat before the doors open. Apparently Boston's nickname is bean town, and I for one am looking forward to a good old plate of beans on toast! Of course, naïve fool that I am, I end up having to settle for a chili dog and not so much as a dab of brown sauce. So, I off-mic burp my way through a good set, and we earn and are allowed to play an encore.

Afterwards, in the dressing room, I find myself talking to John Cale. He's sitting in the sink in the corner of the room, wearing a white boiler suit and an aluminium hard hat. As I towel myself down, we chat about the trend of corporate world domination and the impending collapse of so-called civilization. All good cheery stuff.

"Hey, I'm ready you know." Cale says, tapping the top of his hard hat, "For when the whole stinking deck of cards collapses I mean."

He still has a Welsh edge to his accent and unaccountably I feel a twinge of homesickness. What the hell is that about? I'd only ever been to Wales four times that I can remember: a drug run to north Wales, the gig in a scout hut, and the two Top Rank gigs with The Police.

The Cramps get their lifeblood reverb working and play a great show, Bryan Gregory spitting E major chords and lighted cigarettes into the front rows with equal fervor, wiggling behind his polka-dot Gibson flying V. Nick Knox impassively hammers solid psychobilly beats at the back. Ivy twists and shimmies sex-kitten, cat prowl moves, while boyfriend Lux writhes around spilling his reverb-drenched guts. The Police initially nail everyone in their seats but then have them up and dancing in the aisles by the fourth number. But as the night progresses, that knife blade of homesickness slides itself deeper between my ribs and before I know it I'm pining for the sodding fjords. What a pouff! I moodily decline an after-gig club foray and have Miki drop me off at the hotel. I seem to think that sitting alone in a soulless hotel room all night will cheer me right the fuck up. What a plonker! Don't worry this isn't going to become the poor, alienated me on the road part of the story – well, actually it is, but we can at least try and still have a bit of a laugh at my expense, can't we?

So I'm looking down on downtown Boston from my tenth floor room hotel room and for about fully half a second think about pulling the window open and jumping out. Dickhead! Then I think about giant pizza-shaped guitarist spread all over the pavement. Prat! And then I actually reach out and tug at the window handle just so I can tell myself later that the only reason I haven't jumped is because the window is locked and sealed. Total bollocks! In the end, I go downstairs to the bar for a drink or seven and then phone Symiane back in Bordeaux, whining on about how lonely and misunderstood I am. Total spaz! She listens for a while and then tells me I am a stupid English cunt and that she has to go. Just before she hangs up I hear a bloke cough in the background. So that's all very reassuring, and of course when Annette finds out I've run up a huge phone bill, she calls me all the pillocks under the sun, warns me not to do it again, and docks me three days money. All in all, not exactly another glittering night of drugs and sex-drenched, rock and roll glamour then.

▶▶▶▶

The club in Chicago is called Motherhumpers.

"Very tasteful, I'm sure." Miki says, pointing at the neon sign over the club entrance. The sign occasionally flashes the purple words "Moth hump" at an uncaring world. The inside of the club is a gloomy, low-ceilinged pit of horrors, filled with the stench of stale sweat, beer, cigarette smoke, over-pogoed air, and the usual semi-sticky floor. What's different about this place is that as we walk into the club, Motherhumpers extends like some insane lab rat labyrinth run wild.

"Shouldn't we be roped together or something," I say, as we make our way deeper into the club.

"Oh, believe me, we are." Annette says wearily.

"Just down here," says the promoter, our guide, "and then over there ... left ... watch out for those steps."

A few seconds later there is a crash and muffled cursing somewhere behind me. "And ... here you go."

We troup into a fairly large room where we find the eternal battered couch, a scattering of metal, folding chairs, and a sagging table littered with curling sandwiches and unidentifiable cold cuts. By far the most important furnishings are two huge plastic dustbins which prove to be filled with ice and longneck, green bottles of beer.

"Did anyone leave a trail of breadcrumbs?" Dik asks.

"Got a map, mate?" Mulligan asks the promoter.

"What? Oh, yeah," he says, "no, don't worry. These guys here will take good care of you. Only we had a little trouble recently. Someone got kinda knifed a few weeks back."

Kinda knifed? Four goons in tuxedos loom out of the shadows, looking like they could easily take care of anything you might throw at them.

"These guys will be sticking pretty close. One each for the band. Oh, and the lady as well. So, don't worry about a thing." the promoter says.

"Here, what about me then?" Miki asks.

The promoter eyes Miki.

"I kinda doubt anyone's gonna bother you, man."

"You can borrow mine if you like." I tell Miki and smile at my minder, "Long as I'm not using him that is."

I walk up to Boris, as I'd already dubbed him. He is almost as tall as me but about three times wider.

"Don't worry mate," I say, "None of us are anywhere near as queer as we look. Anyway," I say, turning to fish another beer out of the bin, "even if we were, you ain't my type, are you."

I glance at him as I suck beer. Nothing, not a flicker of expression. Definitely gay, I decide.

"And don't worry," the promoter says (again with the don't worry) "they're armed."

Boris pats at his inside jacket pocket absently.

"Can I at least go to the toilet on me own?" Mulligan asks.

"Wouldn't advise it." The promoter says, "Have a great show." And he's gone.

"Good news anyway," Annette says staring at the door. "I was talking to Dwayne, the promoter there, when we first got here and they've sold so many tickets he's added a second night.

"Oh good. Now I feel twice as safe." I say.

"Ticket sales?" Miki says, "you sure they've got the right band name up outside?"

"Very funny. Least I get a minder." I say.

"Armed minders are for pouffs." Miki say, and skulks off to look for the mixing desk.

Just as Annette has promised, when we hit the stage for our first set, the club is packed to the gills. The beat pounds, the giant yodels, the guitar soars and crunches, the bass thunders, the synth meeps and whooshes, and the electricity flows back and forth in great jagged arcs between band and audience. It's one of those nights, what you might call a jolly good show. After the first set we sit slumped in the Turkish bath heat of the dressing room, grinning, panting, and swigging.

"Here," I say, "You could have knocked me down with a budgie but wasn't that old Rod Steward and Anita wossaname down the front?"

"No, I didn't see them." Mulligan say, "But I did see Goldie Hawn and Twiggy."

"Sylvester Stallone and Rock Hudson." Dik says.

"Blimey, we must be more famouser than what I thought, innit?" I say.

"Celebrity look-alikes. Agency party." Annette says, barely suppressing her giggles.

"What?!"

"Oh for fuck's sake." Mulligan says

"Is nothing bleedin' sacred?" Dik asks.

"Apparently not." I mutter.

"America, eh kids," Miki says, "Ya gotta love it."

"Do I?" I ask. "Very well, have it washed and brought to my tent after the show."

►►►►

And so into Detroit, Murder Capital of the USA that month, according to the radio. I'm more worryied by the fact that it's also known as Motorcity. I'd just spent the last twenty-odd years getting away from a city where they made cars, so excuse me for being more than a little nervous about driving into its American cousin. And sure enough, as soon as I see the clump of skyscrapers on the horizon that denotes downtown, what little countryside there is to be glimpsed out the window runs whimpering for concrete cover. We speed past rank upon rank of eyeless, dilapidated clapboard houses, vacant lots dotted here and there like missing teeth. Occasional banks of smoke drift like wraiths across the freeway. Even though I can't actually see the cars up on blocks, the dirty-faced children, the hard-faced young men gathered on street corners, or smell the defeat in the air, I knows it's there. You can nail up a gigantic painting of a skyscraper here and there, dress some Vauxhall Viva up with fake fins, lace the air with the smell of McDonalds, do whatever you want to infer the American Dream is alive and well and within everyone's grasp, but the truth is that gloom and grime and despair are the true currency here. I slump further down in my seat and start singing *The Passenger*, an incantation, an imprecation, please, by St Iggy, let me not become trapped here,

let the web not close around my face, let the strength to escape
not drain from my limbs. Once the show is over, let me escape.
Miki glances over at me.

"You alright sunshine?" he asks, magicking a lighted B&H
out of his poacket and into his mouth.

"Not really, no." I shiver. He hands me the cigarette.

"Cheer up," he says, "Things could be worse."

So later on, I cheer up, and sure enough things are worse.

Having strutted and yodeled on the splintered boards of
Iggy's youth at Bookie's Club 870, I drink too much and wake up
in a dodgy motel on my own again. I might be anywhere. I could
be anyone. But I'm not, so after a couple of hours of exhausted
sleep in the front of the van, I find myself blinking blear-eyed at
some river we're flashing over high atop a suspension bridge.

"Ohio river." Miki sniffs, as if the dark brown water below
us is sewage.

"How nice for it." I say, "What's for breakfast?"

"After the soundcheck." Annette says, "There will be-"

"Food in the dressing room!" we all yell.

We come down off the bridge and are soon barreling along
streets that look as if they've been frozen in time since the 1950's,
all square, redbrick buildings, dour off-white governmental
buildings, if it wasn't for the cars I wouldn't have know what
year it was. I begin to feel queasy, I don't know it at the time but
I'm allergic to middle-America. I think it's all those American TV
shows set in the suburbs, the McCarthy witch hunts, and the
like. I prefer the crumbling streets of the ghetto, at least through
the window of a moving vehicle I do.

"Where are we going?" I ask.

"That is indeed the question." Miki says.

"Marietta College," Annette supplies, "Entrance is on
Fifth Street."

I pull the tattered map book from the door compartment
and flick to Ohio, find the downtown maps and discover there is
no map of Marietta.

"Make a left at the next light." I say confidently.

Miki slews through a right turn and pulls into a
gas station.

"I know, I know." I say, "Go and ask them how to get to the sodding college."

Ban Johnson Fieldhouse is a great barn of a venue, sitting under the lead weight of the Ohio skies. It's not until I walk in and see the eagle banner and the name on the front of one of the drum kits that I realize who else is on the bill.

"Oh my sainted aunt." I turn to Annette, "You mean The sodding Ramones are on the bill?"

"I thought I'd keep it as a surprise." she says.

I turn to my equally gobsmacked band mates.

"Suck my stump." Dik declares, eloquent as ever.

"Well I'll go to the foot of our stairs." Mulligan adds.

I spent a whole Summer listening to the Ramones first album. Once we're set up, we go to meet our befringed heroes. It's weird, we shake hands, do the old how's it going pleased to meet you, and then sit on opposite sides of the dressing room until it's time to play, grinning almost shyly at each other, like a bunch of fucking punk rock choirboys. I reckon I'll just concentrate on playing a blinding show ... with The Ramones maybe watching from the wings. Oh shit.

Everything is going like a dream, the crowd love us, we've built them to a reasonable lather, and half way into our forty minutes it's time for *Steady Eddie Steady*. I'm glued to the mic, pouring every sweaty ounce of passion I can into my exhortation to the teenage Eddie to hold the gun steady, when I catch movement in the corner of my eye. Movement toward me. I squint round, still asking Eddie if this is the only way out, and see Steward Copeland running toward me holding open a huge pair of stepladders. He plonks these down either side of me and then Sting scampers out, scurries up the ladder and empties a huge box of cornflakes all over me as I'm crooning about having found Eddie out on a railroad track with his eyes burned-out speeded black. A great whoop of laughter wells out of the audience as I'm singing the final *gun barrel trembling, gun barrel trembling in your mouth*, I'm ankle-deep in and decorated with Kellogs. I vow to wreak terrible revenge not only on Stewart, Sting and Andy but also their household pets and children for five generations hence, and while I'm at it, their lawns!

In the dressing room I'm inconsolable, Dik and Mulligan are furious, and Annette and Miki are doing altogether more smirking than is probably good for them. I storm into The Police's dressing room, snatch up a full bottle of Bacardi, wave it at the room and announce to the startled Polizei:

"I'll fuckin' have you lot. You just see if I don't!"

I stomp back to our dressing room. Before my arse hits the legendary battered couch the bottle of Bacardi is already half empty. And no, it's definitely not half-sodding-full, okay.

Chapter Twelve
There's more America?

Atlanta looks great from a distance, a sci-fi downtown shimmering in the Georgia heat. We step off the plane, play baggage roulette and finally win a guitar, a bass, and a kick drum case, have a bit of a wash and brush up in the gents, and step out through whooshing doors into a furnace.

Ten sweaty minutes later, the good old baby shitmobile hoves into view. It's hard to see the original shades of brown as the surface appears to have several layers of desert baked onto it. The windscreen is cracked and one of the wing mirrors is missing. It looks as if it has weathered a meteorite storm which, given Miki's driving, is a distinct possibility. The van doesn't so much pull up at the kerb as slouch to an exhausted halt. I watch as Miki struggles to open the driver side door and as he exits in wreathes of fag smoke and slams the door I fully expected bits to drop off the van, and quite possibly him. He looks as if he hasn't slept or shaved for a couple of days. Kevin, Annette's boyfriend, unfolds himself from the passenger side and stands blinking and swaying beside the van. He also looks as if he hadn't slept or shaved for a couple of days (but then to be fair, he does have a beard).

"You two look as if you haven't slept or shaved for a couple of days." I say.

"Hello darlin', I'm home," Miki says, "Did you miss me?"

"Why did you go somewhere? I thought it had been a bit quiet the last forty eight hours." I say.

Kevin looks at a huge new digital watch and frowns.

"Eighteen hours and forty three minutes," he says. "One thousand two huundred and eighty miles. Door to door. Didn't stop once."

"Unless you count that whorehouse in Kentucky." Miki says.

Kevin grins nervously at Annette. "He's kidding." he says.

"Let's get going then," she says, "We have to be at the gig in an hour and I'm not sure where it is."

"No thanks boss, I couldn't possibly manage so much as a cup of coffee." Miki says, "I had one before we left Minneapolis, day before yesterday."

"Good." She says, "Now get yourselves loaded and let's get going."

"Always willing to get loaded." I say and, smiling beatifically, I throw my guitar into the back and clamber up into the death seat.

"Here," I say, squirming around, "Someone's bony arse has rearranged all the lumps in me seat."

Miki surreptitiously slides me a tiny, round mirror with a couple of lines of white powder on it. I pull out a handkerchief and under cover of snot, hoover up the whiz. His red-rimmed, pupil-less eyes ablaze, he stomps on the gas pedal and swings us out into traffic.

"Have a nice flight did you?" he asks. "Not too tired or anything are you?"

"Well yes, actually, I am a bit knackered. The boss wouldn't let me drink so I didn't get any sleep on the plane. And we were out on the town after the TV show till right up until we left for the airport."

"You poor bastard." Miki says, and sniffs.

"Thanks," I say sniffing for the same reason, "I knew you'd understand."

As the traffic does it's best to get out of Miki's way, my thoughts drift back to new York and what little I can remember about the TV show we'd done the night before. We'd been given a chance to appear on Moogy Klingman's NY cable TV show. We know we're going to be miming one of our songs, so blow and bourbon aplenty are in evidence before the interview. Mulligan and Dik have put their heads together and come up with a half-brained scheme to throw themselves backwards out of their chairs right after Moogy asks his first question. So we hop around mouthing *Product Perfect* for a while, which is great fun and then it's over to Moogy's corner of the studio for a bit of a chat. There

are four chairs set on a dais that looks a bit high off the ground
to me, certainly where throwing yourself backwards is concerned.
Still that is Los Dos Gits problemo, not mine. I have a small stack
of polystyrene cups and a bottle of bourbon to marshall. We take
our seats and while Moogy sings our collective praises into a
camera, I pour everyone a good stiff shot of Jack.

"Cheers then," I say.

"Here's to good old Jack Spaniels." Dik says.

"Bottoms up!" Mulligan says, and he and Dik down their
drinks and promptly throw themselves backwards off the dais,
evidently unable to wait for Moogy's first question. Poor Moogy
looks momentarily at a loss and then, consummate pro that he is,
catches himself and continues.

"Well while the rhythm section are powdering their
noses, let's turn to Luke Sky, lead vocalist and guitar player with
England's latest techno-punk trio Fashion. Luke, welcome. How
are you finding America so far?"

I raise my cup swig down a huge gulp of bourbon and then
calmly bite a chunk of polystyrene out of it. I chew thoughtfully,
then swallow and grin.

"Well Boogie, for a start, I have to say I just *love* this
American food!"

There is an explosion of laughter from the studio crew
and then I hear a clattering and grumbling as Mulligan and Dik
claw their way back up onto the dais and reseat themselves.
Dik is grinning, Mulligan however is grimacing with pain. He
hurt his back in the fall and it will take about a week for him to
stop whining about it. If it had been me, I'd have milked it for at
least two weeks. The slug of bourbon proves to be the straw that
drowned the camel because I don't remember much about the
rest of the show. At some point I think I put my heavily-studded
black leather wrist band over my crotch and proclaim myself to be
Fey Waybill as Quy Lude from The Tubes and sing a quick verse
of White Dopes On Punk, but it's hard to be sure.

The gig before the TV show in NY had been some barn of
theater in Minneapolis with The Police and Moon Martin. (Why
are we now traveling backwards in time? Well, why not – it's
my fucking story, I'll tell it however I sodding well choose). That

particular gig hadn't started well. We were about twenty miles outside the city, running late when a thunderstorm of insane proportions split the sky. This is no photographer's flash lightning like we get in Brum, no pale flickerings behind impenetrable banks of storm clouds. This sucker slashes the sky with huge, jagged arcs of lightning. I see a distant truck, high on a flyover get spiked and swerve off the road. I'm glad I'm wearing my rubber-soled Docs. Just to be on the safe side I slide a few condoms out of my inside pocket, unwrap them, blew them up, knot them, and set about making a rubber insulation cushion.

"What the fuck are you doing?" Miki asks, somehow managing to keep both his attention and the truck on the road. The wind has picked up and the first few splats of rain hit the windscreen.

"Can't be too careful. That truck up ahead just got struck by lightning." I say.

"It did not!" he snorts.

"How would you know? You're driving, so you most likely had your eyes closed." I say.

He blows me a spittle-laced raspberry. Suddenly the road dips and we fly through a pool of rainwater. As the rain stair-rods down like a lunatic, these dips in the road are increasingly filled with ever deeper pools of water.

"Weee!" I say, "This is like one of those roller coasters. Like the ones they have at Alton Towers. You know, with the water."

"Yes." Miki says, accelerating toward a small lake that lies across the road, "I had noticed."

We are slap in the middle of the water when the engine floods, coughs politely once, and dies. We coast to a halt. Rain thrums on the roof. I crack my door and see a black rushing current surge a few inches below my Docs. Annette's head surfaces from the back.

"What's goin' on? Why have we stopped?" she asks, shaking sleep from her ghostly face.

"Stalled." Miki says. "Flooded engine. Water deeper than I thought."

Annette squints at her watch.

"How far are we from downtown Minneapolis?" she asks.

I reach for the map.

"'Bout half an hour." Miki says. Rain beats on the roof like nervous fingers.

"We should be there now. We've already missed sound check." Annette says.

"We don't get this engine going and we'll miss the gig." I whine. "And-"

"I know, I know," Miki yells, "You've all get your fuckin' stage clothes and make-up on and it's raining outside." He wrestles the door open and with a parting, "Buncha fuckin' prima donna poufftas!" he disappears into the downpour.

"What's he going to do?" Annette asks. "Maybe you should go and help him."

"What?! But I've get me gear on." I say.

"Sorry boss," Mulligan says pointing to the roof and cupping his hand to his ear, "What did you say?"

"I'd love to lend a hand." Dik says, "But I'm using them both at the moment." He holds his hands up and then rummages around in the back-combed rat's nest of his hair.

Suddenly the truck lurches forward slightly, then rolls backwards, then forwards a little further, then backwards. This continues in increasing increments for several minutes until finally the forward movement continues and Miki bursts in through the driver's side door and lunges for the hand brake (which, being American, is a pedal on the floor). Looking like a half-drowned castaway, Miki surrenders to a massive bout of coughing that temporarily drowns out the thunder on the roof. He shakes himself like a dog, draws in few ragged breaths, and reaches for his cigarettes.

"Need to sit and let the carb dry out for a few minutes and then with a bit of luck we'll be on our way." He says.

We are all stunned by what he has done, and not a little ashamed of ourselves.

"That was fuckin' heroic" Dik says.

"What would we do without this man?" Mulligan enthuses.

"I taught him everything he knows, you know." I say.

"Shut up Luke."

"Yes boss." Then out the corner of my mouth, "Fuckin' hell man, how did you do that?"

Miki takes a nonchalant drag on his B&H. "Standard Incredible Hulk stuff, innit." he says, "Anyway, the show must go on and all that old bollocks. If I left it up to you bunch of big girls' blouses we'd still be stalled on the way to your first gig."

Five minutes or so later, holding our breaths, silently exhorting the great god Edwin Shirley, Miki grinds the starter motor and after what feels like an eternity, the engine coughs, farts, and starts up. Miki guns us into Minneapolis, scything heedlessly across lanes of traffic, and swerves to a halt outside the theater stage door. We bundle out, guitar and bass in hand, drum sticks at the ready, in through the door, along a couple of corridors, lunge at a door labeled "Stage – Authorized Personnel Only" and stumble out into the glare of stage lights. A voice that sounds scarily like Miles Copeland's booms: "All the way from England ... and about to make a statement you won't forget ... FASHION!"

By this time Dik is seated behind someone's drums, and Mulligan and I have both found someone's amps.

"Good evening," I say, suave as Noel Coward, "Terribly, terribly nice to be here this evening."

And we launch ourselves at *Sodium Pentathol Negative.* As we've had no chance to set-up synths, we play a stripped-down set that seems to be over almost as soon as it starts. The next thing I remember clearly, after being briefly blinded, deafened, and drenched in sweat is sitting in a dressing room, panting. A few people orbit the eternal bettered couch. One of them eventually resolves himself as Miles Copeland. So that *had* been his voice. What's he doing in Minneapolis on a Wednesday night?

"Great show!" he says, "Real venom. You'd have gotten an encore if you hadn't been late."

"Wouldn't have been here at all if it wasn't for him." I say, pointing to Miki. "Pushed us and the truck, single-handed out of a flood."

"Really?" Miles says, and for a second I think I catch a look of real appreciation in his eyes. Not exactly legendary for kindness to roadies, or anyone else he thinks of as "lackeys", is

Miles. Comes of being from a family with far too much power and money, if you ask me.

"This here is Moon Martin." Miles says, as a speccy-faced, blond child of the heartland in an Elvis Costello suit materializes at his side. "Moon was good enough to go on first when you guys were late."

"Thanks very much mate." I say grinning. But my gratitude is tinged with the knowledge that Miles and the promoter had written us of as no-shows, and just put the second act on first. I mean what are they going to do, put The Police on first? Not with *Message In A Bottle* set to follow *Roxanne* into the charts they aren't.

A couple of grinning, midwest punks (they have neat rows of safety pins in the lapels of their jackets) approach. They nervously clutch and waggle backstage passes, pens and programs.

"You guys were awesome!" they say.

"Thanks chaps," I say as Moon Martin hands me their programs so I can add my scrawled autograph to his, "Where you from?"

"Right here in town. We never miss a show."

"Jolly good." I say, "and thanks for coming to see us. Without you guys we'd still be wanking around in a rehearsal room in Brum somewhere. Appreciate it. Here Annette, how about getting these guys a tee shirt or something."

Respect for our fans is something we'd learned from the likes of The Clash and what better mentors could you have than them. Once, I went to Barbs in Brum to see The Clash. The ad in the paper had said one pound fifty to get in. The bloke on the door was charging two quid, which those of us that could, were paying as we grumbled in through the doors. It was hard to go to too many gigs when you lived on the dole. But then there was an announcement from the stage that The Clash had heard about the price hike and were refusing to play until everyone in the packed club has been given fifty pence back. So we all poured back out and queued for our refund. I slipped out twice and was thus able to afford two drinks that glorious night. Always respect anyone who shows even the least passing interest in your band.

So, having gone backwards to come forwards, we're pulling up outside the Agora Ballroom in downtown Atlanta. There is the marquee proclaiming "tonight ... The Police and Fashoon."

"Before anyone gets their knickers in a twist, I'll get it changed right away." Annette promises.

"Yeah, ought to be three o's and an umlaut, innit." Miki says,

Inside the gloomy theater, I breathe the same fabled dust and disinfectant stench that has assailed Elvis's nostrils, Costello that is, and assaulted Johnny and Sid's delicate mucous membranes. I'm standing on the edge of the stage, staring out at the darkened mouth of the auditorium and trying to remember the last time I'd breathed air that didn't stink of sweat, stale booze, smoke, feet, disinfectant, cheap motels, air conditioning, the inside of the van, or the blue exhaust freeway haze. I determine that the very next chance I got to set foot in Nature I was going to take a few dirty great big breaths of the old fresh air. Just to see what it's like. I suddenly realize Dik and Mulligan are standing in front of me grinning up at my face. I'm smiling softly at my thoughts.

"Look at soppy," Dik says.

"Do you think he's in love?" Mulligan asks. "Again."

"Looks more like he's got indigestion." Dik suggests.

"Or constipation."

"Why don't you two tarts piss off. There's not a minute's privacy round here." And I stalk off to find the dressing room.

Then The Police come and sneer through our dressing room door. "Hello ... Fashoon!"

"Fuck off Polis!"

There is a sound check, during which we render our version of "Poxanne", me squawking out *ever since I knew ya, Ya smells just like manure!* It's hard to tell exactly why we're drifting apart, The Polis and poor old Fashoon. True, they have their second single set to assault the US charts, whereas we have a box of tee shirts and about thirty-five dollars each. They have their single on the radio in every town we hit, whereas we're lucky to have a radio in the van that works (and when it does I never hear it play any of our records). Still, I persist in my dreams of planetary conquest. It's only a matter of time, all we've to do is hang in there, keep playing, keep moving, and eventually the pieces will all fall into place, the stars will align, the ducks will all be parallel, and Bog in heaven will smile on these, his favored sons, namely Fashion.

Consequently, I pour every ounce of passion, sweat, soul, and stagecraft I can muster into our performance. Sting grudgingly says "well done lads", and I'm blinded enough by the sweat in my eyes to believe him.

Then something rare happens; I meet someone I actually have a conversation with. I mean, a real conversation, with brains engaged, about music and society and the role of the artist in the latter stages of the twentieth century, sort of thing. His name is Stephen Lester, an Atlanta musician, and I will run into him again, in Brum of all places.

Anyway, all this conversational exertion, pleasant and unexpected as it is, soon has me reverting to git-on-tour mode. I meet this doe-eyed, curvy beauty called Alicia backstage. I give her the old lonely guy on the road routine all the while laying the old English accent on with a trowel and throwing in the odd bit of wacky British humour, just so I don't come over as some sort of depressed Joy Division overcoat. In the middle of the chat some friends of hers approach and ask me if I'd mind carrying a baggy of blow for them as they are worried the cops might do a bit of the old stop and search on their way home. I umm and ahh a bit, and eventually agree to do it, if we can all meet up back at Alicia's place later. She doesn't seem to think this is a bad idea so I tuck the baggy into a slit I long ago cut into the lining of one of my Docs for this very purpose, and off they go. The innocent little lambs. Ten minutes later, I'm sitting in Alicia's car, some monstrous thing with fins, a bottle of bourbon jammed between my thighs, listening to extreme volume Clash as we slice through the peachy Georgia night. I take a look at Alicia's tits, then her profile splashed with oncoming headlights, then her tits again, and take a slug of bourbon.

"Y'all shouldn't be doin' that y'know." she yells, her southern accent simultaneously making me weak in the knees and stiff in the trousers.

"What? Drinking booze in the car?"

"No. I mean takin' a chance on not bein' able to, ah, rise to the occasion. If y'all catch my drift."

Catch her drift? I'll catch her drift alright, right along with her knickers.

"Naw, don't worry darlin'. Just makes it last longer, dunnit." I say.

She has one of those places that are right out of a druggie's wet dream. It's a big, woodframed house with a gigantic deck that is liberally sprinkled with hammocks, swing seats, beanbags, oversize cushions, red lanterns flickering with artificial candlelight, the cicadas are sawing away like old Ludwig's Van's ninth, and the air is scented with equal parts peach blossom, reefer smoke, pheromones, and a dab of Brummie sweat. I lay in her arms while David Byrne warbles something about wanting someone to take him to the river. I feel like a sodding Arab in paradise about to crack his first virgin. Suddenly there are a couple of other people with us. They are asking about a baggy of blow and I hear myself calmly deny that they had ever given it to me, after all I'm in the public eye and prone to police search on account of being a foot too tall and sporting red hair and makeup. They look disappointed but what are they going to tell a six foot nine, dangerous-looking, half-drunk Limey? Eventually they go away. At some point Alicia goes to powder her bottom or whatever, and I dig the baggy out and have a look. It's only about four lines anyway – almost more trouble than it was worth to nick it. Still, I reckon it might come in handy about anytime soon. She comes back wearing a Chinese silk dressing gown that's only fastened up the front in the loosest possible sense of the word. Bobbing on an ocean of foreplay, we gradually float in the direction of her bedroom. Once there, I come up briefly for air and with a look of sudden surprise pull the bag of coke out of my pocket.

"Fuck me. Looks like I did take that baggy after all. Completely slipped my mind. Bit of a turn up for the books that. Still, waste not want not, eh?"

She eyes me suspiciously. "Y'all are just an ole con merchant." she says, but there's a mischievous edge to her tone,

and besides I'm well beyond giving a toss one way or the other.
I grab a hand mirror off her dressing table and chop out two
enormous concentric circular lines of coke. I roll up the only
twenty dollar bill I have about my person and hand both it and
the mirror to her.

"Ladies first." I grin.

The coke works its magic, which is just as well as I'm sans
condoms and she apparently doesn't have any mysterious female
contraception up her sleeve.

She has come three times and it's getting light when she
suggests changing orifices. As the sun rises slow and magnificent
that glorious Georgia morning, every nerve ending in my body is
soaring to climax in one almighty celestial chord (an E7 if memory
serves) as I near the end of a blow job that afterwards has me
crawling about around on all fours whimpering.

We take a shower and then hop into the finmobile so she
can deliver me back to the hotel. Halfway there she suddenly
grabs my hand and jerks me downwards.

"Quick!" she hisses, "Down on the floor."

"What? Now? Do you think that's a good idea while you're
driving, I mean?" I have visions of my head between her legs with
her steering with her feet while peering through a periscope.

"No. Get down. That's ma daddy over there."

I hit the deck, curling myself into a ball in the ample space
of the passenger side footwell. I've slept in smaller motel rooms.

"Be a bit narked to see his little girl with a big bad punk
rocker would he?" I ask. I squint up at her and see her wave
and smile.

"Oh honey, he'd be more than "narked". she says, "Whatever
that means. On account of he's the sheriff."

"What?!" The sheriff. Not just a sheriff, which would be
bad enough. One of the radio stations constantly playing in my
head suddenly has Bob Marley quite clearly singing *"I shot up the
sheriff's daughter."*

Back at the hotel I Groucho Marx out of the powder blue
leather interior of the SS Lustmobile and in through the revolving
door. In the lobby I come to rest firmly against Alicia and start
waltzing her toward what I hope is an empty manager's office. My

groin has risen again and is pressed firmly against hers. Knees, slight bend, and ... quick, slow, quick, quick, slow.

"Will you stop that." she says, "Y'all are getting me hot again."

I grin down at her and says "Really my dear?" imagining she is paying me some sort of stud compliment.

"Yes," she says twisting away from me, "And I don't wanna sit through breakfast with wet panties."

Okay, be like that then. See if I care. But in the end we have a fairly civilized breakfast. For once, all of us have breakfast partners. Even Annette who, if the marks on his neck and the bags under her eyes are anything to go by, is obviously enjoying being reunited with Kevin. Ah love's young dream.

And then quite suddenly it's a mouthful of goodbye and back into the van. It seems I've made a clean getaway, but even so I keep an extra eye peeled for patrol cars until we're a good fifty miles down the freeway headed to Houston.

▶ ▶ ▶ ▶

About the middle of the day second day out of Atlanta, just before the Mississippi border, we almost prematurely end both the tour and our lives.

"I'm bloody starving!" I announce.

"Stop the stop presses!" Miki says, "There's a turn up for the books then."

"Yes, I could eat something." Annette says.

That is it then, officially sanctioned trough time. Miki ghosts into a small town and pulls into the parking lot beside a burnished aluminium diner. We all pile in through the front door. Inside, it's like one of those westerns where everyone goes quiet and the piano stops playing when the strangers push into the saloon. In this case though it's because the moment we set foot door through the door, old Perry Como on the jukebox ends the song *"Don't Let The Stars Get In Your Eyes"*. How prophetic. And the four blokes in the diner look at the door and stop whatever they are saying in mid-sentence. Annette, Dik, Mulligan, Kevin, and Miki slide into a booth and I approach the counter. A waitress looks up from inspecting her nail polish and stares at me as if I'm something she's inadvertently trodden in.

"Six cheeseburgers, fries and cokes. For here please."
I say smiling.

The waitress stares at me for a few seconds more and
then turns and walks to the far end of the counter. She leans on
the counter and starts muttering to two construction workers or
whatever. I wait a couple of minutes and then walk over
to join them.

"Excuse me," I say in my poshest accent, "But might we
please have six of your finest cheeseburgers with fries and cokes.
For here please."

"Sheeeit," one of the construction guys says, turning from
looking at me to stare at the counter in front of him, as if he's just
discovered a turd next to his plate, "What the fuck is that? No
offence Marge."

Marge nods.

"I don't rightly know." his boyfriend says, staring at me,
"But I sure wished I had mah gun."

"Well hell Lester, I got mine out to the pick-up." And he
swings round on his stool and faces the door. Then he looks at
me and slowly smiles. There is absolutely nothing pleasant about
this smile.

I stride back to the booth.

"We're, er leaving." I say. "Now."

"But where's the food ... I'm starving ... what the fuck's
going on ..." babbled all at once.

I jerk my thumb backwards toward the guys at the counter.

"Now." I say and walk to the door.

"Blimey," Dik says, "Must be serious if old lanky is willing
to give up his grub."

Safely back in the van, a few miles down the road headed
back toward the freeway, no pick-up trucks in the mirror, we
whistle along past farmland.

"Plenty of room out here." I observe. "Shoot you in the
back of the head. Bury you and the van and who'd ever know?"

"Or care." Mulligan says and shivers.

"Fuck me sideways Doris," Miki says, "That'd be a hell of a
find for some archeologist five hundred years in the future, then.
A mummified band."

"What? Like the Rolling Stones, you mean?" Dik says as we merge onto 70 West.

Later that afternoon we cross the state line into Mississippi, and almost immediately the countryside changes. Either side of the road huge, tarantula-furred tree limbs hang in loops to kiss mosquito-pricked swamp waters. I gawp at a landscape, alien enough to be another planet, primeval enough to be in a dinosaur movie.

We flash past tar paper shacks propped by the side of the road like ancient invalids. Children and chickens dance in the swirling roadside dust of our wake. We cross innumerable bridges as we thread our way across such exotically named waterways as Buttahatchee River and Catahoula Creek.

A little after midday, we roll into a sleepy little town, down Main Street, past a high school, general store, post office, cop shop, and church, all straight out of a Norman Rockwell painting. We pull up outside a diner Johnny Cash and Elvis had probably stopped at during one of their 1950's tours. At the breakfast counter. Mulligan and Dik are spinning around and around on their stools like new wave tops, Miki pumps quarters into the jukebox and Mr. Cash is suddenly *Walking The Line*. Annette has her head buried in a billboard-sized menu, a slight frown creasing her harassed nanny expression. I take a seat and look around. There's no one else in the place. A trim, middle-aged waitress materializes behind the counter. She is clad in lime green nylon, is sporting bat-wing rhinestone-encrusted glasses, and has a beehive that is in imminent danger of interfering with the ceiling fan. She gawps for a second at the unlikely punk rock vision before her but then, evidently a true professional, she clamps on a smile and asks:

"What c'n ah get y'all. Special's catfish."

I'm halfway through my first glorious mouthful of everything on my plate when the diner door opens and two of Clichéville's healthy, young citizens walk in. He's wearing a highschool football jacket, and is all impossible good looks and radiant teeth, while she's kitted out as a pervert's wet dream come true in a cheerleader outfit. I stop in mid-chew and watch them slip into a booth. They lean toward oneanother and I wonder how they aren't blinded by the combined glare off their teeth. I usually feel like a sore thumb in a finger factory but this high school quarterback and his prom queen girlfriend take that feeling to new heights, to suddenly uncomfortable new heights. Why do *I* have to be the foot-too-tall, Brummie freak with no basketball culture to add a dash of validation if not glamour to my excessive height. No, I have been taunted and teased mercilessly ever since I can remember. One of the reasons – okay the only reason – I wanted a guitar in the first place was because I'd been convinced by everyone, my Dad included come to think, that I was such a freak of nature that no girl would ever be interested in me. But then girls shag pop stars, no matter how they look, I mean look at ZZ Top or Phil Collins for fuck's sakes. So here I am, a new wave dancing bear, a painted frankenpunk, and even though I'm sure I'm on my way to ruling the planet as a megastar, still I'm denied the joy these two perfect specimens enjoy. I resume chewing and manage to swallow a spiky lump of food. Then I imagine them in ten years time; he's a fat, unshaven truck driver married to her, a droopy, alcoholic, valium addict knee deep in debt and screaming brats. Whereas I, well I will be long dead on some penthouse floor by then. I start to feel better.

▶▶▶▶

Texas. It goes go on for sodding ever. And then it goes on some more. And then just when you thought it might be running out, yes, it goes on some more. I mean it's only about an eight hundred mile drive (only!) from Atlanta to Houston but when the landscape never changes it makes it feel further.

"Whoa!"

Miki's apparent delusion that he's driving the Deadwood stagecoach jerks me fully awake. I'd been dozing through a half-dream, pursued by whooping warriors, pushing my arrow-peppered steed across an endless plateau dotted only with Roadrunner-topped buttes. Wakefulness morphs the Deadwood stage into a 1975 Dodge Ram van. Miki slews onto the side of the highway, which is somehow now axle-deep in gory sheep parts. I blink out of the window at the carnage.

"Wasn't me did it!" Miki immediately says, "Whatever it is."

"Bloody hell! Take more than a roll of gaffer tape to put that lot back together." I say.

"Oh I don't know ..." Miki muses. "We could always try."

"Thank you and goodnight Dr. Frankencottrell." I say.

A fair-sized flock of sheep are blocking the road, milling and bleating, the roadside critters are cropping scrubby yellow grass. Thirty feet or so into the flock is a pick-up truck. The front grill is staved into a v-shape and bits of mangled sheep lie in it's wake. Up on the pick-up roof a denim-clad cowboy smokes a leisurely Marlboro, looking for all the world as if he's taking a vacation from his billboard and has chosen this spot for its sheep vista. In the back of the van Mulligan, Dik, and Annette untangle themselves from sleep. Miki and I climb out, careful to stand in the door wells. I'm not about to gore up me Docs, am I.

"You alright mate?" I yell at the cowboy.

He flicks his cigarette at the nearest sheep and slowly turns to look at us. If he's at all surprised to find himself hailed by a seven-foot-tall, black-clad bloke with dyed red hair and eye make-up, his expression doesn't betray it.

"Howdy," he says, "had me a little fender bender here."

I blink. I don't see a Strat or a Telecaster anywhere. Maybe it's in his truck. Terrible thing to happen to a guitar!

"I'll get on the CB." Miki says, "Get you some help."

"'Preciate it," the cowboy yells, "Ain't seen a soul all mornin'."

They don't mess about with this middle-of-nowhere business in the USA, when you are lost, you are *lost!*

"Breaker breaker!" Miki says into the CB mic, "Steady Eddie here. Out on ..." he pauses, "What road is this?" he asks me.

I unfold the map and stab a finger close to the last ketchup stain I left on it.

"Near as I can tell ... we're on 79 ... about a hundred miles out of Henderson ... headed east."

"You just made that up." Miki says.

"As if!"

"Why have we stopped?" Annette's head emerges, blooming like a blonde mushroom from the darkness of the back of the van.

"Oooh, look at all the sheep." Mulligan says.

"Yeah, look at all the *insides* of the sheep." Dik adds happily.

"Oh my God!" Annette dives back to her seat and pulls a blanket over her head. "Let me know when we're moving again." comes her muffled voice.

Miki clacks, fuzzes, static-crackles, and good buddies through a couple of trucker conversations until he is able to let the cowboy know that highway patrol, breakdown truck, and a sheepulance are on their way. The cowboy waves a big country thanks and clambers down into the back of his pick-up for a siesta.

"Well, he should be okay now. Can't sit here all day. Got a gig to get to tonight. Or is it tomorrow?" Miki asks.

"It's always tomorrow somewhere." I say.

Miki bounces the van off the road, skirts the sheep, and has us back on our way.

►►►►

The Austin Municipal Auditorium is a huge, dome of a place that looks like a stalled UFO. We load our gear in through the stage loading bay – the bigger the stage area, the smaller our cluster of gear looks – never mind, we know how to use it to make it make a huge noise.

"Elvis played here you know." I say, struggling to get my cab up onto the lip of the dock a foot or so above my head.

"Costello?" Dik says, clearly impressed.

"Presley, you ignorant git." I say.

"Ancient history, granddad." He spits.

"They don't get much bigger than Elvis, you know." Miki says.

"I know," Mulligan replies, "I saw that picture of him dead on his bathroom floor. Looked pretty big, he did."

After an encore-garnering set in the cavernous auditorium, I repair to the dressing room for a quick towel down and to partake of the freshly-stocked liquid portion of our rider. Everyone else scampers off to watch the Polis's set but, inspiring as it often is, I decide to give it a miss. I'm about halfway through my third or fourth bevy when in walks the Dog Woman. Course, at that point she's just this punk chick with huge eyes, nice knockers, and everything packaged in as inventive a set of black leather and vinyl bondage gear as I'd seen in a while. She sashayes over to me, crop-dusting pheromones as she comes, a salacious smile on her painted face. She climbs directly up into my lap.

"Ah want you t'be mah dawg." She drawls.

As I'm coming to discover, whenever I hear a good-looking female with a southern accent bits of me go limp, while other bits choose to go in entirely the opposite direction.

"Aye lassie," I say, deciding on a Scottish accent as an appropriately exotic foil to hers. It also allows me pause to pursue the doggy metaphor. Indeed, I'm hoping to pursue her until she is down on all four doggy paws.

"Y'all Scotch?" she asks.

"Only from the knees down." I say.

"How 'bout from the knees up?" she drawls.

"One hundred percent Anglo Saxon bastard." I tell her.

Her car is a bright pink aircraft carrier-size convertible with fins you could ski down. As I slide into the spacious front seat *"she drives a Plymouth Satellite, faster than the speed of light"* buzzes like a B52 through my head.

"Ah have a salon." She purs as we slice the downtown Austin night neatly in two.

"A saloon?" I ask hopefully.

"No honey, a hayer salon."

Oh well, at least I might get my hair done. Curled with any luck.

"Why don't y'all let me do your hayer?" she asks before we're halfway through the door.

So I find myself in a candlelit salon, flat on my back, having my hair soaped, with a nice pair of bristols right in my face. Mommy, I think as she rinses me off and then she's doing something decidedly unmommy-like as she climbs up on top of me. After some comic fumbling with a variety of bondage zippers and straps, one thing lead to a couple of others. Suddenly she reaches up over my head and grabs something. Oh shit, a knife, a gun, mace, a set of curling irons? But no, her honeyed voice, rocked slightly by our motion, fills the room.

"Ah lurve mah dawgs." She reads.

I open one eye. She's reading a book?

"Ah lurve the way thayer dicks come out all hot and pink when I strokes 'em."

Okaaaay. I squint up at the cover of the book. *A Girl And Her Dogs*. As the inter-species action become more heated and lurid, so the Dog Woman accelerates her motion on top of me. She begins to moan and grunt punctuation that might or might not have been in the book.

"C'mon," she yells, "ah want you to howl fer me. Lahk the big dawg y'are."

Ever one to oblige a lady, I throw my head back, think briefly of the Hounds of The Baskervilles, and let out as mighty a howl as I can manage. Next door's dog starts barking.

►►►►

The Palace Theater is, like much of the rest of Houston, brand new. I hear tell they built glass skyscrapers downtown that originally reflected such amplified levels of sunlight that it killed all the vegetation for miles around. Sounds about right for Americans. Anyway, having done our sound check, we're crossing the theater lobby when Miles hails us much as he would a cab. We pull over and start our meters. Standing with him is a short, round little man with a great tan, and a huge set of smiling teeth.

"Bob Garcia." Miles says, "Head of A&R at A&M."

"Luke Sky," I say, "Head of gee & tar at Fash & Hun."

He is evidently used to smart-mouthed gits in bands, because he doesn't even blink.

"Miles tells me good things about you guys. A little left of center, I hear. But looking forward to working with you."

"Okay. Working with us?" I ask.

"Gotta a distribution deal for IRS with A&M." Miles says as if talking to a five-year-old. Which as far as being music biz-savvy is concerned, is pretty much what I am.

"Right. Nice to meet ya BG." I say, "Let's do lunch. I'll have my people call your people."

"I'm only in town for the show." Bob says, "Oh my!"

He is looking past me at the spike-heeled, bondage cover girl, punkette, wet dream that is The Dog Woman of Austin, as she sways across the lobby towards us. Bits of her wink at us invitingly from pieces of her outfit that are cunningly missing. Her friend isn't bad either.

"Hello girls." I say, staring right back at her cleavage, "Glad you could make it. This is Bob. Bob this is ... er,"

"Never mahnd, sweet thang," she says, and hands me a hotel key. "We're at the Hyatt." and they sashay off to the ladies to powder their bits.

I turn from watching them walk away, and Miles and Bob are gone, probably off somewhere counting suitcases full of other people's money. Did I mention that I know even less about the music business than the average dead rock star? You should see the contract I'd willingly signed with Faulty.

The gig that night goes according to plan, I come offstage bathed in sweat and excited that the head of Herb & Alpert has seen us at our best. However, I'm in no mood for dressing room ligging. I'm anxious to get to that hotel with those two punk lovelies. Slight hitch in that direction when The Dog Woman's friend walks up to us with Miki in a pneumatic headlock. But how can I be greedy, the poor sod has been working his taters off night after night, and is well overdue for a bit of R&R (rough and ready).

The Dog Woman and I set sail in her pink Cadillac and after a couple of drinks in posh bars, swank in through the lobby of a hotel looks as if it has been built sometime in the twenty third century and time transported back to downtown Houston 1979. Our room is about the size of a football field and there in the middle of it is a circular bed you could land a helicopter on. I'm picking the foil off the top of a bottle of champagne while she sits in the middle of the bed and emptying her purse out. A veritable avalanche of every drug you can imagine – and some you can't – cascades onto the silk bedcover.

"What would y'all like to start with?" she asks, looking up and licking her lips.

The next thing I clearly remember is her pushing me out of the bed.

"Peeeooo boy. Y'all stink. Go take a shower."

Under the stream of hot water I examine myself finding bite and scratch marks that stir fleeting memories, sweet pain.

That night we pull out onto the freeway, Dallas-bound. I doze through the journey, surfacing every now and then to find parts of me erect and other parts numb. Miki whistles for a while, until a barrage of debris from the back of the van silences him. I'm feeling nervous. It's only about two hundred and fifty miles from Houston to Dallas, and apart from feeling a bit like the quarry only slightly ahead of the hunt, I reckon I'll be lucky to have enough energy for the show tonight, much less any further canine cavorting.

I keep a weary and wary eye on the dressing room door after the show, then walk out and grab a cab back to hotel. As I unlock my door I have a horrible feeling she'll be in my room, but she isn't. Of course, lying awake an hour later I find myself wishing she was.

After the successful gigs and excesses of Texas, it's time to head north up into the Midwest, where I've heard you have to set your watch back to the nineteen-fifties. So I'm looking forward to the crack, maybe ruffling a few Puritan feathers, unlocking some daughters, while doing my best not to get tarred and feathered and ridden out of town on any rails, or worse.

We take 35 North and skirt Oklahoma onto 44 East towards Tulsa. I wake up about noon and find something rolled up and stuffed into my jacket inside pocket. I tugged it out and there is the battered copy of *A Girl And Her Dogs*. There's a lipstick kiss on the first page.

"Here." I say, "Why don't I read us all a nice story, eh? Help pass the time, like."

▶▶▶▶

We pull up outside Cain's Ballroom late that afternoon. It's already tending toward dusk and the dying light makes the huge, wooden building look like something out of a gothic horror film. All we need, I think, is lightning crackling across the sky and dogs barking. Please, no, I wince, no dogs barking, eh. So of course, as we walk round the side of the building looking for the stage door what do we find but a gigantic cage full of snarling Dobermans. (Or should that be Dobermen?) A weasel-eyed, cowboy-hatted figure stands occasionally poking the bars with a stick and cooing at the dogs like a doting parent.

"Howdy." He says, "You the band?"

"Er, yes," Dik says.

"We're not dinner." Mulligan adds, skirting the dog cage.

"Nope." The cowboy says and grins some unusually bad dental work at us, "They like a little more meat than that. Name's Floyd. This is my place." He waves at the building.

Cain's ballroom is a listed building which in the US can mean it was built longer ago than a week last Tuesday and is still standing. Inside the cavernous, wooden-floored space, tables and chairs are scattered at the back. We walk toward the stage, kicking up drifts of sawdust as we go. From the walls, gigantic, sepia portraits of the likes of Hank Williams and Dolly Parton stare down at us disapprovingly, as if demanding to know who these painted punks are with their racket, and whatever happened to the Good Old Days. Well, Hank and Dolly, drug overdoses and Hollywood movie careers are a couple of things that happened to them.

The front of the stage is separated from the auditorium by massive sheets of chicken wire.

"Keeps most of the bottle glass from getting through." Floyd says, coming up behind us and making us jump.

"Yes, I can see it would." Miki says, "Here, where's the PA?" and he goes off to do one of the things he does best.

"Hope so." Mulligan says, "You er, get much bottle throwing then?"

"Well," Floyd drawls, "depends how much they like you. Or how much they don't."

"We'll try to play it safe then." I say, thinking back to Brise Norton Airbase. At that gig we'd been told they hadn't had a band for a couple of years on account of what the paratroopers had done to the last band that played there.

"Oh I wouldn't advise that, son." Floyd says, "Man has to take chances every now and then. Well, talkin' of which it's time to feed the dawgs."

"Yeah, right. Good luck." I say.

"Hope to see you later, eh." Dik adds.

After the soundchecks, we have an hour to kill until the doors open. Floyd has thoughtfully provided a good hot meal for us as outside does rather seem to be in the middle of the by now famous nowhere. I'm sitting out in the club, Miles and Sting are at the next table, muttering. Well Sting is, Miles couldn't mutter if his life depended on it. I reckon all that shouting across miles of space on horseback that their ancestors had been forced to do has resulted in the volume level favored by most Yanks. Whereas in England no one was ever much further away from anyone else than muttering distance.

"*Message In A Bottle* isn't moving so well here." Miles says.

"Well fuckin' hell Miles it's still number one in England isn't it. And loads of other places. What's going on here in the States?" Sting wants to know.

"Reckon it needs a little more push." Miles says. "Might have to spend another couple of hundred grand or so on promo. That should do the trick."

I would have thought so. We're still lucky to occasionally hear our single on the local radio station of any town we're driving into. *Another* two hundred thousand dollars? Suddenly the certainty I'm headed for superstardom is looking a little tatty. And here I am, four thousand miles from Pool Farm housing estate, still the boy without the sodding bicycle or train set.

I try to push such thoughts from my mind as we take the stage that night to a half-full, half-hearted mob of a crowd, a strange mixture of good old boys and rural punk rockers, a dangerous mix. I'm not sure I actually hear gunfire during our set, although I'm also not exactly sure I don't. And there's no way I'm going back there to inspect the ceiling. But I definitely catch glimpses of what look like cowboys, up and dancing on tables, and there is a fair amount of "yee-haaw, rock 'n' roll" yelled between numbers. We keep the arty synth stuff to a minimum, get our heads down and blast through *Sodium Penathol Negative, Bike Boys, Die In The West, Burnin' Down,* and the like. There isn't any encore but we do only get a couple of bottles shatter against the chicken wire, although according to old Floyd that's not necessarily a good thing. I mean I've sort of gotten used to being gobbed on and even occasionally bottled, but I don't much fancy a bottle in the gob followed by a couple of bullets in the chest just because I've earned the approval of some western Neanderthal.

For the next two days we drive through, that is around and over, mountains. The magnificent panoramas pasted onto the windshield are far too magnificent to be the usual theatrical flats. Up until now I've often been convinced such flats were being wheeled past the stationary van's windows to give the illusion of movement. The world still has only the same fifty inhabitants who follow us around changing hats and costumes, but I reckon they're all on planes right now getting to California so as to be there when we arrive, the grinning cunts. The sun pinwheels in the shimmering sky like a hippy's halo, as soaring crags draped in ermine snow fields spread themselves before us. But I'm slouched down in my seat, glowering at it all, a right miserable, spoiled, moody sod. Somewhere in Utah I start to hallucinate. The road is following a fast-flowing river that swarms over a rocky bed, bordered on one side by sheer rock faces. Suddenly huge, frowning native American Indian faces are leering at me from the rocks.

"Shit!" I say pulling myself up in my seat, "You see that?" I haven't spoken for a couple of hours which must be a tour record, maybe even lifetime. Miki actually jumps when I speak and the van swerves in a gentle arc across the white line and back.

"What?"

"Faces." I say, "In the rocks. Fuckin' huge Indian faces."

He takes a long squint at the road that loops ahead of us, as if memorizing its curves, and then turns to stare past me at the rock face. Just before we plunge off a hairpin bend and into the river he looks back at the road.

"No Luke." He says and sniffs. "So, where did you get it?"

"Get what?"

"Whatever it is you've snorted, smoked, or poked up yer bum." he says.

"I'm telling you," through clenched teeth, "I've given all that bollocks up. I'm totally straight. And I'm also telling you there are faces in the rocks."

"Okay. How long since you took anything then?" he asks.

"Dunno. Couple of days I s'pose. Seems a lot longer." I say, dripping self-pity.

"Well that's it then isn't it." He says and grins, "That's

reality kicking in. After all this time, it's bound to be a bit of a shock to your system that. You're seeing things is all."

"Very funny, you clever cunt." I say, "I'm telling you I saw Indians."

"Indians?" Dik says, poking his black, rats nest head into the cockpit. "Fuck me Miki, form the van into a circle quick!"

"No prob." Miki says, "We've been driving in one for the last couple of years anyway."

"You what?" Dik asks.

"A fucking dirty great big circle." Miki says, "At least that's how it feels to me."

We come down out of some Utah mountains and spill into the red furnace of Nevada. Miki stops the truck in the middle of a blood-red Martian, landscape and we clamber out to pose and pout with unsheathed guitar and bass on rocky bluffs, scampering and bouncing in our make-up and stage clothes, kicking up red dust, as incongruous as balloons in a razor blade factory.

"Blimey," Miki says as we climbed back aboard dusty and sweating, "you lot looks like a bunch of glam cockroaches out there."

This image actually cheers me up a bit. But not for long. We come across a gas station and while Miki fills her up we buy bubblegum, candy bars, and cheap plastic toys. I see a rack of cassette tapes and there is *Give 'Em Enough Rope* by The Clash. We might as well have been in the middle of nowhere on another planet and here you can get The Clash album. And you still can't hear Fàshiön on any radio station, much less buy their album. What the fuck are those cunts at IRS doing while we're crawling from gig to gig like exhausted hookers. Too busy counting The Police's fucking money I reckon, to pay any attention to the likes of us also-rans, as I'm increasingly starting to think of us.

Later that night, we skirt Las Vegas by a mere fifteen miles or so. I can see it blazing on the horizon like a string of demented Christmas lights. But Annette very sensibly refuses point blank to let us detour through it, damn her.

"We've got to be in San Francisco by tomorrow night," she

says, "and as well as all your gear, you'll also need shirts on your backs."

"But why?" I whine.

"Because you're not Sting, that's why." Mulligan says.

It's true that the golden one seems to be to spending longer onstage with his shirt off as the tour progresses. And their encores are getting longer. Maybe it's another of Miles's directives, like no wives or girlfriends ever being allowed to be seen leaving the gig with their famous other halves, to keep alive damp, girly fan fantasies. And yes, of course I'm jealous, it's part of my job to be jealous of anyone more famous than me. The bastards!

We descend the Sierra Nevada into the lushly wooded garden of California. At the state border there's a checkpoint. A young woman in a green police-style uniform waves us over into a search area. There's some quite audible swallowing of substances noises going on in the back of the van. I'm currently the self-righteous one, out of his mind on sobriety. The nice young blue-haired, blonde-eyed, green cop pokes her head in through the window. I smile at her as if I want to lick her, which I wouldn't have minded. She ignores me.

"Afternoon folks," she says, "You carrying any fruit today?"

Fruit? Do we look like citrus fiends? Banana smugglers? Well maybe it's the tight black trousers, eh? But fruit? We unload the van and stand beside our pile of gear while three officers search the van for illicit limes, outlawed apples, and banned bananas. Eventually, having not been found in possession of so much as a pippin, we're given a clean bill of fruit and waved on our way with a sunny welcome to California. This might have served as some sort of warning as to what we would find in the Golden State, but it didn't.

We are about halfway over the Bay Bridge when I catch my first glimpse of San Francisco. The sun washes magical light across the city and something long dead in me wakes – wonder. It's love at first sight. A hardened bastard who's seen the heartless hearts of most American downtowns, who has sniffed at Manhattan, yawned at metropolitan Chicago, snoozed through the entire Midwest, dozed over the splendors of the Rockies and Sierra Nevada, is suddenly gob-smacked by this jewel of a city.

It tumbles down to the sparkling blue of the bay like a giggling nudist on acid.

We load into the club, The Mabuhay Gardens on Broadway. It's a mid-sized club with a vaguely tropical theme, lots of plastic palm trees as well as the usual graffiti and sticky floored-club smells. As we're a big, bad, New Wave British invasion band I assume we're topping the bill, but I'm wrong. Annette tells us some band called SVT are headlining.

"Never heard of then." Dik says.

"Well I'm sure they've never heard of you either." Annette says.

"That's their problem." I say. "Who are they anyway?"

Annette digs out her notebook.

"Well it says here they're ... Jack Cassady's punk band. From ..."

"Jefferson Airplane." I say and immediately bite my tongue.

"Who?" Mulligan says.

"Never mind." I say, suddenly busy with my amp settings.

"Oh, I get it." Dik says, "Must be one of those hippie bands he used to listen to."

"Didn't. Isn't." I say, muttering to myself that if it's considered uncool to know that Jefferson Airplane was part of the legendary San Francisco scene during the Summer of Peace and Love, then punk or new wave or whatever it's calling itself this week can kiss my hairy, spotty arse.

The dressing room is up a ladder at the side of the stage, in a tiny box room above the wings. How they got the ever-present battered couch up there is anyone's guess, but there it is, large as life and twice as rank. And sitting on it is the world-weary but friendly-looking figure of Jack Cassady. It's obvious he's the old man of the band as the other members of SVT look like a photo-fit line-up of bratty young Yankee punx. They are altogether too well-dressed and healthy-looking if you ask me, but I've already noticed that's California for you. Jack and I chat amiably enough about how I'm finding California. I feel like I'm on the edge of the world, sitting on the edge of this couch, perched ludicrously above the edge of the stage, in a state that's perched on the edge of America, everything feels set to fall into the Pacific at the drop of a fault line. There's a kind of vertiginous exhilaration in this feeling. I'm already thinking about jumping ship.

Fuck it, put a new band together here in SF, conquer the world from here. Why not? There has to be better deals to be had than crumbs from the Copeland banquet table with vague promises of fortune and fame always just somewhere up ahead.

"So what's SVT stand for?" I ask Jack.

"Sex, violence, and television, man," Jack says, waving a hand in the general direction of the whole country.

"Seems a fair enough summary." I agree.

He reaches out, drags over a folding metal chair, and busies himself chopping out a couple of hefty lines. He proffers a fat, plastic drinking straw. I look round guiltily.

"Shit." I mutter. Annette is hunched in the corner of the room with promoter. They look like a couple of conspiratorial mantises, all knees, elbows, and plans for everyone.

"Better not." I say reluctantly. "Least not till after our set. We sort of have rules now."

Jack nods.

"I can't even have more than one fuckin' drink before we go on." I say.

Jack smiles, leans over, snorts up a line and comes up wearing a substantially bigger grin.

"Not all sex and drugs and rock 'n' roll, is it?" he says.

"It's not *even* sex and drugs a lot of the time. Not even that much fuckin' rock 'n' roll either really. Not with all the traveling and assorted other old bollocks we have to do with journos and radio stations and whatnot."

"And you thought it would mean freedom, didn't you?" Jack asks, "Better than a job in a factory or office." It wasn't even really a question.

"Well yeah. Course, I grew up in the slums of a car town. I saw a lot of my mates swallowed by those factory gates." I say.

"Hey man, you're a poet." Jack says.

"Yeah. Only problem is, I'm the only sod knows it." I say. "I mean, I thought being a pro would be way more exciting than all those years I spent struggling to get a deal. Y'know, no one telling me what to do or when. I actually used to laugh at all the sheep.

What was it Jimi said – *go ahead on Mr. Businessman you can't dress like me.* Well maybe not but we've all got fuckin' bosses. Schedules. Places we have to be. Things we have to do."

"Come on lanky," Dik says, sticking his head round the door, "Leave the natives alone. We're on."

I shrug at Jack and clamber to my feet.

"Have a good one, man." he says.

After a great show the first night at The Fab Mab, I am a little disappointed to find myself sharing an all-night diner with Dik, Mulligan, and the single groupie we're all trying to bed. Then again, once the booze and coke wear off, she takes on a decided Fido aspect and I can't be bothered. I decide to let the little gits fight it out or share her, who cares, and I carry the remains of my bucket of 7-up out onto the fabled streets of North Beach. Maybe it's the cold air but one of my back teeth that has been aching on and off for the last few days now chimes in with the occasional stab of sharp pain. Back at the hotel room I lie awake the rest of the night listening to Miki snore and growing my toothache.

▶▶▶▶

I swallow half a bottle of PMS medicine and spend the rest of the afternoon vaguely numb, wandering around Fisherman's Wharf with a stomach ache, scaring tourists.

That night the Mab is packed again. During our set I look down and I see this Mexican-looking bird dancing away at the front of the crowd. Well into the old bump and grind she is, with plenty of the right shaped bits. Mulligan and Dik spot her about the same time I do and the stage is suddenly knee-deep in drool. She looks a bit like that Victoria from *The High Chaparral* TV show, even has white cowboy boots under her Mexican peasant mini skirt. We play the fastest encore version of Sodium Pentathol Negative since the night we did all that speed at the Brum Odeon gig. Then all three of us run for the dressing room. There's a flurry of furious toweling down, followed by hastily sprayed clouds of Rive Gauche, and we're jammed shoulder-to-shoulder in the dressing room doorway, fighting to be the first to get out and get at this exotic bird. I win.

Her name is Sady and I hit her full force, mouth going fifteen to the dozen. It's one of those times when the patter is just so, the stars are aligned, I can't put a foot wrong, and I wake up the next morning, one arm still tied to the headboard, with sore tackle and a phone number written in lipstick across my chest. I free myself and stagger down to breakfast. My snot has a white crust and my brains feel like they've been scooped out and shoveled back in through my ear sideways. And of course, I get all sorts of shit from Annette about the extra room I booked on the band's account.

Later we drive over the Bay Bridge into Berkeley where we're booked to play an afternoon outdoor show at the university's Sproul Plaza with Devo. But when we get there, there's no sign of a stage, no posters for the gig, no promoter, and so no gig. Someone has bollixed things up. I look around but don't see any Mormons with flower pots on their heads wandering around looking lost, so it looks as if Devo haven't shown up either. Which is a shame, as I really like them and was looking forward to playing a show with them.

While Annette disappears into the campus bowels to find out what happened, we repair to a student bar called The Bears Lair. Tempted as I am to call the phone number on my chest, I manage to resist. Anyway, I'd had a bugger of a time reading it backwards and upside down in the bathroom mirror that morning. I reckon I might give her a jingle next time we're in San Francisco, if she's lucky. Annette comes back as we're on our second round of beers and about our fifth round of trying to separate preppy college girls from their knickers.

"Gig's off." she announces, puffing out her cheeks. "Student union promoter nowhere to be found. Sorry."

"Can we at least have another round or five of these," I ask draining my glass, "As compensation and seeing as we don't have a show now till night after next."

"LA." She says, "And no you can't. I managed to get you an interview on the college radio at two o'clock."

We peer at our new digital watches – we're all so fucking modern – and head for the bar.

"Just to lubricate the old tubes." Dik yells.

"Tooth aching something rotten." I say, brandishing my empty shot glass.

"Just a papaya juice and 7-Up for me." Mulligan says –which he'll no doubt use to wash down a handful of pills.

"No more for me." Miki says, "Not till we get to LA tonight." Since Kevin has gone home to Brum and the pursuit of the yuppie dream Miki's the only one with a driving licence, poor sod.

Eventually, Annette manages to shoo her pack of punk puffins in the general direction of the university radio station. The DJ comes in and introduces himself. He looks a bit like Dustin Hoffman from The Graduate, which is a bit unfortunate for him because Dik immediately takes to calling him Dustbin. To his credit, even though we're obnoxious and often totally out of order, the kid manages to stay cool and conduct some semblance of an interview. At one point, he announces that we're doing an in-store at rather Ripped Records by the north gate of the campus . Which is news to us. We thank him and offload a copy of *Product Perfect* and some Police merchandise. Our merchandise ran out weeks ago and we've given up expecting IRS to ever ship us any more.

Ripped Records is a small corner shop opposite the university's north gate. We introduce ourselves to the owners, and produce a couple of copies of *Product Perfect*. Again, it's too much to expect IRS distribution to have our record on sale in a store in a town where we're supposed to play a show that doesn't happen anyway. A couple of punks and the occasional student drift in and out. They peer at us, until I feel like I should have a "Do Not Feed The Guitarist" sign round my neck. At one point some kid asks me to sign the new SVT album. Later, I deny for the umpteenth time that I am Rick sodding Okasek from The sodding Cars. By the time the record store closes I'm quite depressed. We drive away still clutching our two copies of *Product Perfect*. As Miki tries to figure out how to get to 101 South and I bid farewell to my San Francisco dreams, I might be forgiven for finding all this "it's your turn to be famous any second now" guff more than a little wearing on the old patience.

▶▶▶▶

I doze through the night as Miki makes the Fashionmobile gobble up the three hundred and fifty miles to LA. Sometime just before it gets light he bounces us into a service station for gas and breakfast. To Dik and Mulligan's delight the breakfast shop is calls Julie's Pantry. They loudly order pelican pie, and a crocodile sandwich ("and make it snappy!"). I just know that for the rest of the day they will boast to anyone who will listen, not to mention everyone who won't, that they had a big breakfast in Julie's panties. I reflect that as the tour progresses we plumb new depths of puerile childishness – just in case you hadn't noticed. Not that I've turned into Mr. Maturity or anything, it's just that sometimes I can't be bothered to join in and watching our typical behaviour I almost feel sorry for Annette. Almost.

Miki peers at our map, trying to determine position and ETA among the impressive collection of stains I've assembled over the last few weeks.

"It's sodding huge." he says at last, "and please, there's nothing you can possible say that not only isn't true, but that I haven't heard at least a dozen times."

"I was just going to say that's what I heard. About LA I mean." I add, dogging my fag in a pool of bacon grease.

"I reckon we're only about thirty miles from the outskirts. We're playing Madam Wong's West tonight. Boss says the hotel is in Chinatown. But Chinatown doesn't seem to be marked on this map." Miki says.

"Let's have a look." I swivel the map round. "Got an address?"

"Yeah," he says, "But not an A to sodding Z of LA. I mean, looking at the size of LA on this map I don't reckon the van's big enough to carry a comprehensive street map."

"Not to worry," I say, "I'll do what I always do and–"

"—get us lost." Miki says.

"Yeah, get us— hey, wait a minute. No fair. I'll have you know I've got an unfailing sense of direction." I say.

"Or is that a non-directional sense of failure?" Miki asks, and lights a Kool. He takes a drag, pulls a face, and sniffs. "Stone me, they even manage to get sugar into the bleedin' fags?"

"What I mean is, I'll just look for a clump of skyscrapers and that'll be downtown." I say.

"Time to push on." Annette says, herding a giggling Dik and Mulligan ahead of her with her briefcase.

An hour later Annette, Dik, and Mulligan are asleep in the back of the van and we've driven through what seems like hundreds of square miles of surburban-sized buildings and strip malls without so much as a sniff of a skyscraper.

"I can't understand it." I say for the umpteenth time.

"Here I've just noticed that the billboards have changed." Miki says.

"What?" I glance up from the map.

"Well, a while ago they are all pictures of black people grinning about booze and cigarettes. Now they're all Mexicans grinning in Spanish about booze and cigarettes." Miki says.

"Well let me know when they're grinning in Chinese about booze and fags and we'll be there." I say.

I peer over the top of the map and suddenly there's a bright flash in the distance.

"Unless they've just dropped the bomb," I say, "and unless I'm very much mistaken, yonder glint will be the sun reflecting off the elusive downtown skyscrapers."

But as it turns out I am very much mistaken and whereas it is indeed the sun, what it's glinting off appears to be the Pacific Ocean. Somehow we've driven right through LA and reached the ocean!

"I'm not going to do it and you can't make me." I say.

We're parked on the forecourt of a 76 gas station. Annette has crawled from the back of the van to join the land of the living and the lost.

"Look," she says, "you're the one who failed to find the middle of one of the biggest cities on the planet. Now get out there and go and ask where LA is."

Grumbling, I approach a bullet-proof glass booth that houses a cash register and a teenager riveted to a comic book.

"'Scuse me mate." I say, rapping on the glass, "Er, where's LA?"

The kid looks up, clearly annoyed by the interruption. I immediately notice that he's the kid who bussed our table in a Howard Johnson's in Nevada. And before that he was a toll taker on some bridge in Utah. I don't know how much longer these fifty people think they're going to get away with pretending they're the entire population of the USA. Of course, every time I accuse one of them of traveling ahead of us changing clothes, hats, and jobs they just blink at me as if I'm stark, raving bonkers. But then they would, wouldn't they?

"What?" the kid asks, frowning.

"LA." I say, "Where is it?"

"Where is it?" he sighs and sets his comic book aside. "You're in it, you Limey fruit."

"Yeah, yeah, but where's the middle? Y'know, downtown." I ask ignoring the insult.

"Which downtown?"

"LA's downtown."

"Where d'you wanna get to?" the kid asks, already starting to stray back to his comic book.

"Chinatown." I glance down at a scrap of paper Annette has given me, suddenly feeling unaccountably like a kid with a note from his Mom excusing him gym class. I shake my head and I'm back in Santa Monica. "Royal Pagoda hotel. North Broadway. Mission Junction."

"Mission Junction? Take 10 back to 110 North." he says and yawns.

▶▶▶▶

"This has to be someone's idea of a fucking joke." I say. We're standing outside a red roof-tiled building that wouldn't look out of place in downtown Shanghai, waiting for Miki to bring the van round from the parking lot.

"So, I have my own room, which is nice." I say, "But the shower is so small the water only reaches my navel. If I lie flat on my back on the bed, my knees hang over the end. We're talking feet flat on the floor. I practically have to limbo dance to get in the door. If I'm lucky enough to pull tonight, unless she's a fucking midget contortionist I'm going to end up putting either her head or my foot through the sodding wall!"

No one is listening. I'm not exactly unused to this, although I can see that Dik and Mulligan now have far away looks in their eyes (the one that makes me wish they are far away) thinking about fucking a midget contortionist. What the fuck, I decide to join them in fantasy land. I mean I might as well for all the good my bitching is doing. To make matters worse, in the last couple of hours we've all come down with stinking colds. All, that is, except Fagsmoke Von Cottrell, who seems to be immune to puny earth germs.

"Ad wod abow dis sobbin code?" I ask with exaggerated congestion, "How'm I spose to sink when by dose is tobally block up?"

"Will you stop sodding complaining." Annette yells and promptly sneezes.

Madam Wong's West isn't just above a Chinese restaurant, it's actually *in* a Chinese restaurant. We come up a long staircase into a big room that's the restaurant. There's a small stage on the left and a huge bar on the right. The stage has some kind of Pacific Island theme with fishing nets, shellaced fish and bamboo all over the place. It faces a dirty great big carved Chinese bar.

"Stone me," I say, "Looks like a cross between Billingsgate market and the Hong Kong waterfront."

The "dressing room" is behind several fiendishly arranged paper-paneled screens. The stage floor, on closer inspection, is just a few large sheets of thick plywood balanced on what look like soy sauce barrels. The room is filled with large circular tables, each with a huge, wooden serving turntable in the middle, and ringed by about twenty chairs.

"Look at that," Dik says, "The DJs must be enormous."

"Extended mixes." I mutter.

We're behind the dressing screens dabbing at our makeup when Annette shows up with Bob Garcia. He's wearing one of those pleasant, I-have-more-money-than-God smiles. He's also carrying three cellophane-wrapped gift baskets.

"This is Bob Garcia." She says, "He's with A&M."

"Looks more like he's with the Red Cross." I say, noticing that the gift baskets are full of cold medicine, throat spray, bottles of aspirin, cough syrup, and the like.

"Annette tell me you guys are feeling a little under the weather," Bob says, "So I had these care packages put together."

"What a nice thing to do." I say, touched, "Thanks mate,

you're a life saver. Here, wait a minute weren't you at that Texas gig?"

He nods and smiles.

"Well done that chap!" I say, and take a basket. I rummage around until I find the Chloroseptic. I spray half a bottle of numbing relief onto the old inflamed vocal chords, and then screw the top off and swoosh the other half around my throbbing molar for good measure. I spit into a handy fire bucket.

"You, er, wouldn't happen to have anything a bit stronger handy would you?" Dik asks.

"Yeah, I've get a terrible pain up me nose." Mulligan says, "Could really do with something to numb it."

"Sorry guys," Bob says, "Y'know, Miles has a pretty strict policy about that sort of thing."

"Yeah," I say, "We know. Your body is a temple or at least a living room and you don't shit on your own carpet or some old bollocks."

"Evidently Miles didn't grow up in a council house full of stray dogs." Miki says.

"I'll thank you not to talk about my family that way thank you very much." I say with mock outrage.

"No," Dik says, "Miles probably grew up in a house full of stray money!"

The show at Madam Wong's West is another of those weird set-ups where I feel like some New Wave version of a 1950's crooner, singing *Technofascist* at tables filled with well-to-do, designer punks who pay only occasional attention to the band while they're busy wolfing down rontons, flied lice, and other assorted racist delicacies. Backstage after the show, there is some serious thera-flu-chloroseptic-nightnursing going on. Dik is sitting ankle- deep in balled-up tissues, while Mulligan is looking for his chest so he can rub Vicks on it. Annette and Bob Garcia approach with some Dame Edna chick in tow.

"You guys were fabulous!" Bob says, and finds his critique greeted with mass exhalations of phlegm.

"This is Renée Wayne Golden." Annette says.

"Wotcha Reenie." Dik say, grins, and sneezes.

"Don't come too close missus. We might not be quite as dangerous as usual, but we're definitely infectious." I say and smile weakly.

"Infectious music that's for sure!" Renée says. "Great guitar! So original."

"Oh yes," Dik says, "most guitar players would give their left arm to sound like old lanky here."

"Where are you guys playing next?" Renée asks, totally missing Dik's insult to my guitar playing.

"Hollywood Palladium tomorrow night." Annette says, "Then Riverside College. Both with The Police."

"Too bad, I can't make the Palladium show. Maybe Riverside. But if you guys are free tomorrow afternoon I can pick you up and we can visit one of my companies in the hills."

We obviously all look far from enthralled at the prospect of visiting some lawyer's company.

"Future General," she says, "They're doing the special effects right now for the *Star Trek* movie."

And that perks us right up.

Later that day I'm sitting in Jay Boberg's office at IRS Records on the A&M Records lot on La Brea and Hollywood. Jay is a fresh-faced kid who's smile is all surf boards and perfect health ... makes me feel quite ill. He's telling me:

"Yeah this lot is where Chaplin came to establish United Artists after he left Niles."

I glance out of the window as a black limo glides into the courtyard. I assume it's bringing some super fly soul star or mayhap Herb himself to the main studio, but sit up and take notice when Renée Wayne Golden clambers out wielding a size twenty seven handbag.

"Here, there's that lawyer bird," I say and we all clatter down the rickety wooden stairs to say hello.

Ten minutes later, we're in rock star fantasy land again, stretched out in the back of the limo, passing around an ice cold bottle of vodka, as LA flashes past the tinted windows and we climb into the Hollywood Hills. By contrast, Renee sits perched on the very edge of her seat like a bird, occasionally dipping her beak into a large gin and tonic.

"So where are we headed again?" Dik asks. He passes me the bottle and I suddenly remember passing the voddy on the back of that number sixty two bus after having the crap beaten out of us before our first gig. Was that really only eighteen months ago?

"Future General." Renee says, "I own twenty five precent of it."

Everyone I've met in Hollywood seems to own at least a percentage of someone else.

"This *Star Trek* movie is gonna be huge. It's what the world has been waiting for." she states, confident as she is matter-of-fact.

The limo whispers to a halt before an impressive pair of barbed wire-topped, wrought iron gates. The driver leans out, presses a button, exchanges a few words with a crackly little speaker and the gates swing open. We follow a driveway until we come to a compound worthy of a small mercenary army. Renée is out of the limo, waving at people, saying "It's okay. They're with me." Before I've managed to upend the dregs of the voddy bottle.

"Like I said," she says as we stand around her like the

world's most unlikely tourist group, "this is the movie the world's been waiting for. We have to be careful."

"Why?"

"Industrial espionage. Sabotage even." she says

Inside the main building we're greeted by a bloke who looks like Brains from Thunderbirds, only he's sporting a chin beard and wearing Bermuda shorts.

"This is Doug. Future General is his baby." Renée says.

We're herded into a dimly-illuminated, cavernous room where a range of different-sized models of the Starship Enterprise hang by invisible threads. There are several complicated-looking, multi-jointed armatures, each holding a movie camera, ranged around the starship models.

"We're real proud of this." Doug says, "The camera booms have complete three hundred sixty degree movement through a three-dimensional plane and they're computer controlled."

I know what computers are, this is 1979 after all. Computers are big boxes with spinning reels of tape and lots of flashing lights. They fill entire buildings. They are what enable NASA to fly to the moon, and the government to keep track of who's thinking the wrong thoughts in sci-fi movies. In that *2001 A Space Odyssey* film the bloody thing even talked back. Doug flips a couple of switches and with a smooth purring sound one of the cameras starts a graceful sweep around the Enterprise. I'm wondering if I can somehow get hold of a couple of these arm things and see how well they can be programmed to play keyboards, bass and drums. Luke Sky backed by a kind of robotic Shiva sort of thing. My dreams of fronting an accurate and obedient band are interrupted by Doug.

"In the movie this little beauty over here is called V'ger. The planet eater."

We're looking at something that looks like a hollowed-out turd that might have (eventually) been produced by a severely constipated Brontosaurus. Hanging in front of it is a tiny, perfectly-detailed Enterprise.

"V'ger swallows the Enterprise while it's on its way to destroy Earth." Doug confides. "The script calls for lots of high voltage electricity crackling across its maw. Let me show you how we solved that problem."

As Doug leads us into the next room I look back and see Mulligan has one arm inside V'ger up to his shoulder. I scoot back to him.

"What you doing?" I hiss at him.

"I stuck a badge in there, didn't I." He extracts his arm and taps the side of his nose.

"What?"

"Well if this thing swallows the Enterprise and that's the Enterprise," he points at the tiny model, "I reckon one of our chrome Fàshiön badges will look hundreds of feet long. Great ad for the band."

I'm not sure I care anymore whether he's serious or not. Catching up with the others we find them standing in front of a thirty foot square of chicken wire.

"We filmed this and superimposed it on the V'ger jaws. Better stand back." Doug advises and reaches out to throw a big electric chair-type switch. We all jump as jagged arcs of blue electricity snake back and forth across the chicken wire grid. Mulligan's hair starts to stand on end.

"Hey boss," Mulligan yells above the crackling and phutting, "Could we --?"

"No." Annette says, "You couldn't."

She knows Mulligan well enough by now to spot a request for a stage set when she hears one coming. Just as well really. I wouldn't fancy stumbling into that halfway through *Die In The West*, no matter how sodding spectacular it might look.

▶▶▶▶

San Diego is way too fucking hot. We play a crap set, middle of the bill in some restaurant inside a huge towerblock hotel. I don't get laid or drugged, so I drink a bottle of vodka and pass out on the coffee table in my room. The next morning I sit on a beach for ten minutes feeling like a fucking ant under a magnifying glass and then take my hangover back to the hotel. As we're bouncing out of the hotel parking lot, we're dopplered by a cacophony of sirens. San Diego's fire department are swerving a couple of battleship-sized fire engines past us and into the hotel parking lot. I peer back at the hotel and see black trails of smoke billowing out halfway up the tower.

"Er, boss," I ask Annette, "What floor were our rooms on?"

"What? I don't know. The ninth, I think."

One-two-three-four-five-six-seven-eight ... nine. Oh dear. Do the Yanks count the ground floor as the first floor? Is that the ninth or tenth floor that's on fire, and did I leave a fag burning on the edge of the dresser?

▶▶▶▶

Back in LA, when we come out of the hotel the next morning there's a limo parked next to the van. Miki's standing, arms folded, leaning against the van and he looks far from pleased.

"Mornin' Doris." I greet him.

"Don't you mornin' Doris me, you great streak of piss," Miki says, "Just get in your limo with the rest of them and follow me to the gig."

"Limo?" I say, "Alright." And I stumble over to the bowling alley-sized bugger and tug open the back door. Inside Mulligan, Dik and Annette are already installed.

"Fuck my old boots," I say, slumping onto the back seat and stretching out my legs "Leg room. Who'da thunk it. This is a bit more like it then. Did someone kidnap Annette in the middle of the night and replace her with an exact replica that likes to spend money?"

"Very funny. Renée rented this to take her new preciousneeses to the gig." Annette says.

"Nice old boot really." Dik says.

"An aunty to the stars." Mulligan adds.

"So that's how come Von C has get the hump. He has to drive the truck while we lounge and glide in luxury." I say. "Any chance of a drink?" I reach for the bar. Annette slaps my hand away from it.

The drive to the Riverside gig takes about an hour and whereas it's a bit of a luxurious novelty for a while, I soon grow restless. It's not the same as riding the death seat with my best friend. An uncharacteristic silence settles over us. I don't like that at all, so I take a nap.

The gig is huge – these universities obviously have more money than brain cells. The Police roadies have already set up, as have the opening band, some local, big hair band. I help Miki haul our gear onstage and we set up in an odd silence that is anything but fun. In the dressing room, I find a cacophony of hair dryers as the big hair band make their hair immense. Dik whips out a gunslinger's array of combs and joins in the back-combing fest. Once the hairdryers have done their work and we can hear ourselves talk, we discover the opening band to be a splendid bunch of chaps. If their tuning and warm-ups are anything to go by their two guitar players are no slouches. But then I've come to find that most American musicians seem to be big on technique, while a bit less so on originality and ideas. I'm not sure just why English bands are in such favor in the States at the moment, but I doubt it's the playing or singing. I doubt anyone would give most English bands a second glance if it wasn't for originality, make-up, smoke and mirrors. But then I've always thought half an ounce of style is worth a pound of ability.

"I am an English punk rock star who can't really simg." I drone at myself in a monotonous Lancashire accent. I'm peering into the mirror, imagining film clips again, while daubing hi-lighter on my cheek bones.

"I'm not happy with the sound." Mulligan says.

"I'm only joking Mulligan." I reply, "I'm not really going to start singing like the fucking Human League."

"No." Mulligan says, "I mean the live sound. Our sound. Our mix."

"What the fuck would you know about the mix?" I ask, "Miki does his usual great job and everyone gets to hear what we sound like."

"I think we should let Kim have a go tonight." Dik suddenly chimes in.

I smell a conspiratorial rat.

"Why the fuck would we want to do that?" I ask, "He doesn't know the songs. You think he's ever out there listening to us?"

"That's where you're wrong." Mulligan says, "I've been having a word with him."

Oh shit, not the famous Mulligan word. Annette bustles into the room.

"Right," she says, "I've talked to Miles and The Police and Kim and it's okay for him to do sound tonight."

"What! Wait a minute, what happened to Miki being the fourth member of the band? Remember, he's the whole reason the punters get to hear something other than a wall of banging and crashing with a few meeps and synth farts thrown in around an ocean of undefined flanged guitar." I say.

"Blimey, he sounds like he's been reading the *NME* again." Dik says.

"Sorry Luke," Annette says, "It's all set."

"Don't I have any say in this?" I ask. The ensuing silence gives me my answer.

"Well I think it's a mistake." I say. I can feel a surge of anger rising and so I decide to get out and walk it off. I'm halfway through the door as Miki breezes in past me.

"Board's all set." He says, "When are we on?"

And instead of storming back in there and yelling that if Miki doesn't do the sound, I'm not singing or playing a note, instead of standing up for my oldest and closest friend, I betray him. I go for a piss instead and then walk around the hall lobby, buffeted in a sea of perfect teeth, sun tans, and college jackets.

We're halfway through the third number, *Red Green & Gold*, when something flies through the light's glare and smacks me in the head. Ouch. Fuck, that hurt. Then there comes a small fusillade of missiles, arrowing in untrackable through the lights, peppering my face and hands. I can't be sure but it feels like I might be bleeding. I scoot back from the edge of the stage and almost skid into Dik's drums. The stage floor is littered with ice cubes, and more are on the way. We gallop to the end of the song and are greeted with scattered, muted applause, but mostly catcalls and boos. I dodge up to the mic.

"Well, I'm sorry you don't seem to be enjoying yourselves." I say as calmly as I can, "Shame really, 'cos I'm having a great time!"

Whether taken by the crowd as sarcasm or optimism these comments do nothing to lessen the barrage hurled at the stage, a few bottles and plastic cups are now added to the ice cubes as we wheel into *Citinite*. Some of the sweat running into the corners of my mouth now definitely tastes of blood. An ice cube might as well be a lump of glass if thrown hard enough. We emergency blast through to the end of the set, ditching synths or any attempt at subtlety in favor of two and half minute versions of *Sodium Pentathol Negative* and *Die In The West*. Back in the dressing room everyone is kicking chairs and swearing. I'm peering at my forehead in the mirror, It looks like I've taken a load of buckshot in the bonce, I'm peppered with small cuts and one of my cheekbones is gashed.

Annette trudges through the door.

"Look at this!" I howl.

"Sorry," she says, "But you did sound pretty horrible. Nothing was clear, it was ..."

" ... like a wall of banging and crashing with a few meeps and synth farts thrown in around an ocean of undefined flanged guitar?" I ask.

"I thought Miki said the board was set." Dik says, throwing his soaked shirt onto the floor.

"It was." Miki says. No one has noticed he's come into the room. "But seeing as you lot decided you don't want me to do sound. Seeing as you apparently just want me to drive you around and hump gear, I went out and zeroed the board. After all, Kim is such a great sound man, I didn't think he'd want any of my crappy settings getting in his way. Now, you lot can do what you like but I'm breaking down that stage and taking the truck to the motel. If you want to talk to me about sound for tomorrow night's gig at the Hollywood Palladium I'd be happy to do that. Otherwise I'll be flying back to London and you can hire yourselves another fucking driver."

He slams the door on his way out, and given the way we've treated him, I must admit I admired his restraint.

Out in the auditorium, after another stirring set from The Police, I'm talking to Renée, explaining that Miki hadn't done the sound (although not why) and that is why we'd been a bit off that night. I have several Jack and cokes under my belt and my face has stopped bleeding. Some passing college kid yells (from a safe distance) "Hey, you guys suck!"

"Yeah mate, I know," I yell back, "And so does your sister!"

By the time we leave – not so much as a sniff of a groupie tonight – me and Dik are well tanked up and both dying for a piss. We're out in the parking lot reveling in the fact that our limo is a bit bigger than The Police's. I see the golden ones head out the stage door toward their limo. They're batting off fans as they go.

"Oh look, it's Fashion." Andy says.

"Hey Andy," I yell, "Look. Mine's bigger than yours!" I point to our limo.

They scowl, all except Stewart who's smirking, and clamber into their limo.

"Come on lanky," Dik says, "Time for that piss, eh?"

We stand behind The Police's limo and wait until they settle into their seats. Then we hop up onto the fender, Dik leans over and raps on the glass, and as three faces turn, we whip our dicks out and piss all over the back window.

▶ ▶ ▶ ▶

Outside the Hollywood Palladium gig it's full-on Hollywood-stylee cliché night. There's a crowd milling around outside trying to spot anyone who looks even vaguely famous (as opposed to famously vague), and there are two of those big searchlight things on the sidewalk, looking for low flying disco planes no doubt. Cars, trucks, taxis, and the occasional limo buzz the front of the theater, and then take off like flies from a papier mache turd. We skulk in with our gear, barely catching a jaded LA eye in the process. The stage is huge, which is just as well as we need to set-up our drums in front of three other kits. The bill has changed and now runs (in order of appearance): Fashion, Hazel O'Connor, XTC, The Police. We're waiting in the wings to see if we'll get a five minute sound check (unlikely). Sting has one of those new radio bass rigs that eliminate the need for a cable between instrument and amp. But in these early days of wireless guitars you do run the risk of picking up bursts of passing cop cars and taxi cabs right in the middle of the old ee-oh-ee-oh-yo-yo's. Sting is down on the main floor, roller skating in great swooping loops while they run through *Can't Stand Losing You* ... buzz, crackle ... *"car 54 where are you?"*

Once they're finished, we watch XTC and Hazel get their sound right and then are given five minutes to lumberthrough bits of Citinite before being herded offstage. We head for the dressing rooms. But there are separate dressing rooms for each band and they're locked and/or guarded by gorillas in silk bomber jackets with "Staff" lettered across the back. So the atmosphere, far from being one of wild and crazy punk rock excess, is more like that find in a maximum security wing of Broadmoor prison than anything else. I'm finding things I'd expected to be highlights – playing the Hollywood Palladium for fuck's sake - are turning out to be a bit of a visit from Aunty Climax and Uncle Ho-Hum. But the sound is crystal clear, all is apparently forgotten if not exactly forgiven. We play a tight set and the cocaine is back after the show, so the next clear memory I have is Annette telling us next day that Miles is taking us to dinner. We have a night off but an evening spent with Miles as opposed to cruising the flesh pots of Sunset Strip is greeted with less than enthusiasm.

"Aw, do we have to?" I ask Annette.

"Yes you do." she tells us, "And try to behave. Some more A&M execs will be there. I think they want to discuss your future."

"Oh bugger." I say. Last time I heard that someone wanted to discuss my future was from my parents when I was sixteen, right before I went to see the career's officer at school. I seem to recall he'd suggested I join the police force, on account of my height. "Very fuckin' funny." I told him.

Dinner turns out to be more of a late lunch as we suddenly have a gig that night, at some place called The Cuckoo's Nest. We decide to bring the truck to the meeting so we can drive across town to the club right after and have a leisurely set-up for once. The meeting is in a mid-priced, French restaurant on the border of Beverley Hills and somewhere a little less sordid. Miles is accompanied by two suits and amidst the old steak pommes frites and coq au vin there is a lot of vague talk, and a complete lack of any specific talk, about us moving to A&M and becoming the saviors of modern music. At one point Miki grows bored and wanders outside to check the van. He comes back after only a couple of minutes and leans down to mutter in my ear:

"Er, I think we've got a problem."

I look up at him and see he's not kidding. My stomach sinks slowly into my groin and presses down on my balls. I get that feeling that something pivotal is about to happen, something pivotal that I'm not going to like one little bit. I suddenly have those horrible twin thoughts that not only does life not have a rewind button, but reality is not, after all, a movie projected onto my retinas to keep me from getting too bored. I get up and follow Miki outside, the jabbering promises fading behind me. Once outside, he points to the driver's side quarterlight window. It's hanging by one twisted hinge at an awkward angle. Like a broken wing. I run round to the back of the van and tug open the doors. I clamber up behind our gear and my hand finds the empty space where less than an hour ago I'd placed my guitar case. This guitar is not some production line model. It's one of a kind, the only one of its kind in the world. This guitar has become my arm, my friend, my dick, my shrink. I have pictures of it in a baby crib in a Mississippi hotel room. It's been onstage with me for more than two years. It has had its picture in the national and international press. This guitar is in my heart, my dreams, my future, and now some cocksucking LA junkie cunt has stolen her. I am beyond anger, beyond words, hurled suddenly into a pit.

Later that afternoon, I stand in Guitar Center on Hollywood Boulevard with a blank, signed check from Miles Axe Copeland III in my hand. I'm surrounded by custom Les Paul goldtop deluxes, vintage Strats, Parker Fly this that and the others, Rickenbackers et-fucking-cetera, and I don't want any of them. I want my guitar. Eventually, I numbly buy one of the latest Ibanez models, a black thing called an Iceman, just because it's the weirdest shaped guitar in the store. I sleepwalk off to play my first gig in over two years without my guitar.

Everything inside Cuckoo's Nest is, astonishingly enough, painted black – how original. But it's a sunlit meadow compared to my mood. I hate my new guitar, it's a stupid piece of shit that's the wrong shape, the wrong color, and wrong guitar. I don't give a flying fuck how it sounds, although as it happens it sounds alright, I suppose, if you like that sort of thing, which I don't!. I'm so pissed off that I barely nod at much less listen to the opening band, The Flyboys. A right snobby cunt they must have thought, me and in this they are at least half right. No one has ever accused me of being a snob.

Halfway through *Red Green & Gold* three drunken skinheads clamber onstage and start moonstomping drunkenly around. Security is either asleep or doesn't care, Miki's on the mixing desk at the back of the club, and I could give a toss anyway. Between numbers, one of the clodhopping oi merchants bellows down my ear that they're from Liverpool. Towards the end of *Bike Boys* we veer out of the reggae into a fairly straight ahead rock section, the rhythm change throws him, and he falls headfirst off the edge of the stage. His two pals dive after him and administer a good kicking, first to him and then to anyone foolish enough to be slam dancing near the front. And that's it. I spend another lost night in a hospital ward-colored, LA motel room, and the tour is suddenly over.

M.I.A. 1979

Chapter Thirteen
America Finishes Us Off

The flight from LAX to Gatwick is uneventful. I get so wired on voddy and speed that it isn't until I get to Gatwick and peer, blear-eyed at my ticket that I realize my connecting flight to Paris is from Heathrow. The only way I can make the connection apparently is to take a helicopter shuttle.

"No way. Far too expensive." Annette says. "You'll just have to stay in London tonight and get a flight out tomorrow. You can crash at Faulty or somewhere. I'll take care of the tickets for you."

She stalks off toward the Air France counter, clutching my ticket. There are no fond farewells, no declarations of what a great tour it's been, what a great time we had. Everyone is exhausted and/or hungover. I take my new ticket from Annette, promise her I'll be back in Brum in exactly two weeks, and dodge off to take a much needed piss. When I come back everyone has gone. At first it feel s a bit strange, being on my own, but then it feels fucking great. I saunter around the airport leering and winking at young women to absolutely no avail and then realize I'm stuck at Gatwick with a ticket for the next day out of Heathrow, and as yet I have nowhere to stay.

I rummage through my wallet and come up with a handful of crumpled dollar bills of various denominations. The bureau de change certainly don't hand me enough to be booking into any airport hotels. I have some money in a bank in Bordeaux but a fat lot of good that does me now. I dig out the trusty old black book and after half an hour can't find a single female in the great metropolis who's willing to put up with me, much less put me up. Ah, what it is to be popular and loved - I wish I knew. Finally, I call Nick Jones at Faulty Products and he agrees I can crash on his settee. I grab a shuttle bus to Heathrow, then the tube and snooze all the way to Ladbroke Grove. When I get to Nick and

Dee's flat on Blenheim Crescent, they're out. It's mid-morning
and the pubs are shut. My stomach is feeling too delicate for a
greasy fry-up at Sid's Kafe so I decide to take a nostalgic stroll
up and down Ladbroke Grove. After ten minutes, not only am
I thoroughly depressed I'm also soaked through. I've forgotten
about that sneaky bastard drizzle, doesn't quite feel like it's
raining until you suddenly realize you're drenched to the bone.
I shuffle back to Nick and Dee's, trot down the steps to their
basement flat and huddle in the doorway, sucking on a
damp Marlboro.

Nick and Dee show up with a bagful of groceries and booze
and usher me into their haven. There's a faint odor of cat box,
cigarette smoke, and Indian joss sticks. I take a deep breath. It's
almost good to be somewhere that smells a bit like home used
to. A couple of neurotic cats play ringaround the Lukey legs then
take themselves off for a wash as I install myself in the kitchen
behind a large glass of vin very ordinaire.

"So, how was the States?" Dee asks, pulling vegetables out
of a shopping bag and lining them up on a chopping board. She's
in her early thirties, with one of those shortish, don't-mess-with-
me, alternative executive, career women's haircuts. She starts in
on the vegetables topping carrots, like Madame Guillotine with a
full tumbril of French knobs to get through.

How the fuck do you begin to answer a question like that?
I reckon she's just being polite so I tell her what I think she
wants to hear.

"Brilliant. Encores every night and shagging aplenty!" I
say. "Miles is very pleased with us (hah!) I reckon we'll be going
back next year with a hit or two under our belts."

Nick smiles weakly and starts to roll a joint.

"So, has Miles actually talked to you about a promotional
budget?" he asks.

"Er, well him and Annette probably have. I just handle
the front end, you know. Riffing and yodeling and generally being
adored." I say.

"Right. You know what's been happening here while you've
been away?" Nick asks. He lights the joint. He takes a toke and
passes it to Dee, who does likewise, somehow without stopping

chopping onions, and hands it to me.

"Same old stuff I expect." I say.

"Ska," Nick says, "Y'know Two Tone, man. Feckin' huge. The Specials, Selector, The Beat, all on Top of the Pops. *Ghost Town, Stand Down Margaret.* Half the fuckin' country's running around decked out like mods."

"What about punk?" I ask. "Post-punk, New Wave, or whatever the fuck they're calling it this week?"

"Not really." He says, "I mean the Pistols are long gone. The Clash have had a hit in the States but not really here. No, Two Tone is the big new thing here."

I start to feel a little uneasy.

"What's been going on here for us?" I ask, naïve as a learner driver at a stock car rally.

"For you?" Nick asks. He sighs and refills my glass. "I've had that same question from The Cramps. They got stuck here in town with no gigs or money for a month-and-a-half. And Squeeze have been asking what's next after *Cool For Cats.* There's been a lot of meetings behind closed doors and dodgy looking geezers coming and going carrying briefcases. Things have changed since *Message In A Bottle.*"

"You still haven't answered my question Nick."

"Well, you know how it is, man. This business is ... how can I put this delicately? Fucked up! Every penny Miles is making from The Police is going straight back into promoting The Police to make more money. So in all honesty, I'd have to say that we've done nothing for Fashion. Or anyone else. He just won't give us any promotional dosh, man."

A cat jumps into his lap and he strokes it absently. He looks like a beatnik villain from a James Bomd film.

"No," he says and sighs, "No press coverage of your tour Stateside. No press coverage for you at all. I did manage to plant a small mention in The Daily Mirror about the master tapes for Product Perfect being seized by the bomb squad, dunked in a bucket of water, and then blown up."

"Er, why?"

"It was all I could think of at the time and this journo

owed me a favor. Look, let's have a few more drinks, bite to eat. Get some sleep. Go on your holidays. Take a break. I'm sure Annette will fill you in when you get back, eh?"

The next day I wake up on the foot too small couch with what feels like knife wounds in the small of my back and a cat on my face. Just for a second I think I'd gotten lucky with some S&M punkette, then I smell Whiskas and spit Tiddles across the room. I brush my teeth, rinse with the dregs of a bottle of Chianti, scribble Nick and Dee a note of thanks, and stagger out into the freezing morning murk. I tap dance between the frozen dog turds on Ladbroke Grove, breathing the bus fumes along with my first cough and choke of the day, and make it to Sid's Greasy Spoon. After a reviving, artery-clogging fry-up and two cups of scalding tea it's back on the tube to Heathrow.

At Heathrow, I start to feel like one of those evacuee kids in World War Two. You know, clutching a suitcase tied up with string and a gas mask, standing on a platform next to a steaming locomotive, looking forlorn with my name and new destination written on a label and tied to my lapel with string. But a quick squint in the mirror in the gents where I refresh my eyeliner reminds me that I'm just the future King of Pop, dressed all in black, in the world's biggest airport on his way for two weeks of rumpy pumpy with his young French bit of crumpet. I hit the duty free and stock up with fags and vodka. Then waltz down to the gate for my noon flight to Paris.

By the time I get to Charles De Gaulle airport I'm well out of it, wondering along the tubular corridors and up and down the tube-encased escalators. I start to feel as if I'm being flushed down some gigantic bog. I stop at a phone and give Symiane a quick call. She sounds less than enthusiastic to hear from me, but then it's hard to tell whether that's for any specific reason or if it's just because she's French.

So I lug my black leather hold-all to the gate and doze in a plastic seat fiendishly designed to cause curvature of the spine in the average giant. Ten minutes before we're due to board they announce a three-hour delay. So it's off to the phone box again. The new ETA is greeted with a muttered "merde" followed by a slightly exasperated "boff" and a dial tone.

It's about 9PM local time in Bordeaux as the plane starts it's descent into L'Aeroport de Bordeaux. This flight is continuing on to Dakar in West Africa. We've all done the seats upright, tray tables at attention, seat belts routine, and down we go. We're literally at that point where they cut the engines, a second or two before the old bumpity- bump welcome to La Belle France, when they power the engines back up and the whole plane does a forty five degree upswing as we're all pressed back in our seats by face-distorting g forces. As soon as we level out and I can lean forward, I tug a bottle out of my hold-all and take an enormous swig. If I'm being hijacked or slammed into the ground, I'm definitely not going sober. We fly around for about twenty minutes, everyone including stewardesses, firmly strapped into seats. There are no announcements from the flight deck and as it's now dark I can't see anything out of the window. Then we descend and bumpity bump bump bump we're down. In one piece. Still there are no announcements about what happened. But then what are Air France going to say: *"Ladies and gentlemen, we apologize for trying to land without the landing gear down"* or *"We apologize for almost landing on the wrong runway and colliding with another plane. Please fly Air France again."*? I don't think so.

Symiane greets me in a detached, almost cold way. At first I think it's just one of her famous French moods. We go back to her place, riding in silence, have some fairly spectacular but somehow insectile sex, and it's at this point that I decide not to bore you by going on and bloody on about my two week holiday that ends up being only ten days. Suffice it to say that she remains mostly aloof, mentions some Irish bloke she'd met while I've been away far too many times (do I babble to her about the Dog Woman of Austin? I think not.) There is a good deal of great food, amazing sex under bone-white ceilings or azure-blue skies, long siestas, and moody silences. Ten days in, I decide to fly back to exotic Brum early and get ready for the next phase of my assault on the dizzy heights of stardom.

When I turn up on Annette's doorstep, Kevin makes it abundantly clear that he's not having any more pop musicians kipping down in their attic spare room. So, I spend three nights back at my Mom and Dad's place in the shadow of the dreaded Longbridge car factory. I lie in my old bed and stare at the faded image of Jimi peering down at me from the ceiling through several coats of failed emulsion. How is it that just a couple of weeks ago I was rampaging around Hollywood and now I'm lying in the freezing darkness of a Rednal bedroom listening to next door's cat fuck its brains out, while the distant rumble of the traffic on the Bristol Road mingles with the distant rumble of the night shift at British Leyland? Well, for a start, I was so certain I was off to become a huge star that I, foolishly, thought I'd be living in villas, penthouses, or presidential suites at top hotels. Why would I need a one-bedroom flat on Woodstock Road?

▶▶▶▶

Dad rattles his black cab through the miserable, freezing sleet that is Brum's main Winter decoration, and drops me outside the Birmingham Arts Lab. That's where the band are to reconvene, to spend a couple of weeks in a rehearsal studio writing the next album.

There's a distinct "not that glad to see each other" atmosphere, more of an "oh well, here we go again, I suppose" sort of an atmosphere. Not even Dik's ribbing or Mulligan's exaggerated holiday exploits can relieve me of this uneasy feeling. We haven't even played note one before a rather attractive, arty-looking, young lady, who is singularly uninterested in any of these painted punky perokeets, sticks her head round the door and says there's a phone call for Luke.

"Didn't know he knew anyone far enough up the food chain to use the phone." Dik says, then to the arty young lady "Here love, I hope you don't mind me asking, but where do you get that arse, because..." but she's already fled back to culture and I'm following her, at least as far as the phone.

"Yello." I say, thinking myself terribly modern in an American sort of way (what a prat!).

"Blithers," a voice says, "It's Dithers."

"Dithers, you old bigot strangler. How the blazes are you?" I ask Miki.

"Well enough, old fruit fly, well enough."

"We are just about to embark on a frightful din or five. Would appreciate your hand on the tiller don't'cha know."

"Fraid not Blithers. There' been an uprising in Tonga. I leave on the evening husky team from Euston." he says.

"You don't mean ..." and suddenly this isn't funny, if it ever was.

"Sorry mate," Miki says, reverting to his usual voice. "I'm not coming back. Too much bullshit. Too much hard bloody slog. There are other things I want to do with me life besides working my knackers off hauling the Copeland wallet around."

But you're my only ally, I want to say. What about our plans to open that naturalist, teenage girls bronzing academy in St. Tropez? What about the bright new tomorrow? But I bite my tongue and just mutter,

"Are you sure?"

"Sorry, yes, I'm sure. I've thought it over the last couple of weeks. Be careful out there, alright? And don't forget to send me a postcard from paradise. If you ever find it."

"Yeah. Okay. Well then. Tarra." I say. I hang up and stand staring at the phone.

The arty-looking, young lady comes into the office.

"You okay?" she asks, "Bad news?"

"Yes," I say, "And yes."

"Blimey, lose a bollock and find a fingernail?" Dik asks.

"Miki's quit the band." I say glumly, and to my horror and disgust Mulligan and Dik dance a little jig, whooping "thank fuck for that's". The little shits. I realize I'm on my own. It's just me against everyone else now.

▶▶▶▶

I don't think I've fully realize until now that all the booze, drugs, and sex pursued after every gig has a more fundamental role, beyond the centuries-old tradition of the troubadour getting his jollies after entertaining the king and queen. As I've already mentioned, playing a successful show is so intoxicating, so wonderful that if it wasn't for that time onstage I wouldn't put up with all the other shit you have to do. The booze, drugs, and sex are all just ways to try and continue that amazing feeling, that feeling you bring from the stage to the dressing room, the crowd thundering for more, that feeling that evaporates with your sweat the minute you're not on that stage.

And it's when that wonderful feeling isn't there onstage any more that the pursuit of booze, drugs, and sex becomes more frantic, more desperate. And then anger starts to surface. How dare that feeling not be there any more. It's not my fault, I'm still doing the same things, singing and playing my heart out, or at least trying to. I haven't changed, everyone else has, I'm not to blame, they are. All of them, Annette, Mulligan, Dik, Miles, all the record company and agency people, the bastards in the audience. It's a fucking conspiracy, and no I'm not paranoid, I don't think everyone is out to fuck up my life, my career, my fun, my time onstage – I *know* they are!

After the wide open spaces of America, the low, heavy skies of Rednal are like a blanket over the face just prior to being buried alive. Claustrophobic doesn't begin to describe how I feel. All through that Christmas I feel as if I'm stuck in a time warp. Some bugger with a time machine has conspired to dump me back at my parents flat in mid-adolescence. Only with no access to the simple childhood pleasures I'd originally enjoyed. No, I'm stranded, timewrecked, the great god TV twitters the Morcambe and Wise show, the only difference being they are now in colour. Mom is shackled in the kitchen, trying to do a Dr. Who Tardis number on a turkey too big for the oven, cauldrons of boiling potatoes, cabbage, cauliflower, and carrots Turkish bath the kitchen with foul, steamy odors that wisp occasionally under the kitchen door and into the living room. Dad dozes in slippers, his paunch ceremonially covered by the Santa hat-wearing tits of Samantha Fox in the Christmas edition of The Sun. My brother Roy, the poor sod, is also stranded, only he's down in Devon where he's working as an assistant green keeper on a golf course with Uncle Brian. A daunting prospect in the dead of English winter. He's no doubt suffering his own seaside, version of Xmas hell.

I'm missing the road. There is no tour. There are not even any Xmas or New Year's Eve shows, no sodding shows full stop. Every afternoon I'm on the blower to Annette, my inquiries about upcoming gigs increasingly punctuated with heavy sighs, muttered curses, and outbursts of foul-mouthed abuse.

"It's not my fault," she explains for the umpteenth time, "We were away in America too long. There's been no follow-up here. Some of the agencies even thought you'd split up."

"But we were only gone three and a half months for fuck's sake! It's not like we were shipwrecked on a sodding desert island for twenty years."

"I know, I know," she tries to console me, "I'm working on something early February—"

"February? That's fucking weeks away." I say, "Do you know what it's like rehearsing with a bass player I have to continually teach the bass lines to? With a drummer who's spending more time in the bathroom each rehearsal than any bowel or bladder necessitates? With a sound engineer who doesn't know how we're supposed to sound and couldn't make us sound right even if he did. With a fucking roadie that doesn't know how to set-up a back line and who never stops fucking whistling?! On top of which I haven't written anything new for sodding weeks."

"Yes," she says when I pause to draw breath, "Miles has been asking about the next single." I can hear her bite her tongue even as she says this.

"Miles should be a little bit more worried about the next fucking gig. And so should you. And how many fucking records have we sold? No one will tell us, will they. I'm totally brassic, skint. Nowhere to live. I don't have a pot to piss in. No woman. My guitar was nicked. I don't think I'm being unreasonable. How would you feel?"

I hang up the phone until it's time to have the same conversation again tomorrow. I take may parents' dog, Pip, for an unwilling drag round the frozen block so I can get a fresh breath of the Bristol Road and Pip can freeze his willy to a couple of lampposts. I haul him past the dead-eyed windows of British Leyland and into the wasteland of Cofton park. The park is deserted, everyone is nailed safely in place behind locked doors this Boxing day morning. There are no birds, singing or otherwise, in the skeletal trees and the squirrels are very sensibly hibernating. At least they've get their nuts to wake up to, the lucky little buggers.

Afternoons I spend fruitlessly trying to wrestle a hit single from my ampless Ibanez Iceman. From time to time I try a bit of wardrobe mirror guitar posturing just for old time's sake, but it all seems so pathetic.

Mid-January, I get to housesit a friend's flat on the other side of town, just outside the city center. The band decide to throw a welcome home Fàshiön party and word is spread through the Brumvine. Ah, it's such a relief to see everyone togged and tarted up like something from one of Marie Antoinette's indigestion nightmares. There's *Product Perfect* blasting out of the stereo, lots of bonking going on in the bedrooms, snorting in the bathroom, and jaded philosophical musings in the back yard.

The party proves to be a turning point for my depression, albeit a temporary one. Annette's promise of a welcome back gig (we've been back almost two months!) comes through at Aston University. We're booked into the main hall, two thousand capacity, for February 2. Mulligan goes into high publicity gear and you can't move in town for gig posters. BRMB radio announces our triumphant return (ha!) and puts our records on primetime rotation. *The Birmingham Evening Mail* runs a half-page feature on us the Saturday before the show and even *Sounds* is persuaded to give us column inches.

The night before the show, Annette reports that new gigs have been booked, including a couple of possible guest spots on the Squeeze tour, as well as some London club dates. Mulligan has relearned his bass lines, Dik is spending more time behind his drums than in the bathroom, and whereas we still don't have our hit single yet, we do have a few lengthier, brooding, weird pieces of music. *Fiction Factory*, *The Use of A*, and *Bad Move*, and we've also come up with a longer dub version of *Silver Blades*.

The Aston University gig is sold out. There are people hanging from the rafters, some of them looking, appropriately enough, like bats. We open with a bit of recorded *Also Sprach Zarathustra*, loads of dry ice flooding the stage, then under lots of moody blue lighting we open with the seven minute, baffling instrumental *The Use of A*. I'm not sure how this will go down and I'm not sure that I care. It's just so good to be facing a crowd again, and a home one at that. It turns out I have nothing to fear. As *The Use of A* cruches to the halt that's meant to be symbolic of the fall of Babylon, the whole auditorium goes collectively barmy. After a gleeful *"thank you very much, it's great to be home"* I peer at the back of my hand and mutter my name (off mic) just to make sure I'm not dreaming. We run through a selection of what have become local hits and dance back to new weirdness with *Artificial Eyes, Fiction Factory,* and *Bad Move,* wrapping up with *Technofascist* before bouncing back for a *Bike Boys* encore. Then off we go, leaving them wanting more.

"Now is that a boy or a girl?"

"Mom! That's George" I wave a hand at George O'Dowd who is sitting next to Martin Degville. They are both dressed up to the nine-and-a-halfs.

Much to my initial mortification and embarrassment, my brother has decided to drag Mom and Dad to the show, and they are now ensconced backstage. Dad is watching the Bacchanalian revels with a wary eye but Mom seems to be having a great time. For years to come she will gleefully tell people how she "met" Boy George and that he used to come and see her son's band all the time. So with the familial unit in attendance, I barely manage a few drinks and by the time they toddle off home, the bar is shut, the dressing room rider has been scoffed, supped, and hoovered up, and nary a dealer in sight.

I'm sitting in the front seat of the van. Outside it's started snowing. Our new roadie, Pedro, clambers up into Miki's driverside seat. The only thing even remotely Mexican about Pedro is his Viva Zapata moustache, his Brummie accent is as wide as The Bull Ring. He's an experienced, all-round roadie with some sound-mixing experience, a good lad, reliable, but he can't hold a candle to my best mate Miki. I miss the old sod, it doesn't seem right being in a van without him and the sound certainly wasn't as good, even though we'd had one of Steel Pulse's sound engineers to run the board.

Outside, the pubs are all shut, I can't face any of the two or three clubs that might be open, we have no backstage booze or drugs stashed, I'm not stoned, and I'm about to be driven back to the flatsit in Erdington, alone. The all too brief time back in the heat of things is gone, I feel hollowed-out and strangely betrayed. Pedro settles behind the wheel, fishes a joint out of his pocket, and hands it to me.

"Fire that up ferrus would yow Luke," he says.

I light the spliff, take a couple of half-hearted tokes and hand it back to him as he pulls out onto the Aston Expressway. Great, now I'm going home stoned as well as alone and depressed.

►►►►

I have to wait almost two weeks for our next gig, by which time I've lost the flat sit and am back at Rednal with Mom and Dad. But the good news is that it's off in Chaucer's footsteps we go, to the Odeon in Canterbury for a one-off gig with Squeeze. We check into a hotel that looks to have been originally opened by Mr. and Mrs. Shakespeare sometime back in the late 1500's. The usual miserable old sod at reception gives us the usual warning that this is a family hotel. He makes it abundently clear that he does not like strangely-dressed, makeup-sporting weirdoes compromising his nice safe version of reality. He makes a point of warning us twice that there are no visitors allowed in the rooms after nine.

"Don't worry mate," Dik tells him, "We'll be right back after vespers."

"Yeah, just as soon as we've finished raping the cattle and stampeding the women, we'll be home for tea and tiffin." I say.

The old hotel clerk scowls at us. "And the bar closes at ten sharp!" he says, as if pronouncing a death sentence.

It's really great to see Squeeze again, they are probably my favorite band to share a bill with, diamond geezers and stunning musicians. There's lots of good natured banter and it's almost like old time. Almost.

Sounds 2/22/80
Squeeze/Fashion, Canterbury
"... In 'Citinite' Fàshiön released one of the diamond singles of last year. Gallingly this time round the song turns out to be the aggregate of all their problems, self-inflicted and otherwise.

Mulligan's vocal is a classic "Oh-Christ-now-what's-happened-to-the-monitors?" job. Any resemblance to tunes living or dead is purely coincidental and this is the night's low point in an erratic performance by sound man and equipment which undermined Squeeze as much as their support band.

But the circumstances within Fashion's control are pretty chaotic too. The beautifully created movement of moods and rhythms from bleak tension to humorously romantic tropical tango seem to have been dumped in favor of shapeless carving about on synthesizer and guitar.

It is a black hole in the middle of their set and all my doubts go gurgling into it. Are they reacting to a hectic life on the road by making changes for the sake of it rather than focusing on optimum presentation of their material? Is Dik's drumming too hyperactive and is Mulligan far too busy switching from synthesizer to bass and back to put across the unique flavour of their music? In short, is it time they took on another couple of members to ease the various strains which seem to have crushed their best songs like a hydraulic junkyard press?

Well the answer to the last question might well be 'Yes' but in fact much of the rest of their set is far more encouraging and I remain quite sure they are one of the bands to pay attention to for the duration. Old favourite 'Product Perfect' teased as ever, almost pop, almost catchy, almost toe-tapping, perversely pleasing. New songs to me 'Fiction Factory' and 'Do It In The Dark' are full of Fàshiön freshness and challenging to orthodox song-making. Primitive sophistication? A new theorem: 'People who play in garages don't have to have mundane brains.'

Ultimate proof is 'Artificial Eyes'. A manically feverish reggae, a white nightmare in a black night, it featured the lengthy Luke whose salient vocals and inventive guitar playing has kept Fàshiön's music in motion when all else is in turmoil. From punk buzzsaw to John Williams harmonics he's the most exciting instrumentalist I've seen since the last time I said: "He's the most exciting instrumentalist I've seen since..."

It's truly depressing when sodding journalists start to notice that things are going awry – and they are right. It takes Annette another three weeks to get us a gig. In the meantime,

we've relocated rehearsals to The Rum Runner on Broad Street
in the middle of town. Mulligan's cousin (so he claims) owns
The Rum Runner and is about the only persone allowed by The
"name-deleted-for-safety-of-kneecaps" Brothers, Brum's very own
Krays, to run another club in Brum.

We take a cab across town from The Arts Lab while Pedro
and Whistling Pete haul our gear over to The Rum Runner. Once
there, Mulligan, Dik and I cross the road to the Broad Street Kaff
for a band meeting. We settle round chipped mugs of scalding tea
and jam donuts.

"So what are we going to do then?" I ask.

"About what?" Dik says round a mouthful of donut.

"About the price of fish," I say, "About no gigs, no new
record, no sodding press."

"Annette's doing her best." Mulligan says with uncharacteristic
charity, "I don't think it's her fault."

After a pause for thought and a quick slurp, Dik and I
agree with him.

"No, I blame Miles." Mulligan says.

"Safe bet, that." Dik adds.

"Well they did sod all promo while we were in the States,"
I say, "There or here for that matter. I told you what I overheard
in Oklahoma. About the kind of dosh they're pouring into making
The Polis even bigger."

"Yeah." Dik says, "It's not just us either. The Cramps are
stuck down The Smoke again with no gigs or dosh. Even Squeeze
are having problems getting paid their royalties. From hit records
for fuck's sake!"

"Royalties?" I ask, "What are they when they're at home?"

"People who ought to have their heads cut off." Dik
declares, "Again!"

"Vive La Republique!" I yell, and a couple of dour Brummie
lorry drivers glance our way.

"Yeah, money is a problem." Mulligan says.

"'Specially when you haven't got any," I say, "I mean it's
not exactly as if we can sign on the dole again. Or want to for that
matter."

"I think we need to look at replacing Miles." Mulligan says.

Dik and I nod agreement.

"Who with though?" I ask.

"Good question, big nose." Dik says, "We haven't exactly got people queuing up to sign us, have we."

"And then there's our contract." I say.

"Oh, don't worry about that," Mulligan says, "Contracts are meant to be broken. Look, I'll see if I can get us a meeting with my cousin." He nods over the road at the Rum Runner.

"I thought he was all gung-ho to manage Duran Duran." I say.

"Well yes, he is. But he might be interested in us as well. We can pitch ourselves as being part of a stable of bands he handles." Mulligan says.

"I suppose." I say, "Although the way our luck's been going lately, the only stable we're likely to find ourselves a part of is the kind you muck out. And us with the shovels and buckets."

"That's one of the many things I've always liked about you." Dik says, "Well alright, about the only thing actually. Your sodding optimism."

"We *are* all doomed." I remind him, "It's just a question of how and when."

The next day when I show up at rehearsal I find Dik and Mulligan already there. They're standing staring at a spanking, brand new back line – drums galore, stacks of amps, new basses, guitars, and keyboards all over the place. There's even a sodding saxophone on a stand.

"What the ..." I ask, "Don't tell me Miles finally came through with a sponsorship deal."

"You must be joking." Mulligan says, "This all belongs to Duran Duran."

A gorilla in a suit two sizes too small for it steps out of the shadows.

"That is all off limits." He growls, "Boss's orders. That belongs to Duran Duran, that does."

"Or to a music shop with a hole where the back door used to be." Dik says. Mulligan grins and shushes him.

Later that afternoon Mulligan gets us our meeting with his supposed cousin. To be honest it's a relief to get away from all the smug this-is-our-not-yours lording it that various Durans have been doing since stumbling into their new Aladdin's cave of gear. In a small, lushly-furnished office upstairs we sit and face Mulligan's supposed cousin.

"Thing is, Miles isn't doing anything for anyone much except The Police." Mulligan says, "So we were wondering if you might be interested in taking us on. I mean, I know you're busy right now with John and the lads downstairs, but we're not exactly unknown. Plus old lanky here has been writing some sure fire hits."

I have? Oh yes, of course I have. This is Mulligan's universe and he'll say anything to try and get what he wants. Sorry, I forgot for a second.

"Well, the thing is," Mulligan's Supposed Cousin says, "you, ah, must be under contract, right?" Weasel sharp this one.

"Well yeah. We're working on the second album right now." I say and Mulligan glares shut-the-fuck-up daggers at me.

"Contracts." Mulligan says, "Not exactly watertight are they. Well, not this one anyway."

MSC looks thoughtful, steeples his fingers and stares up at the ceiling, as if praying to the great god Decisions Decisions.

"Thing is," he says at length, "I'd like to help you. It's very tempting. Hey, I love you guys. And you definitely have a following."

I'm marveling at the way so much positivity can be leading up to "but" or "the thing is".

"But the thing is," he says, "Right now all my investment capital and time, well they're pretty much tied up with Duran Duran. And running this place, you know. That costs an arm and a leg." He spreads his hands, a helpless look on his face, probably designed to elicit sympathy. We stare at him.

Costs and arm and a leg does it? And there was me thinking you ran it solely for the benefit of the pretty, painted few, and never a thought to the wacking, great profits you must be coining in charging people five quid in and two quid for a lousy bottle of Pils.

"Well. I'll let you know if anything changes." he says.

The interview is over, we're back downstairs in the club. There are people loading lighting rigs and cameras into the club's main room. My old friend Suzy Varty appears.

"Hello darlin'" Dik says, "What's occurring?"

"The Beat." she says, "I've been doing their artwork for them. They're going to shoot a video for their new single. *Mirror in the Bathroom*, it's called."

She indicates the mirror-tile covered walls and ceiling.

"Seems a good enough place for it." I say miserably. I slump into a booth, wondering just when I'll get to shoot a video, just when this boy-without-a-train-set curse will ever be broken.

▶▶▶▶

So after two years that feel more like ten, we're back at Outlaw Studios. Phil and Ebba are still there, the eight-track is now sixteen-track, and the main studio floor is twice as big as it used to be. In the glaring absence of a single to launch at chart success, we decide to re-record *Steady Eddie Steady*. Talk about flogging a dead suicide. Don't you know you can never go home boys, there's no road back.

I've been messing with a new song that won't come right called *Emotional Blackmail*. Maybe that's because it has more to do with the sporadic and accusatory arguments I'm having with Symiane, than it does with a decent chart-bound song. We decide to abandon vinyl suicide à la *Citinite*, what we need now is vinyl resurrection. We dutifully grind out two versions of *Steady Eddie Steady* that somehow manage to have none of the original's spark or bounce. True, the arrangement is a lot more sophisticated, plus we spend a couple of days doing dub reggae mixes in attempts to kick poor Eddie's corpse back to life. There is no excitement or enthusiasm, so how the fucking hell we ever think we're going to lay down great music is a mystery to me. It's more like working your way towards an exhausted orgasm just for the sake of the final spasm.

Later that week we head down to London to play a new club calls Billy's on a Tuesday night, and practically no one shows up.

"Long way to drive for a rehearsal we don't need."

Mulligan says.

"I wouldn't go so far as to say we don't need rehearsal." I say, but I'm too exhausted to even get into it.

Two days later Annette tells us that the newly-equipped Duran Duran want us to play a showcase gig with them at The Rum Runner.

"They'll open the show,." she says.

"Yes, and I'm sure we'll manage to finish it off." I say.

For some reason DD's management has taken to grilling me about their vocalist. Is he any good, they want to know. Does he have what it takes to be a star? Why would I even care, and how the fuck am I supposed to know? I've lost my way, I'm no longer convinced of the inevitability of my own stardom. I'm on treadmill, going through the motions, it feels like I'm trapped on some stairway to nowhere.

Anyway, Duran Duran bang through their set with lots of dash and fresh-faced enthusiasm. I, on the other hand, play the whole set collapsing back against the mirrored wall, staring out at the crowd with a bored and fixed expression. Who knows how the show goes, most of the poseurs there probably weren't even listening. I know I barely was.

Two days later, we go back down to London and play The Rock Garden and by the next afternoon I've forgotten everything about the show. I just want to be asleep most of the time. Once again Annette supplies the vital cardiac paddles to my ailing career by announcing that she's got us two nights opening for The Stranglers at The Rainbow Theater. This is all part of the grand old theatre's fiftieth anniversary celebrations. The Stranglers! And suddenly there's the old urgency deep in the guts, a chance to play a gig with one of my favorite bands.

Stranglers frontman Hugh Cornwell had gotten himself arrested after the Old Bill searched his car and found a few grains of speed in amongst the carpet fluff and fag ends. In court, and later in appeal court, his lawyer argued that banging poor old Hugh away in Pentonville Prison was too harsh a sentence for such trace amounts. But the senile old tosser on the bench declared that an example must be made, for the sake of teenagers and musicians everywhere (what? We don't need examples, we all know how to roll a fiver and snort a line thanks very much all the same yer 'onour.) So old Justice Bollocks risked a stroke by hefting the book at Hugh and banged him away for two months. The Stranglers, however, decide to cock a snoot at the authorities and go ahead with The Rainbow shows. In a rare display of solidarity, the musical community rallies around the singerless band and so the proposed line-up for the two nights is variously:

> Ian Dury, Toyah Wilcox, Hazel O'Connor, Nicky Tesco, Phil Daniels, Peter Hammill, Jake Burns, and Richard Jobson on vocals. Wilko Johnson, Robert Fripp, Robert Smith, Steve Hillage, Basil Gabbidon, Larry Wallace and John Turnball on guitar.
> Matthieu Hartley from The Cure on keyboards. Nick Turner (Hawkwind) and Davey Payne (Blockheads) on sax, and Steel Pulse are providing the rhythm section.

There are rumors that Paul McCartney, Elvis, Mozart, and Jesus might show up as well. The support bands are Fàshiön, The Hazel O'Connor Band, and Joy Division.

▶▶▶▶

We get to The Rainbow early afternoon and as soon as I step out on the stage I get the old magic feeling. We set up our gear in front of everyone else's and then set off to wander the labyrinthine backstage corridors in search of our dressing room. This turns out to be a small room, but one steeped in the atmosphere of generations of luvvies, red nose comics, rock 'n' roll singers and guitar slingers, slapping on the old pancake and sallying forth to face the stench of the crowd. I slump down on the eternal battered sofa and make a start tuning guitars and bass. Makeup is, as ever, already applied and will only need minimal touching-up before we go on. There's such a flurry of bands and musicians involved in the show that we already know we won't be getting a sound check. In the past, with Miki at the helm, this would have caused me minimal concern, but I'm not so sure about Pedro. The door opens as I'm underlining my eye liner and a familiar semi-comprehensible voice greets us:

"Wey aye Fashion, y'buncha feckin' queers!"

It's Richard Jobson of The Skids. Now I feel everything is in place for a great crack. I haven't seen Richard since the night he leant me his Strat at Barbarellas back in '78.

"Any chance I can sing yon *Steady Eddie Steady* with yez?" he asks.

"Fuck yes!" I say, "Ta very much, eh lads?"

Dik and Mulligan nod and grin.

"It's the .. er," I squint at the set list "... fifth song. I'll give you a big intro."

"Aye, well make sure you fuckin' do an all." he says, "See yez later then." And off he goes.

Dik and I decide to go for a bit of an explore while Mulligan tries to decide what to braid into his newly-dyed platinum dreadlocks.

"Bit like Hampton Court maze, this." Dik says.

We're walking along a low-ceilinged, dusty corridor and all the doors along the way have thus far proven to be locked.

"Just like it." I say, "Especially the privet hedges."

"You know what I mean, lanky. I mean it's a maze innit."

"Alright then." I say, "In that case, if we always keep the outside wall to the left we'll soon reach the middle."

"Thank you and goodnight Alice in Blunderland." he says, "Here, look at this."

He's pointing to a door labeled "Artists Bar" in gothic script.

"You don't suppose ...?" I ask.

"Only one way to find out." and he tries the door knob. In we go to find ourselves in a large, oak-paneled room dominated by a long Victorian bar.

"Nirvana." I say.

"Dunno 'bout that," he says, "Looks more like heaven to me."

As we make our way through crowd I start to recognize people, people I've been looking at in *NME, Sounds, Melody Maker* and *Record Mirror* for the last couple of years, a few I'd even seen in *The Sun* and *Daily Mirror*. With a large gin and tonic in my paw, I turn to survey the room.

"Feels like ... like, I'm home." I say.

"What? Oh, yeah." And Dik is off into the crowd, cutting a shark's path toward a small cluster of young lovelies over in the corner. I decide to just enjoy the view and keep myself to just one drink. I chat to a bass player (who isn't interested in joining Fàshiön), and also someone irritatingly familiar that I can't place. I finish my drink, set the empty glass on the bar, stop by the dartboard on my way out to grab a stub of chalk. I intend to mark my path back to this wonderful room. Sod staying at a bed and breakfast or kipping down in the van, I'm going to spend the night here, even if I have to hide from the cleaners in the bog. Wouldn't be the first time. Back in the dressing room, I pocket the chalk stub, having left a trail of arrows behind me that lead back to the bar.

"We've been talking." Annette tells me.

"Oh yes. That's nice." I say.

"Thing is," Mulligan says, "The Stranglers are a bunch of hard cases. Their bass player is a black belt karate. Hells Angels show up to do security for them. And their fans are a bunch of nutters."

"Hmm," I say, squinting at my perfection in a mirror, "So?"

"Well," Annette says, "You know how you get sometimes. After shows. A bit, er over-excited. So we don't want you going into their dressing room after, shooting your mouth off, and getting crippled."

I stare at them, smiling.

"Well, your concern is as touching as it's unexpected," I say, "How can I put this delicately? Oh, I know. Piss off! Yes, that's it. Piss off!"

Pedro comes in to tell us he's checked out the sound desk. He's fair salivating.

"Fookin' berilliant." He says "There's effects racks up the wazoo. And a lorra buttons, got no idea what they're for!"

Oh bog. Miki, Miki, wherefore art thou Miki?

"That's great Ped." I say, "But let's not try anything too adventurous with the PA, eh? Big night. Let's just give 'em a good, crisp, clear mix."

"Yeah," Mulligan says, "None of them soddin' Pink Floyd

tricks, okay?"

"Come on now." Pedro says holding up his hands, "You can trust me."

"Yeah." I mutter, "I bet you say that to all the girls. Just before you come."

We're crouched in the wings, ready to jump out and the excitement is almost overpowering. A full house, the DJ has Siouxsie and the Banshees wailing out the old *Hong Kong Gardens*, and then it's "ladies and gentlemen, welcome to fiftieth anniversary week at The Rainbow."

A cheer rises and echoes round the auditorium. "

"Tonight's first band are from Birmingham."

Don't tell them that you prat! There are a few boos and groans peppering what is now just a smattering of applause. The lights slam on and I run out, plug in, and am on the mic with a

"Good evening. This is *Product Perfect* ... for your perfect occasion!"

And I'm gangling loose-limbed into the spastic giraffe dance for the intro. My joy at being back onstage in front of a big crowd is short-lived. This is no welcome back to Brum Aston University gig and even before the end of the first number a few odds and ends are being chucked at us from the front rows. The rest of the set is an escalating nightmare. From what I can tell, a couple of hundred people at the back like us, but it's hard to tell really, as the front fifteen hundred or so clearly do not like us and are letting us know in no uncertain ... er, fashion.

Back in the dressing room we're all slumped in sweaty despair. Even Jobson had failed to materialize for his guest vocal on *Steady Eddie Steady*, although none of us are exactly blaming him for that.

"What are we going to do?" Mulligan asks, the unmistakable glint of terror in his mascara-smeared eyes, "I mean, we have to go out there again tomorrow night."

"They fuckin' hated us." Dik says miserably.

"Well I know what I'm going to do." I say, and I set off down the corridor following my trail of chalked arrows. It doesn't take long (about five Bacardi and cokes) for things to start to feel a little blurry and better. Jobson apologizes for not showing for his guest vocal and sympathizes, I hang around a conversation about recording studios with Godley and Crème of 10cc, fail to get off with some German tart, and by the time I encounter Robert Fripp I'm so out of it that my attempts to talk to him about the Moogy Klingman TV show we both did last year only elicit a curt:

"Yeah? Well, catch you later."

He scurries off, leaving me befuddled enough to not feel embarrassed until his brush-off sinks in half an hour later.

I wake up, stiff and cold, on the floor under a table. I know I'm under a table because I bang my head when I sit up. I grope my way to a light switch and groan at the sudden flood of light. I get up and trudge over to the bar and mix myself a hair of the dog.

I stumble back along the corridors to find the dressing room locked. The theater seems deserted. My watch tells me it's almost midday. I'm too hungover to be hungry. I make my way to the stage and in the glow of the fire exit signs I sit and dangle my legs off the edge of the stage. I finish my bloody Mary and heave the plastic glass out into the auditorium.

Perhaps, if we stripped out the synths, all wore black leather, and played *Sodium Pentathol Negative*-type songs, we might just about survive another night in front of a Stranglers crowd. I'd have to find a way of getting Mulligan to agree to no synths, not easy, he loves them almost as much as, well anything else he purports to love. I climb down into the auditorium, let myself out through a fire exit and, after a quick stop at the chemists for aspirin, find a kaff and have breakfast.

By the time I return to the gig it's two o'clock, my hangover's gone, and I have a new set list for that night's show: *Sodium Pentathol Negative / Burnin' Down / Die In The West / Steady Eddie Steady / Bike Boys / Big John, Hanoi Annoys Me, The Innocent.*

Twenty five minutes tops and nothing too evidently arty in that lot. Sod art, this is about survival.

Back in the dressing room, Mulligan, Dik, and Annette listen to my plan and one by one they nod agreement. Mulligan is obviously a bit reluctant but pain, and the threat of more pain to come, can be great persuaders.

"And if you try anything fancier than a bit of reverb on old big nose's vocals tonight," Dik warns Pedro, "we'll set Mulligan on you with a pair of tweezers and have that fuckin' stupid moustache off one bristle at a time."

Pedro wisely concurs. That night there are no backstage drinks and consequently a somber, determined mood. We strap on black leather armour and steel ourselves for what's out there. We re-swear our oaths of ganghood, of us against the rest of the bastards, come what may. It feels good. We hit the stage with a swagger and bludgeon our way through the set in just over twenty minutes. Jobson joins us for a gleeful vocal contribution to *Steady Eddie Steady*. As the last notes of *The Innocent* echo around the auditorium we run for it. Somehow there seems to be a great roar of approval coming from the crowd and we're called back for an encore. Unbelievable. Last night we ran off stage dodging a hail of missiles and abuse, and tonight they fucking love us. Say what you like about the great unwashed British public but if you ask me they're a bit easier to fool than I thought.

Dik and I are standing in the wings watching Joy Division. Well, actually we're more glaring daggers at the buggers. It's not that we're ones to bear a grudge – well, okay, yes that's exactly what we are. We haven't forgotten the argument and punch-up we had with them at Manchester Free Trade Hall on the John Cooper Clark tour. They're grinding their way through their now legendary set of "we're-miserable-buggers-in-overcoats-and-love-will-tear-us-apart-and-then-jump-up-and-down-on-what's-left" songs, when singer Ian Curtis suddenly jerks backwards and falls into the drum kit. There's some major strobe lighting going on so it's a bit difficult to tell what's happening. It all looks quite impressive though, and I'm just thinking that perhaps Joy Division have decided to use a bit of stage craft beyond standing around whinging and looking sulky, when it occurs to me that Curtis has half-demolished the drum kit and the rest of the band have stopped playing. A roadie runs onstage as the strobe lights die and I see him jump on Curtis and jam something into his mouth. He's having a sodding epileptic fit, I realize, brought on by the strobe lights, and the roadie's jamming a pen or something under his tongue so he won't choke. Two other roadies join the fray and carry the still thrashing singer from the stage.

"Looks like a Milwall fan being ejected from the ground." Dik observes.

You can call us callous, hard-hearted little shits (you wouldn't be the first, you won't be the last) but this is too much like poetic justice to warrant anything other than gales of hysterical laughter.

While the Hazel O'Connor band are on, I swing back by the bar to top up my buzz, then back to auditorium via the bog for a quick line of whiz, before making my way to stand next to the sound desk (best sound in the theater) to listen to The Stranglers. There's a right cavalcade of guests trooping on and off for each number so it's hard to keep up, but I do recognize Toyah Wilcox on vocals for *Peaches, Duchess, Bear Cage* and *Something Better Change, with* Hazel O'Connor joining her to compete for the honors on *Peaches* and *Bear Cage,* before then having a bash on her own at *Get A Grip* and *Hanging Around.* But the real star of both *Peaches* and *Bear Cage* is Ian Dury. And then there's The Cure's Robert Smith giving it some welly on guitar on *Grip* and *Hanging Around.*

I also spot Nicky Tesco (The Members), Jake Burns (Stiff Little Fingers) and Wilko Johnson (Dr. Feelgood), as well as old hippies Robert Fripp (King Crimson) and Steve Hillage (Gong). Richard Jobson does a number on *Bring On The Nubiles* and *No More Heroes,* while Basil and David from Steel Pulse lay down various wicked grooves on bass and drums. The cherry on the cake comes when after the encore, Billy Idol swaggers onstage, having had nothing whatsoever to do with the show, to take a bow. Jean Jacques Burnel takes exception at this and strides across the stage and decks him. Lovely! Even without poor old incarcerated Hugh Cornwell, it has been a great show by one of my favorite bands. It has been a snoot cocked at authority.

I take absolutely no notice whatsoever of Annette and Mulligan's warnings about keeping my big, fat mouth out of the Stranglers dressing room and as soon as the encores are over that's exactly where I head. Therein, I find a smattering of stars, a possel of groupies, a huddle of hangers-on, and three very sweaty Stranglers. Over in one corner, I spy a young lovely who seems to be on her own. I wonder over and say hello and imagine my delight when she turns out to be French. I hunker down in the corner next to her chair and start to give her a bit of "le vieux chat" (and I don't mean the old cat, either) Things seem to be going well, she's from Toulouse (I've been there) and she's with someone in one of the bands who has abandoned her backstage while they're off furthering their career. (oh the irony!) We're just getting around to her telling me where she's staying that night, when some old hippie comes over, all agitated that a painted New Wave lothario is chatting up his young bird. Blimey, it's Steve Hillage and he's twittering about having to get the guitars in the van and get back to the hotel. With a slight smile and my suavest "C'etait vraiment plaisir de faire ta connaisance" I slide slowly up the wall until I'm on tip toes, a good seven feet tall. Poor old Steve, who is probably bollixed out of his bonce on acid, stares gape-mouthed up at the freak who would usurp his bint. She's covering her mouth, trying not to laugh out loud as I coo "'voir" and stride off.

Deciding to keep the French theme going, I plonk myself down next to Jean Jacques Burnel.

"Wotcha mate. Brilliant show." I say.

"Sanks." he says, just a trace of the old frog accent still there, "You were in that first band, right?"

"Yeah. Least, last time I looked I was."

You were great. Really rocked."

"Thanks. That's what happens sometimes when you cut out all the arty shit and that and give it a bit of welly."

"You are from where?" he asks.

"Birmingham," I say, "Or Brum, as the inmates call it."

"That is a huge conurbation."

"Yeah," I say, "It's definitely what you might call a mass conurbation all right."

He almost spits out his drink laughing, and we settle down for a bit of a chat. I tell him about Symiane and Bordeaux, he tells me about his karate, I compliment him on decking Billy Idol. We move on to our respective bands upcoming plans. This starts to depress me – well, it's not as if we have any plans I'm aware of beyond the ones I'm about to make up. Annette and Mulligan bustle up doing the world's worst impression of the Seventh Cavalry come to effect an entirely unnecessary rescue.

"Er, time to go. Van's loaded." Annette says.

"Is he?" I ask, "I didn't even know he was here."

"Sorry if he's been bothering you." Mulligan says to JJ.

"Bozzering?" he asks.

"Take no notice JJ. They're with me. Harmless for the most part, clueless for the rest. Well, it's off back to me mass conurbation innit. Been a pleasure chatting and thanks for the gigs. They were bostin'."

In the miserable van on the miserable way back to miserable Brum, somewhere around Leicester, I finally manage to put myself out of my misery with the half bottle of voddy I've got hidden in my tour bag. I wake up next afternoon on the settee at Mom and Dad's with a hangover the size of British Leyland. The flat's empty, so I go upstairs, have a bath, and go to bed.

▶▶▶▶

Things start to get a little sketchy around this time. My booze and speed use has escalated (not a good mixture, especially when it comes to mindless rage) although to be honest I'm taking more or less anything I can get my hands on.

We drive up to Scotland to play four gigs. Glasgow is as scary as advertised. I remember Jools Holland telling me how, dazed and exhausted from a brutal US tour, Squeeze played Glasgow and after the third number he made the mistake of saying it was great to be back in England. Needless to say that was as far as that particular show went! So we have every right to be nervous, a bunch of tarted up sassanach poufters. After the gig, we grab our sheckels and make a run for Edinburgh. Annette has booked us a gig at The Nite Club (how do they think these names up?) with The Photos, who are among my favorite people in bands. We first met them aeons ago back along the trail when we played some club in Worcestershire. They have signed to Epic and are doing rather well, so we open for them. Not that I mind, the night is one of those increasingly rare times of calm in the turbulence, I have a great time, and both bands play blinding sets.

In Dundee, I decorate the ladies bog (where I've taken to pissing these days) with large drunken magic marker proclamations that Fàshiön is going to die and Luke Sky is the laddie to kill it.

And so on to Aberdeen and some college where, after an unmemorable show, I end up back at some vaguely hippie young bird's student flat. She spends half the night rabitting on about astrology and my chart while I drink and smoke everything I can find. This takes so long that it's several hours before I've got her knickers off and HMS Sky is steaming up Muff Cove. I'm just starting to enjoy the ride when there comes a furious pounding on her door and Pedro and Whistling Pete barge in and literally drag me off her. They cart me out to the van, where early morning bits of Fàshiön sit dozing, and we're off without so much as a piss, much less a climax. I sit in the van, nursing blue balls. About half an hour south of Aberdeen I insist we stop on a coast road at a historical site so I can have a slash. There's a small, square building on a slight rise next to a ruined castle wall. The wind off the North Sea is batting seagulls around like feathers in a hoover. I find a plaque on the small, rough stone building that says over two hundred families, men, women and children, were imprisoned in this building for over a year by the garrisoned English army. All crammed into a space smaller than our first rehearsal room. When I point this out to Dik he says,

"Well, they got a bigger crowd than we did last night then."

"Yes. Quite." It's easy to see why the Scottish still hate us. I still hate us. I might only be Scottish from the knees down, but it's enough to stir my blood and add another level of dissatisfaction and loathing to my opinion of my band mates.

▶▶▶▶

The next week it's business as usual as we completely fail to come up with a hit single. At the end of the week, Annette shows up at the studio and tells us she's got us a gig for fifty quid opening the show for Chelsea at Notre Dame Hall in London.

"Opening?" Dik asks, incredulous.

"For Chelsea?" I add.

"Fifty quid?" Mulligan says.

"It's a gig, guys." Annette says, grinning with embarrassment, like a dog caught eating its master's shoes.

"For them, yes. I'm sure it's a big gig for sodding Chelsea!" I yell. But then I'm too depressed to be angry any more, so I slump in the corner and play automatic rubbish on my unamplified Iceman.

▶▶▶▶

We go to London and play the show, without swallowing, like the well-trained little whores we've become. The next week's reviews, that mostly pan Chelsea, don't even mention us. Apparently we don't even warrant a bad review any more.

▶▶▶▶

"I've got us some free studio time." Mulligan says.

Dik and I barely look up from our fry-ups at Greasy Sid's. It might well have a new awning and be called The Moseley Café these days, but it will always be Sid's to me. Certainly the food does nothing to change my mind.

"How long have we got to pay for it this time?" Dik asks.

"No, no. Nothing like that." Mulligan says, "It's over in Pete

King's cellar. He's built a studio under his house. They're just fine-tuning the set-up so he's letting us use it for free."

"Okay. Pity we don't have anything worth recording." I say.

"Let's have a bash at *Fiction Factory*." Dik says, "And *Bad Move*."

These are both songs that Dik sings. I've even switched to bass for *Bad Move*, as the bass line is beyond Mulligan.

"I suppose." I say, dragging an unwilling sack of unconscious enthusiasm up the cellar steps of my depression, banging its head as I go.

We're halfway through *Fiction Factory* and it's going surprisingly well. Pete King is manager of Steel Pulse and has built a tidy, compact but state-of-the-art studio in the basement of the house that sits atop Moseley Road hill. Up there, the old Victorian houses are either still single occupancy or else have been converted into large luxury flats. Not like the rat hole me and Miki used to share at the bottom of the hill years ago. Being up on top of the hill, recording new material, I'm almost managing to convince myself that we're still on some sort of path that will lead us to the big time. In between takes, Dik is playing a dangerous, flirting game with one of Steel Pulse's girlfriends, a sloe-eyed South American-looking beauty.

"Hello darlin'" he says. She looks away unimpressed. "I wanted to ask you something. I'm wondering where you got that beautiful arse. Only I've got to get a new one. Mine's got a crack in it."

She yawns and drifts away. I breathe a bit of a sigh of relief. Last thing we need is to get thrown out before we've done a mix and got our sweaty hands on the tapes.

"See you haven't lost your touch then." I tell him.

"Oh she'll be back." he says, "Watch and learn, big nose."

"Have you ever thought about varying your approach?"

"Why would I do that?" he asks, "It works."

"Apart from anything else, so I wouldn't have to listen to the same tired shit over and over again." I say.

Annette ducks into the cellar studio. If she has to duck, as you might imagine, I'm spending most of my time either sitting or doing bad Groucho Marx impersonations.

"I've got you a tour." she says.

"Funny." Mulligan says, "My hearing must be playing up. For a second I can have sworn she said she'd got us a tour."

"What's that then?" Dik asks, "Only I've forgotten."

"You know. It's where we slog all over the place working our taters off for little or no money and then everyone thinks we've split up." I say.

"Very funny. Do you want to hear this or not?" she asks.

"Okay boss. Spill the Heinz then." Dik says.

"It's with U2." she declares.

"What, just the two of us?" I ask, "Which two?"

"No, no. U2." she says.

"Well I'm glad it's with us as well. Otherwise it wouldn't really be much of a tour. For us I mean." Dik says.

"The band." she says. "From Ireland. Letter U, number 2."

"I'm sure they can't be as bad as that. No need to describe them as number twos." Mulligan says.

"Wait a minute." I say, "I've heard of them. They're good! I suppose that means we're going to opening again. What is it, fifty quid a night and a bag of chips?"

"No, it's a split bill." she says.

"Sounds painful." Mulligan adds.

"Means one night you open for them, the next night they open for you. We split the door fifty fifty."

"Might be alright." I concede, "What sort of gigs."

"Only clubs." she says, "But they're definitely a band on the way up. Can't do any harm, being on tour with them. I hear Island Records are interested in them."

"On their way up, are they? Better than where we seem to be headed." Dik says.

"That's the gratitude I've come to expect from you lot." she says, "I've been on the bloody phone for two weeks getting you this."

"Oh, we're ecstatic. Don't let the lack of jumping up and down fool you." I say morosely.

Before we start out on the U2 tour we squeeze in another Brum club gig at The Holy City Zoo. The Zoo is a mid-sized club tucked away under the brickwork of Victorian railway arches near the city center. Mulligan comes up with a great poster but this time Annette actually provides money for a couple of other poor sods to put them up. So there's no shinning up lampposts at two in the morning with freezing buckets of wall paper paste for me, which in a sick sort of way I almost miss.

The Holy City Zoo is bursting at the seams with punters but even so I'm still pissed off. I'm not even sure exactly why any more, it just seems to be one of my common states these days. I alternate between rage and lethargy, sometimes in the space of a single sentence. Other than that, I'm pretty sure I'm reasonably sane, thank you all the same. An old friend called Kinch is at the club. I haven't seen him since our second ever gig at The Golden Eagle a couple of (hundred) years ago, at which time he declared himself happy to see me in the hottest band in town with the hottest French chick in town. Both now, alas, long gone.

"I hear on the grapevine you're not happy." he says. He's wearing mechanic overalls with "Blockhead" stenciled across the back.

"Shows does it?" I say.

"Just a bit. So, what's the plan?" he hops habitually from one foot to the other, casting occasional nervous glances behind him, as if worried someone might sneak up on him.

"Dunno. Play the show. Get pissed off. Get pissed. We're out on tour again tomorrow."

"Yeah? Who with?"

"Band from Ireland. U2." I say.

"Hey, I hear –"

"Yes, I know." I say and sigh. "They're great."

After the second encore I'm in the dressing tomb, my face in a towel, when Kinch appears.

"Man," he says, "that was fuckin' scary. *You* are fuckin' scary. That was anger, right there. Great show though."

"Yeah. Thanks." I say, "Pity we can't bottle it, eh. We could sell it down the Villa."

"Gotta go. see a man about a dog, y'know. Look after yourself, alright?"

"Yeah." I say, reaching for a bottle of vodka. "I will."

▶ ▶ ▶ ▶

The thing about U2 in England in 1980 is that they are a

great band. They are vibrant, passionate, energetic, they are on a mission they believe in. And then there's Fàshiön – exhausted from two years on the road, a road littered with broken and false promises, going through the motions with very little new material, slowly being devoured by internal dispute and dissent. Apart from that we're doing just fine!

But U2 have great songs and put on great shows. It's a bit like touring with a bunch of really nice, well-behaved boys next door. They don't do any of the booze or drugs. If there had been any groupies I'm fairly sure they wouldn't have done them either. No, they show up, treat everyone with courteous respect, play amazing music, then say goodnight and drive their battered old transit van back to their bed-and-breakfast.

The U2 "tour", with only a couple of provincial exceptions, turns out to consist of gigs in London's smaller clubs, clubs we'd first played back when we thought we were on our way up. First stop, May 22, is The Hope and Anchor, Upper Street, Islington.

"I see we're back playing in someone's mouth again." I say, eying the red painted walls and dangerously low ceiling.

"Some of my happiest moments have been spent playing inside someone's mouth." Dik says.

"Pity we didn't all become dentists instead," I say.

"What's he moaning about now?" Annette asks.

"Oh, the usual," Mulligan says, "Everything."

I watch Whistling Pete and Pedro try not to get squashed lowering bass cabs through the pavement trap door.

"I was just saying, we were here two years ago, that's all. Remember there was that journalist bird from Record Mirror. Gave us a great review she did." I say.

"That's not all. She gave great h—", Mulligan says.

"Yes, alright, alright. Spare us the grizzly details. True and otherwise." I say. Then to Annette, "So is there going to be any press here tonight?"

"I'm sure the usual will be here. *NME, Sounds, Melody Maker.*"

"*Tractor Breeding Monthly?*" I suggest. "*Wasp Farming Quarterly. The British Journal of Dung.*"

"Shut up Luke."

"Yes boss."

"Hello. Are you Fashion?" asks a fresh-faced lad, "I'm Bono. I'm the singer with U2."

"Very nice to meet you Bongo." Dik says.

"Yeah, welcome to the big time mate." I say.

"Take no notice of them Bono." Annette says to Bono, who has a slight smile on his face. "No one else does."

She squints at her schedule.

"We're opening the show for you tonight," she says, "So we'll get set up and if you can have your back line ready at the side of the stage—"

"That postage stamp-sized thing over there," I say. "That's the stage."

"Shut up Luke.."

"And next to it, that alcove where they stack the mops and sawdust, that's the dressing room." I say, "Watch your head on the ceiling."

Along with the fifty or so punters jammed into the cellar, U2 watch our set. Something happens, I don't know if U2's good-natured enthusiasm is infectious, maybe it's that it's good to be up-close and personal with a small group of punters again after playing to the blinding stage lights and mile distant seated crowd at The Rainbow, but halfway through *Red Green and Gold* I catch myself having fun. Now there's a novelty, I tell myself, and promptly play a wrong chord. We all have a good sweaty time and bang through *Bike Boys* as an encore – there's nowhere to go at the end of the set so we just stand there, wait a respectable amount of time just to where the applause is dribbling to silence and give them the old thank you very much here's our encore routine. Bono, The Edge, Adam and Larry are down the front bopping up and down seemingly having a great time. I decide to return the favor and have a bit of a dance when they play.

The gear having been switched without too many collisions, a voice announces,

"From Dublin, please give a great Hope and Anchor welcome back to U2!"

They launch into *11 O'Clock Tick-Tock*, and fuck my old

boots if after only the first minute of so I don't find myself on my feet dancing away, and a minute later smiling. This is the most fun I've had, clothed or not, for a good long while.

The next night is the Moonlight Club, a room over a pub in West Hampstead, just off the High Street. It's our turn to headline and it goes as well as can be expected; given that I spend a good deal of the set thinking about how often this U2 mob are going to play sets that have everyone on their feet having a great time. I've got a horrible feeling they might just do it every night. We're all crammed into the tiny dressing room waiting for our respective vans to be ready to leave. Theirs to some dodgy, local bed-and-breakfast, and ours back up the motorway to Brum. The "crowds" at the shows so far are just about paying for petrol and chips all round, so Annette decrees no bed-and-breakfasts, much less hotels, unless we start packing them in. (And probably not then either knowing her.) We're playing Sheffield University tomorrow night, so at least I might get fed, it being a university.

"'Ere the Sex Pistols are outside." Dik bursts into the tiny dressing room and the door almost knocks Bono off his chair.

"What, all of 'em?" I ask.

"Probably just the ones who aren't dead." Mulligan says.

U2 look a little nervous.

"Well whatever they want, we haven't got it." Annette says.

"Right." I agree, a little stumped as to what exactly, if anything, we do have.

In the end Jones and Cook try to barge in, being boisterous, but there's really not enough room and once they see there's nowt going on beyond a bunch of knackered Brummies and Paddies sitting around waiting for their vans, they do a bit of yelling and cackling (as you would expect) and piss off into the night.

And so it becomes a grind of banging up and down the motorways, back to Brum after every gig for a few hours exhausted kip at my folks place of an afternoon before catching the train into town to join the van.

We play Sheffield University where we get fed and open the show for U2. There's a big, half-drunken crowd of future middle managers in attendance, and the lads from Dublin go down a fucking storm.

The next night we trek all the way south to Brighton to play the New Regent. It's a pleasant enough little theater but a long way down the ladder from the last time we were in Brighton opening for The Police at The Dome. By now I'm actually feeling a little embarrassed every time U2 open for us, I mean they are basically so much better than us. And who ever though the future king of new wave would admit that anyone was better than him?

The next night we're back in London at The Rock Garden where we've played a tepid warm-up. While U2 are waiting to go on, I'm discussing the band's future with Annette.

"But I'm telling you the cunt came straight out and told me that *Silver Blades* won't be a hit. He even said it was a great record but that old money bags isn't willing to spend any dosh promoting it. So what is the fucking point of me living on chips and spending my life in a sodding transit van if all it's going to lead to is more of the same?"

Bono leans over.

"I know whatcha mean. We've the devil's own job getting CBS to do anything with our single over here. And the bugger of it is, every time there's record execs at the show, we play like puddings. So how are we supposed to get a better deal?"

"Well, I know what you mean Bono, but I've never actually heard you play like puddings. You lot are great. Night after night."

He looks at his feet. I swear he's embarrassed by the praise.

"And another thing," I ask Annette, "Is there any danger whatsoever of some sod from the press actually turning up and reviewing a show. I mean for U2 as much as for us."

I know her well enough by now to see that she's hiding something.

"What? " I ask.

"Well, you'd probably have seen it sooner or later." She hands me a copy of *New Music News*. "Moonlight Club review," she says, "page twenty-three."

FASHION/U2
Moonlight Club, London
There are plenty of medals for bravery but how many of these daring rocky types deserve them?

Not a lot, of course. Heroism usually comes cheap these days and all manner of glib entertainers can easily disguise their ordinariness with an array of manufactured noises, manipulated sufficiently to claim a noble art of implication, depth and, above all else, a boldness truly deserving to be treated as something very special. Indeed.

The two groups here tonight make a neat distinction between an honest integrity and this habitual conceit – U2, being former occupants of a desert Ireland but now future suppliers of Island discs, and Fashion, still at sea but doing quite "well". (Pardon? Miles Copeland).

And why not! Fashion's grim greyness has been perfected to reflect an ugly moderne world and yet it's these decaying standards which ultimately permit such soulless garbage to be effective. There are always enough wallies around just waiting and wanting to trust pseudo pretence.

This Fashion show is a bald front really, a hollow conceit of implausible monotony by three stubbornly indifferent posers wandering in their own empty mystery of dressed up assumptions as to some kind of outrageous supple subtlety. Reward inevitably follows such inanity.

I ball the paper up and throw it on the floor.

"I mean it's not even written in English, is it!" I yell.

"Course not," Dik says, "It was written by a fucking journalist, wasn't it."

"Who hires these people?" I demand.

"Other hacks who can't write." Mulligan says. "So they can write bollocks for people who can't read."

"Ah come on now lads," says Bono, "you shouldn't be believing everything you read in the papers. It's just someone's opinion. What is it your man says, it doesn't matter what they say about you as long as they spell your name right, eh?"

I stare down at the crumpled review and notice that the band name has none of the accents or umlauts, so strictly speaking they haven't even spelled it right.

Trinity Hall in Bristol is a blur. I only stay sober enough long enough to play the set, we top the bill and get no encore. U2 open and they do get an encore.

And then it's back to home turf and The Cedar Club on Constitution Hill in Brum. Even though we headlined the night before, U2 are generous enough to let us headline in our home town. There's a good-sized crowd jammed into the old Cedar Club, friendly and faithful faces dotted here and there among the crowd, dedicated followers of Fàshiön.

U2 start of with a blinding version of *I Will Follow*, then segue into *11 O'Clock Tick Tock*. Bono has his arms out at shoulder height, doing a bit of the old mock Irish country dancing. He's magicked a red rose from somewhere and during the guitar solo he jumps down into the crowd and presents it to a bashful young punkette. As the vocals wallop back in at the end of the solo, The Edge and Adam decide to join their front man, and jump down off the stage. Only they've forgotten their guitar cables aren't long enough and so they both come uplugged from their amps. Suddenly there's just Bono's voice and Larry's drums, soaring and pounding,while Adam and Edge clamber back onstage and shamefacedly plug back in. And fuck my old boots if the drum/vocal breakdown doesn't sound like they meant it, and when the guitar and bass come back in they almost blast the roof right off.

▶▶▶▶

In the next ten days we play nine gigs, criss-crossing the country from London (Nashville Rooms) to Nottingham (Boat Club one night, Beach Club the next – and me all at sea both nights) to Nuneaton (The 77 Club where we'd played with The Skids back in the 19th century), to Leeds (Fan Club) back to The Midlands to Dudley (JB's) and finally back to London for The Marquee and The Half Moon.

The tour ends, we shake hands with U2, who steer their battered transit van back to the ferry home and future superstardom.

A few days later I find myself sitting in Annette's kitchen reading *Record Mirror*. All the previous joy of raiding Annette and Kevin's fridge, of bouncing on their Scandinavian designer furniture, of watching Blondie videos and The Kenny Everett Show on their colour TV while sipping Pernod and smoking

Gauloise has long since evaporated. I might as well be sitting in a railway station waiting room, an operating theater, or any other blank, sterile environment. Mulligan comes into the kitchen brandishing Annette's curling iron like a sword.

"Anything in the papers?" he asks, "About the tour?"

"No." I say, "Not a sausage."

"Typical." he says and goes off to try and change the way he looks for the third time that day.

I'm thinking about the tour, I'm thinking about the passion of U2 and the jaded puppetry of Fashion. I read again part of an interview with Bono. It comes right after a review of the Half Moon gig where the reviewer is raving about how unexpected U2's music is, how it often veers off into unexpected territory when you least expect it, how whole songs break suddenly into great swirls of echo and harmonics before ending with a frenzy of emotion. I could have been reading about what we were trying to do two years earlier. But I'm not.

And then there are those lines of Bono's, burning into my mind. I know he's not taking the piss, he's not petty, not the sort of bloke to do so. No, he's just being honest. And I find myself agreeing with him:

"U2 is not about fashion. We don't want to be in fashion, because being in fashion is going out of fashion, you know?".

June 18th 1980
-Fàshiön vocalist Luke has disappeared, leaving a note that read "Gone to America".
Post Punk Diary, 1980-82 by George Gimarc

www.ingramcontent.com/pod-product-compliance
Lightning Source LLC
Chambersburg PA
CBHW031833090426

42741CB00005B/229